PRAISE F

HOW YC
SAY IT

"*How You Say It* takes readers on a personal and experimental journey that will be appealing and informative to a general audience and scientists alike. A gifted writer, Kinzler displays that rare ability to engage readers with many intricate, yet highly accessible, scientific details."

— John Baugh, author of *Black Street Speech* and *Linguistics in Pursuit of Justice*

"'An Englishman's way of speaking absolutely classifies him / The moment he talks he makes some other Englishman despise him.' In this timely and engaging book, Katherine Kinzler shows how Henry Higgins's observation applies to all of us. She presents the fascinating new science of linguistic prejudice, much of it her own, and spells out the implications for education, parenting, and our understanding of one another."

— Steven Pinker, *New York Times* best-selling author of *The Language Instinct* and *The Sense of Style*

"A compelling journey into the science, and essence, of what it means to be human — that is, how we communicate with each other. *How You Say It* is an incredibly timely book, revealing the power of speech beyond words alone, and pushing us to confront our biases and to understand the biases of others. By learning to understand the nature and effect of verbal communication, we can help our world become more equitable, constructive, and positive for everyone. A highly recommended read for all of us!"

— Dana Suskind, author of *Thirty Million Words: Building a Child's Brain*

"Kinzler explores in this revelatory and thought-provoking debut the social assumptions people attach to accents and speaking styles, to sometimes devastating effect . . . Well-written and entertainingly told, Kinzler's persuasive exploration of linguistic-based differences will awaken readers to potentially unrecognized biases."

— *Publishers Weekly*

"A fascinating book, *How You Say It* will intrigue you, surprise you, and maybe even provoke you—but above all else, it will make you think!"

— Carol Dweck, author of *Mindset*

"Katherine Kinzler is a phenomenon — one of the most brilliant young psychologists of her generation. She is a clear and lucid writer, a brave and creative scholar, and her discoveries about how language shapes the social world are truly groundbreaking."

— Paul Bloom, author of *Against Empathy* and *Just Babies*

"An articulate examination of an underrecognized aspect of human communication."

— *Kirkus Reviews*

"A powerfully original, eye-opening book about the many ways we misjudge each other when we open our mouths to speak. A smart and delightful treat for you, youz, yins, and y'all."

— Daniel Gilbert, *New York Times* best-selling author
of *Stumbling on Happiness*

"In the multifarious ways the sounds of language tumble out of our mouths, Katherine Kinzler brilliantly detects questions of identity, personality, and social relations. This book is for anybody who is intrigued by the uniquely human sounds of language — the subtle messages they convey and the impressions they conjure up."

— Mahzarin R. Banaji, *New York Times* best-selling
author of *Blindspot*

HOW YOU SAY IT

HOW YOU SAY IT

WHY WE JUDGE OTHERS BY THE WAY THEY
TALK — AND THE COSTS OF THIS HIDDEN BIAS

KATHERINE D. KINZLER

MARINER BOOKS
HOUGHTON MIFFLIN HARCOURT
Boston   New York

First Mariner Books edition 2021
Copyright © 2020 by Katherine D. Kinzler

For information about permission to reproduce selections from
this book, write to trade.permissions@hmhco.com or to
Permissions, Houghton Mifflin Harcourt Publishing Company,
3 Park Avenue, 19th Floor, New York, New York 10016.

hmhbooks.com

Library of Congress Cataloging-in-Publication Data
Names: Kinzler, Katherine D., author.
Title: How you say it : Why we judge others by the way they talk—and
the costs of this hidden bias / Katherine D. Kinzler.
Description: Boston : Houghton Mifflin Harcourt, 2020. |
Includes bibliographical references and index.
Identifiers: LCCN 2019049915 (print) | LCCN 2019049916 (ebook) |
ISBN 9780544986558 (hardcover) | ISBN 9780358172239 |
ISBN 9780358305248 | ISBN 9780544987425 (ebook) |
ISBN 9780358567103 (pbk.) |
Subjects: LCSH: Language and languages — Variation. |
Linguistic Change — Social aspects. | Languages in contact. |
Second language acquisition. | Sociolinguistics.
Classification: LCC P40.5.L54 K56 2020 (print) |
LCC P40.5.L54 (ebook) | DDC 302.2/24 — dc23
LC record available at https://lccn.loc.gov/2019049915
LC ebook record available at https://lccn.loc.gov/2019049916

Book design by Kelly Dubeau Smydra

Printed in the United States of America
ScoutAutomatedPrintCode
$ScoutAutomatedPO

For Zach, Taylor, and Nate

CONTENTS

INTRODUCTION: IT'S NOT WHAT YOU SAY   ix

CHAPTER 1: HOW YOU SPEAK IS WHO YOU ARE   1
Your Language Is Your Tribe. Burnouts and Valley Girls.
Peers vs. Parents. Who's Afraid of RBG? Remembering in
Russian.

CHAPTER 2: NATIVE TONGUES   28
Nabokov's Nanny. Give Me a Sign. The Wonder Years.
Ghost in the Machine. "I'm Just Not as Funny in English!"

CHAPTER 3: HOW LANGUAGE DIVIDES US   54
Scarlet Letters. Shibboleth. Toward Babel.
Ugly Americans. Are People Nicer in the South?
Linguistic Insecurity.

CHAPTER 4: DEEP TALK   80
Organisms of Nature. Calls of the Wild. Out of Africa.
Who Said What? Flurps and Zazzes.

CHAPTER 5: LITTLE BIGOTS?   101
Mother Tongue. Social Animals. When in Rome.
"Julie Isn't Racist!" Aladdin's Accent.

CHAPTER 6: ON THE BASIS OF SPEECH   125
"They Can't Even Speak English." In Talk We Trust.
Living; Wage. Communication Skills. Speak Truth.

CHAPTER 7: A LINGUISTICS REVOLUTION   152
The Monolingual Myth. What Language Do You Use to
Brush Your Teeth? The Bilingual Bonus. Polyglots Preferred.
It's Elementary.

AFTERWORD: IT'S ~~NOT~~ WHAT YOU SAY   177

Acknowledgments   187

Notes   190

Index   225

INTRODUCTION

IT'S NOT WHAT YOU SAY

Humans are joiners: we band together to create social groups. But in the process, we also cause social divisions. This will come as no surprise to anyone who follows national politics or who has attended middle school. Your race, your gender, your nationality, and your religion all help determine whom you associate with and whom you steer clear of, whom you know and whom you don't, whom you like, whom you love, and perhaps — sadly — whom you hate. For better or for worse, social groups are an unavoidable feature of human life.

Psychologists like me have spent a lot of time studying social group membership, trying to figure out why people feel that they belong with some groups but not with others, and why they vilify people whom they perceive as belonging to other groups — that is, people they perceive as *other*. Decades of social psychology research on intergroup and interpersonal relations suggest that we just can't seem to turn off our "category detectors," which divide the world into *us* and *them*. It is simply human nature.

Yet something is missing from the study of social grouping — and from public discourse about tribalism in particular, and human nature in general. Researchers and many other people largely overlook a key factor that determines whether people find common ground: language. More precisely, I'm referring to the way you talk, which often means the accent you speak with. (Yes, you have an accent! Everyone does. It pops up every time you speak.) As the saying goes, it's not what you say, but *how you say it.*

Where we belong, whom we connect with, whom we love, and whom we hate: almost every aspect of social life is shaped by the way we speak. This is true in personal relationships: babies choose to approach people who talk in certain ways, and employers hire those whose spoken language fits their expectations. A similar dynamic is present across all levels of society. The way we speak plays a fundamental role in cultural and national life.

By dint of the way you speak, people think of you as a member of an in-group or an out-group, and it is incredibly hard to prevent this from happening. Convincingly faking an accent other than your own is extremely difficult. This is the paradox at the heart of human speech: we are linguistic geniuses and linguistic dunces all at once. The sensitive period of human language acquisition during infancy and early childhood is well known. Babies and young children are able to master language (or languages) with ease — taking on the native-sounding accent in whatever languages they hear. Yet as adults, we muddle through formal language classes with tremendous difficulty. Apart from the rare linguistic genius, most adults simply cannot replicate a non-native accent when they learn a new language.

Thus, when people hear the way you speak, they infer a lot about you (which may be right or wrong) and treat you accordingly. If you speak American English, some people might have a higher regard for you if you use what's often called "Standard American English" (think of the dialect you might hear on the news, which is generally heard in parts of the Northeast, the Midwest, and the West Coast — though these categories and geographical distinctions are imprecise). If, on the other hand, you don't or can't speak Standard American English, people might treat you poorly. Speaking a nonstandard dialect* can be stigmatizing. People who speak variants

---

* This book uses the terms "standard" and "nonstandard" because these terms are often used in the literature. This is not, however, meant to imply that "standard" should be interpreted as "better."

of Southern American, New York, or African American English can be subtly — or not so subtly — taught that their speech has less value. Likewise for British English. To my American ear, its multiple variants sound similar, yet a British person can instantly distinguish posh from cockney and the many shades of English spoken in different parts of the British Isles.

When people talk about voices from, say, the Southern United States, you may hear them refer to the "dialect" of Southern American English, as I just did. They may also refer to a Southern "accent." I'll use both terms in this book, in part because they're closely related; both refer to differences in the way that words sound. Different dialects of English are spoken with different pronunciations, or accents (in addition to having subtle differences in grammar and word choice). Likewise, when adults try to learn a completely new language, they take the sound structures of their native language with them to some degree; hence, they speak with what others hear as a foreign or non-native accent. This unshakable, easily detectable quality of accent is what gives it immense — if under-recognized — social power.

The thing is, it's not unreasonable to assume that you *can* deduce something about a person's background based on the sound of their speech. Because many linguistic patterns are so firmly established during childhood, accent forever betrays our origins. Try as we might to avoid it, when we speak, we are inadvertently telling the world who talked to us during our childhood. In some ways, language changes as our lives evolve — for instance, when we transition to adolescence or adulthood, when we move to a new place, when we join a new community, or when we develop new social desires and ambitions. In this sense, our language is constantly morphing throughout our lives. Nevertheless, a good deal of our speech — and hence, large swaths of our social identity — is baked in, showcasing our early upbringing, which is very difficult to escape.

For ages, humans have been using language in general, and accent specifically, as an important marker of identity — this was already the case when the Bible was being written. For example, the

Hebrew Bible contains a story about two tribes; one defeated the other in battle. To identify survivors of the defeated tribe, the victors performed an unusual ritual: they asked suspected survivors to say the word *shibboleth*, which in Hebrew means something along the lines of "ear of corn." Members of the enemy tribe were unable to pronounce the word correctly. In this way, the victors were able to identify, round up, and execute their remaining adversaries.

The story of *shibboleth* is a bloody reminder of how accent reveals native group membership. But less dramatic, yet significant, versions of this story play out every day, in encounters whose consequences we often fail to appreciate.

How you speak is, in a very real way, a window into who you are and how other people see you (perceptions that sometimes may be correct, and sometimes may be prejudiced and inaccurate). For too long, we have failed to grasp its importance and the impact of linguistic prejudice on our lives. With this book, I hope to change that.

My interest in the way language creates and divides social groups began when, as a newly minted college grad, I spent the summer of 2003 in Croatia. During that time, I also had the opportunity to travel to Serbia, Bosnia, and Slovenia. What I saw there changed the way I thought about human speech and the way language can reflect the past and shape the future.

In the 1990s a brutal civil war, characterized by interethnic conflict, had led to the breakup of Yugoslavia. In 2003, unresolved feelings related to the conflict still lingered. I got to know a Croatian woman who at age nine had been injured in the war. She was crossing the street when — *bam* — out of nowhere she was hit by a Serbian mortar shell. Fortunately, she survived. When I met her, she was a happy, productive adult, engaged to be married. But remnants of the conflict were still palpable: I could perceive it in the way that my friend reflected on her childhood, and I could hear it in the way that people spoke.

I signed up for an introductory language course, and the textbook that I purchased was called *Introduction to Serbo-Croatian*.

Yet I soon discovered that Serbo-Croatian was not a unitary language, as the book's title suggested. Croatian and Serbian were mutually intelligible — sure, people could speak to each other (though they used different written alphabets). But I was told that you shouldn't say "Serbo-Croatian" anymore. People said they spoke Croatian or Serbian. (Or Bosnian.) In the language class, the instructor often corrected us: "Don't say it like this — that's a Serbian way of speaking."

Even as an outsider, I quickly came to understand that the languages of the Balkans were not static entities. Serbian and Croatian were indeed diverging. Languages are dynamic, and they morph with the social lives of the people who speak them. When a group of people separates from another group, language follows suit. Likewise, when a group unites with neighbors, language changes. This is also true at the national level. The more that people of one nation feel united, and differentiated from their neighbors, the more their language changes to reflect this.

Returning to the United States, I realized that I didn't need to travel to the Balkans, or even venture outside my own country, to see how the way people speak unites or divides them. For instance, in the northern United States, where I grew up, people tend to think that their counterparts in the South speak in a homogeneous way — that is, with an accent that immediately brands them as Southerners. Yet I knew enough people from the South to know that there are many further divisions within the region's speech, and that you can tell a great deal about someone's background based on whether they speak, for example, Appalachian English, or English with a Georgian drawl, or Louisiana's Cajun English.

As a PhD student in psychology at Harvard, I started to study the psychological underpinnings of how speech can structure social life. I wanted to probe the origins of people's language identities. Where does it begin, this role that speech plays in uniting and dividing social groups? Thanks to extensive research in psychology and linguistics (which has confirmed something that many parents learn firsthand), we know that infants come into the world ready to learn language. But do babies also enter the world ready to prefer people who are in their own linguistic group?

Through a series of studies with infants and young children, my collaborators and I discovered that from the very beginning of life, humans appear to care about the social meaning of language. Right away, children seem to sense that differences in language demarcate different social groups — and they prefer people in their own group. As I quickly learned, language doesn't just serve as a marker of social divisions among people in the Balkans, or in the American South and North. Rather, it is a fundamental part of human nature. Even at this early stage in my research, I knew that the roots of language identity must run very deep.

Since then, as a professor of psychology at the University of Chicago (and for a few years at Cornell), I have done a lot more research concerning how much the way we speak matters to the social lives of children — and hence, the lives of the adults that children grow into. Children, I've observed, can care about how people sound more than how they look; for instance, in some studies I've seen that young children can evaluate how they feel about unfamiliar people based on spoken accent more than skin color. Children also start to pick up on society's messages about which ways of speaking are valued and which are stigmatized (which is similar to how they also come to pick up on messages about bias in other domains, such as race). In this way, they absorb society's biases and bigotry from a very young age. And often, biases based on language and race are intertwined. American society's linguistic prejudice against speakers of African American English is an insidious aspect of systemic racism.

My training is in psychology, yet to fully understand how language affects social life, I've had to immerse myself in a range of other fields, from linguistics to anthropology to law. This inquiry took me far from my academic comfort zone, but the more I discovered, the more I felt compelled to push forward on this intellectual journey. To my knowledge, no book has tied together all of the different academic disciplines that touch on language and its social function — a fact that is remarkable and unacceptable, considering the urgency of this issue in our time.

The way we speak shapes life in ways that we're only beginning to understand. It can make the difference between getting hired or being passed over for a job. It can be a tool for political oppression and a driver of social and economic marginalization. We may think that one accent sounds nicer or smarter, more polished or pristine; we may think that someone speaking in a certain way sounds taller or more attractive. Simply having an accent considered more prestigious or higher in status can grease the wheels of interactions with individuals and with public and private institutions; having what people perceive as the "wrong" kind of speech, conversely, can have the opposite effect. The law and the courts try to protect citizens from discrimination — yet without a thorough awareness of how much accent matters, they often fall short. Language also shapes how we think and process information. The language we happen to be speaking in — whether our native tongue or a different one — can influence our emotional experience and even the decisions we make on issues related to finances and even morality.

Language defines who we are, and where and how we fit into society. This matters for everyone — monolingual and bilingual people, native-accented and foreign-accented speakers, and anyone who is interested in educational policy or who is parenting a child. Understanding the social significance of how we speak matters in all realms of our personal, professional, and civic lives.

Knowledge is power. One of the goals of this book is to empower people who use language — which is to say, almost everyone. I want to help anyone who has moved to a new place and felt out of place, anyone heaving a sigh of relief when returning home and basking in the comfortable familiarity of a native tongue, anyone facing discrimination due to their accent or dialect, or anyone wanting to understand the implications of bilingualism for their children, grandchildren, students, or friends. By knowing more about the intricacy of language, we can better understand the power it has over us, and in turn use that power wisely when we interact with others.

We need this power not only as individuals but also as a society. Language is personal, yet people speaking together create families, groups, and nations. As social groups in the broadest sense, we create the educational and social policies that determine how much and what kind of power speech has over individuals. Debates over bilingual education and immigration are two familiar examples; linguistic discrimination in housing, employment, and our legal system receives less attention. If we had a better understanding and awareness of language's social power, this could be changed.

While writing this book, these issues grew even more relevant to me. I became a parent and began to see this research from a personal rather than a scientific perspective. I started to better appreciate the struggles parents face — wanting our children to experience kindness and appreciate diversity and thinking about the kind of world we want our children to live in and how their lives are touched by the language or languages they learn.

Around the time that I had my daughter, my colleagues and I made some new discoveries in our lab about the social benefits of being exposed to more than one language early in life. For example, we found that children who have had this experience are better able to consider the perspectives of others, which may lead to better communication and social connections. Needless to say, this research impacted the decisions I made for my daughter — but it also convinced me of the necessity of educating adults, not just children, about the importance of multilingualism in any society. And it energized me to share these findings with the world.

Language can divide us, but it can also bring us together. Experiencing different ways of speaking and thereby different perspectives can broaden our horizons and make us more creative, more intellectually expansive, and perhaps even kinder. My hope is that by revealing the power of speech in defining our lives, this book also will demonstrate how we can take this power in hand and use it for the good.

HOW YOU SAY IT

HOW YOU SPEAK IS
WHO YOU ARE

G rowing up in the Bible Belt in the 1980s, David Thorpe learned that homosexuality was a sin. He did not know anyone who was openly gay, nor did he understand gay identity in society. Going to college was liberating, and in this new, accepting environment, David was able to discover himself. Still, it took him until his sophomore year of college to get up the courage to come out.

But by the time he was in his forties, David felt dissatisfied with where he was in life and, in particular, mystified by his voice. When he listened to himself speak, he thought that he "sounded gay." But he was not sure why. When he thought back to his childhood, David didn't think that he sounded gay then. And what did that mean anyway, to sound gay? Was it sounding effeminate, or something else? Did he articulate his vowels oddly? Did his gay friends sound gay? Amid this swirl of questions, David knew one thing with certainty: he felt self-conscious about how he spoke.

So David, a filmmaker, turned his camera on himself. In the process, he uncovered something unexpected about his identity — and the origins and power of speech itself.

For his film project, which eventually became a documentary called *Do I Sound Gay?*, David interviewed friends from high school who knew him before he came out. They reported that he came home from college a changed person. It wasn't just his newfound sexual identity. Something about the way he spoke — about how his voice sounded — was different too. His speech had changed, along with his understanding of his sexual identity.

Speech and language experts Benjamin Munson and Ron Smyth talked to David about the changes in his speech that his friends had noticed. Contrary to the common stereotype, gay men do not tend to lisp; if anything, they are more likely to *hyperarticulate* their speech, meaning that their *s* sounds may be a little clearer, rather than muddled with a *th*. These effects are small (and certainly not all gay men speak the same way), but as the linguists have shown, some American gay men speak with vowel sounds that may be held slightly longer or are more clearly articulated.

So yes — after David came out, he really did begin "sounding gay" to others. But what caused that change? It couldn't be anything biological; after all, David's vocal tract was the same before and after his initial years in college. Linguists who have studied gay speech agree: although sexual identity, preferences, and behaviors may stem from a complex mix of biological and sociocultural origins (a topic of continued scientific research), gay and straight individuals have vocal tracts that are the same length. On average, their voices do not differ in overall pitch.

If biology does not explain the linguistic differences between gay and straight men's speech, it stands to reason that these disparities must be caused by social factors, rather than physical variations in the way that sound emerges from the body. And it is here that David's quest to understand his voice intersects with a revolution sweeping the fields of linguistics and social psychology: an explosion of research that is giving us a new understanding of the complex relationship between speech and social forces. In investigating the source of his discomfort with the way he spoke, David put his finger on a little known but hugely important aspect of human speech: the way you talk is a window into who you are.

YOUR LANGUAGE IS YOUR TRIBE

Dividing into social groups is a recurrent aspect of humanity. We humans are constantly organizing ourselves and others by nationality, race, gender, age, ethnicity, religion, politics, and even sports team affiliation. And whether these groups draw upon a deep sense of shared identity, or seem slightly arbitrary, our groups matter to us and to the people around us — a lot.

People define themselves by their social group affiliations; other people define them that way too. Social group membership determines whether and how people connect — or how they fail to find common ground. And our perceptions of each other's social groups have a huge impact on first impressions, which can have lasting consequences when people are asking themselves, for instance, "Whom should I hire?" or "Should I help this person in need?" or "Would I feel comfortable if my child married someone like this?"

Social psychologists have spent a lot of time studying social group membership — why we feel like we belong in one group instead of another, and how we judge others based on what group they are in. Our attention to people's social group identity seems to be both automatic and unconscious. Often researchers discuss gender, race, and age as primary grouping variables that jump out at us when we meet someone. In fact, if you meet someone new, you can't help but notice these characteristics.

To see what I mean, consider this classic example included in many introductory social psychology classes:

Imagine a woman who moves into a new apartment building. She is a little overwhelmed and frazzled, and is precariously carrying a bunch of boxes. As she walks in, her new neighbor opens the door for her and kindly says, "Hello, welcome to the building. Nice to meet you." She glances at the neighbor quickly and replies, "Hi, nice to meet you," then makes it to her new apartment without dropping her boxes.

Later on our new tenant goes to the mailroom, checking out her new mailbox. It dawns on her that she is nervous she won't recognize the same neighbor she just saw, hours earlier. She really can't remember what this person looked like at all. She imagines that if this were a legal trial, she certainly couldn't pick her out of a lineup.

Yet she does have some faint recollection of this person. She remembers that she was a middle-aged white woman. As to which particular middle-aged white woman? No clue.

Now, there are indeed research studies on how we remember a person's appearance, especially when picking someone out of a lineup. (News flash: People make errors! Errors are worse across racial lines!) But this isn't the point of my anecdote. Rather, it's meant to show that we tend to remember features that have nothing to do with people as individuals and have everything to do with their social group.

When we are busy or not paying careful attention, we typically forget a person's individual features but do recall gender or race. This is because we view our social world through the prism of *categories*. Dividing up a social environment in this way can be a really effective strategy: categories are easy to deal with quickly. They are simple heuristics that guide thinking and help us parse a busy, stimulating, overwhelming world.

Yet categories can also be pernicious, often leading us to make mistaken assumptions about the people we choose to place in certain boxes. We assume that people who share a social category (for example, the same gender, or the same race) are *like* each other, even when they are not. This type of overgeneralization — this assumption of similarity or of difference — is where a lot of stereotypes and prejudices come from.

One group you may not hear about much in popular discourse or think about much in private is your *linguistic* group. Yet it is paramount. Who we are as social actors and beings, where we fit in socially and where we do not, depends on our language. Language is a major vehicle and indicator of social identity.

Replay that "new neighbor" anecdote, but this time, add a detail or two about how the woman spoke. I would bet a lot of money that if that neighbor spoke with a British accent or a non-native accent and said "Hello, welcome to the building. Nice to meet you," the overloaded woman moving in would remember this too. She would recall that she met a nice middle-aged white woman with a foreign accent. And nevertheless she would still not be able to recognize that woman's face in a lineup.

Think about all the people you know, and all the people you feel close to. They probably speak your language, right? The answer seems obvious. How would you communicate if they didn't? But let's dig a little deeper. Do these people not just speak your language but also sound *like you* in a broader way? Perhaps you grew up in the same region and have a similar accent. Perhaps you say *soda* and not *pop*. Perhaps you round your *o*'s in a similar way. Perhaps when watching TV, you find the same accents funny. If you are a native speaker of English, most likely the way you talk with your close friends and family who are also English speakers converges at a very subtle level. You probably speak English in the *same way*.

My (white, highly educated) friend Mike recently provided me with a great bit of anecdotal evidence about this phenomenon. He grew up in Texas, in a cosmopolitan area, with parents who were transplants from the Northeast. Describing his childhood, he reports being surrounded by people who denied they were "from Texas" in any real sense — they were all from *somewhere else,* just currently living in Dallas. Mike himself does not have a pronounced Texan accent, to my ear at least. He now lives in New York City and has an eclectic and racially diverse mix of friends. Staunchly progressive, he is someone who takes living an inclusive social life seriously.

But Mike's friends all sound just like he does. If you heard a recording of them, they would all sound like New Yorkers. And they would all sound like posh and educated New Yorkers too. You probably would not be able to guess that Mike's friends have different geographic and racial backgrounds — and just hearing them talk, you would not be able to pick out who was white, Asian, Latinx, or Black. These individuals are part of a common social circle, and that circle shares a common language, which they speak with a common dialect.

When I pointed this out to Mike, he was genuinely befuddled. Although he values diversity, he had never considered that *linguistic* diversity might be a category. To him, diversity was all about race, or perhaps gender and religion too. He had never thought about the value or challenges of associating with people who spoke differently from him. It had just never come up.

Language can be a critical marker of who we are and who our friends are — yet it can fly beneath the radar. Like Mike, many people do not realize how the way they sound is critical to their social lives.

The way you speak can signal who you are and who your group is in a way that can transcend all other categories. But as David Thorpe discovered, speech isn't static. It morphs as people change, and it can also be aspirational. How you sound can signal both who you are and who you want to be — where you came from, and also where you are going.

Bill Labov, a famous sociolinguist, has conducted seminal research that shows the subtle ways in which speech can signal and reflect your social group. Among other things, he has demonstrated that people can infer details about who someone is — and maybe even who they want to be — by how they sound. They can also hear specific vocal clues providing insight into someone's identity.

Imagine a seemingly homogeneous large group of people — say, all the English speakers in New York City. Do they all sound alike? Not at all. Some might speak with a foreign accent, revealing that English is not their native tongue; others might project the characteristic sound of Brooklyn or Long Island; still others might use a mix of languages or a dialect such as Spanglish. Laypeople in a place like the Big Apple intuitively know that a random sampling of people there will be full of linguistic diversity, but as a linguist, Labov can exactly define these differences in speech and explain what they mean.

Labov's analyses of people's speech — especially their vowels and *r*'s, which tend to show characteristic patterns of variance — lead to the conclusion that people sound like the groups they inhabit as their own. Seemingly random variation in the roundness of vowels, in the length of *r*'s, turns out to not be random at all. Rather, it reflects the social forces that guide people's lives, their friendships, and their social desires.

Even seemingly subtle linguistic variations map quite reliably onto people's class, religion, and ethnicity, revealing a surprising key to their identity. People's voices are both a clue to who they are and to their innermost desires about who they want to be. Labov demonstrated this with astounding clarity in a linguistics study set quite close to New York, geographically speaking. Socially speaking, however, it was worlds apart: Martha's Vineyard.

You might think of Martha's Vineyard as host to ritzy summer get-togethers for the liberal elite. But it was also the site of seminal linguistics studies from the 1960s. At the time, Martha's Vineyard had a fishing community, real "up-island Vineyarders" who did not always relish it when their island swelled with summer guests. Labov went to the island and talked to these people. He didn't ask about their language directly. Instead, he made small talk about unrelated topics, and in doing so he quietly studied people's diphthongs — sliding vowels, or two vowel sounds quickly combined to form a single utterance (as in *found* or *fight*), which vary somewhat across speakers.

Modern New Englanders say the vowel made by the *ou* in *house* as you may hear it in your own head — starting in the back of the mouth, like that *a* in *flat*, and then moving to the front, like the *oo* sound in *caboose*. Or the *i* in *fight*, which quickly moves from the back to the front of the mouth as well. When you pronounce diphthongs, your tongue moves across your mouth; you start with one sound that then morphs into another. Labov found, however, that some of the local Vineyard community would begin these diphthongs with a vowel produced more centrally in the mouth (rather than in the back), like the *u* in *cut*. *Fight* became something more like *fueet* (said quickly). This centralizing of the vowel space was the classic, older Vineyard way of talking.

Crucially, Labov found, not all people on the Vineyard spoke with exactly the same vowel space. Some older people centralized their vowels — but strangely enough, they weren't the Vineyarders who centralized the most. Many older adults had dropped this pattern and sounded more like typical modern New Englanders, whose English does not have this particular vowel feature.

Instead, it turned out that young people were more likely to cling to the linguistic past. Young men who had a strong sense of identity as Vineyard fishermen were the ones most likely to centralize their vowels. One interpretation is that they wanted to hold on to this distinctive community and their sense of being a part of it — and to push back against the rampant tourism that was changing their hometown. Their language was serving as an outward signal of their deeper social desires.

BURNOUTS AND VALLEY GIRLS

Speech delineates our chosen social groups — who we identify with and who we want to be. Someone's language can shift and change over the course of a lifespan, reflecting the evolving social self. It can reflect our aspirations, since sometimes, when people want to be different, they change the way they speak. Thus, for anyone who attended middle school, it should come as no surprise that these shifts in language are particularly noticeable among adolescents, whose evolving social identities engender continuous, and dynamic, changes in speech.

Adolescents tend to use slang, or vernacular language, rather than the standard language that is mainstream in their community. Penelope Eckert, a sociolinguist at Stanford, calls adolescents "linguistic movers and shakers" in part for this reason, and it's not hard to see why. Most adolescents are searching out their place in the social world while also rebelling against the old guard. They are defining and creating their own social lives on their own terms — and this rebellious spirit may be part of the reason why adults often don't like the words adolescents choose to use.

In his book *The Sense of Style*, Steven Pinker adeptly captures — and skewers — adults' inclination to lambaste teenage speech. "As people age," he observes, "they confuse changes in themselves with changes in the world, and changes in the world with moral decline — the illusion of the good old days. And so every generation believes that the kids today are degrading the language and taking civilization down with it." Older adults, he notes, have objected to younger people's use of English since at least the invention of the printing press, although "moral panic about the decline of writing may be as old as writing itself."

Adolescents' ways of speaking might not make their elders happy, but as Pinker knows, this linguistic rebelliousness is a fact of life. Those young people — with their verbal trailblazing — are unstoppable. Youth want to identify as their own group, and in order to do that, they must create new language to mark a new social identity.

And really, who can blame them? We can all remember the heightened importance of social groups during adolescence, and if any readers forget, or just are feeling nostalgic, I recommend reviewing Tina Fey's *Mean Girls*. (Unsurprising confession from an academic: I was never cool enough to be a "plastic.") In part because of the newness and intensity of the social pressures they are facing, young people care a great deal about social affiliation — which helps explain why their language morphs as easily as it does.

Eckert, the Stanford sociolinguist, conducted an ethnographic study in an American high school in the suburbs of Detroit in the 1980s. She found that you could tell who was who by the way they spoke. In the high school she studied, she identified two major groups that competed for status — what the students there called the "jocks" and the "burnouts." The jocks were generally oriented toward school and extracurricular activities. They were the "good" kids and sometimes teachers' pets. The burnouts didn't like school.

Eckert noted that the jocks and the burnouts competed for legitimacy. They wore different clothes, listened to different music, and shared a mutual dislike, even an open hostility. They also *sounded* different.

Tracking phonological variables in the teenagers' speech — subtle twists in vowel sounds signaling different forms of the vernacular — Eckert showed that the jocks and the burnouts tended to speak in distinct ways. For instance, do you say *lunch* like *lunch* or like *launch*, pronouncing the vowel farther back in your mouth? The use of these vowels varied based on group affiliation (burnouts were more likely to use *launch;* jocks were more likely to say *lunch*).

Interestingly, Eckert also found that the most relevant factor in predicting the way the kids spoke was their current social group identity, an expression of where they were going rather than where they came from. Whether their vowels sounded jock-ish or burnout-ish reflected their present group, not the socioeconomic status of their parents. Adolescence is a time of transition, and as young people find their path and their group, their language morphs into slightly different formats. Girls, Eckert observed, were the leaders in these vocal transformations — a gender difference that has been found repeatedly in more recent languages shifts too.

"Jocks" and "burnouts" are not the only adolescents who shift their speech to match their social group. Adolescents from all backgrounds and places do the same. So it should come as no surprise that each new generation is, in terms of its speech at least (and often in terms of many cultural variables), different from the one that preceded it.

Among other examples of language changes across generations are upspeak and vocal fry. You may be familiar with them; both are hallmarks of recent generations' speech. Adolescents (and often adolescent women) drove these developments — and both ex-

emplify the ever-changing connection between language and social groups.

If you are from my generation or thereabouts (born in 1981, I'm
on the cusp between Generation X and millennials), watch the
movie *Clueless* to reexperience your high school exposure to upspeak. It's that Valley girl kind of talk — you end a sentence as if it's
a question. (And since it is most common among younger women,
it may unfortunately be interpreted as a lack of certainty.)

For instance, Claire Danes was one of my generation's cultural
icons. Immediately before writing this sentence, I rewatched a clip
of Danes being interviewed by Jared Leto, her co-actor and onscreen crush in *My So-Called Life*, in 1995. He says, "So you've been
doing what, like six or seven or ten movies?" She coyly responds, "A
few?" Danes makes her answer sound like a question. As an adult,
playing a hard-charging CIA officer on *Homeland*, she has apparently kicked this vocal habit.

As a member of the generation that contributed to creating it,
I'm conflicted in my own views about upspeak. Since I was a teenager in the 1990s, many of my social role models used it, and thus
I find that I am prone to upspeak myself — even if I don't necessarily want to be. Now, I'll note that no way of speaking is inherently *good* or *bad*. Language reflects human social life, and there is
no right or wrong way for language to evolve. Thus, based on that
logic, upspeak should not bother me. Nevertheless, I see how it can
project a false sense of insecurity about what you are saying; also,
older adults deride it. Hence my conflicted feelings when I find myself using upspeak.

I spoke with Mahzarin Banaji, an expert on implicit attitudes,
about how easy it is for older adults to negatively evaluate upspeak. She immediately provided an example. A student stopped
in during her office hours to question a finding that the professor
had presented in lecture. The student made this comment sounding like a Valley girl, and Banaji suggested that the student rethink her idea. The student then left the office and made it as far
as the elevator when a research assistant sitting in the adjoining

room, who had overheard the conversation, suggested to Banaji that there was merit to the student's idea. Realizing her own bias and her responsibility to correct it, Banaji followed the student, asked her to repeat herself, and ultimately invited her to join her research laboratory group. Banaji reflected on her initial failure to perceive the student's keenly insightful comment; she had erroneously judged the student based on how she sounded — not on what she was saying.

Another example of the changing landscape of youthful speech — which older adults similarly deride — is vocal fry. It is that low-sounding, creaky, gravelly, back-in-the-throat trailing off of vowels. Imagine Kim Kardashian or Britney Spears saying "soo cuuute." Millennial women do this a lot. (Men do it too — but research suggests that listeners recognize it more when women do it.) Unsurprisingly, many older adults don't like the sound, and some say that using vocal fry may undermine professional success.

Yet the interesting thing about vocal fry is that to younger women, it doesn't sound bad. When I ask my undergraduate students their opinion, they say it sounds normal, perhaps even educated. Someone who trails off her sentences in a growly fashion sounds to them like a person who is going to succeed professionally when she graduates from college. A person who is going somewhere. Once a way of rebelling against the linguistic establishment, vocal fry seems to have joined its ranks — at least as far as younger listeners are concerned.

PEERS VS. PARENTS

A mysterious aspect of language learning is how immigrant children grow up to sound like other kids rather than like their parents. Think of children of immigrants growing up in the United States (or whichever nation you live in). And think of their parents — coming to a new country despite the difficulties they surely will face, so that their children can have a better life. A child of immigrants in the United States may have years of exposure to their parents' non-native accent in English. Yet what happens when that child goes to school? Poof! They end up speaking American English just like any other kid in the local community.

The Netflix comedy *Master of None* aptly captures this dynamic between a child and his immigrant parents. The parents sacrificed their familiar language and culture so their children would have a better life. And what do they get for their troubles? They are scared to answer the phone because they think no one will understand them. And who are their children? Their kids are American. They act American and they speak English with an American accent. They are embarrassed by their parents' funny accents.

My former college roommate Joey can surely relate. She was born in Hong Kong and moved to suburban Chicago as a toddler. When she talked to her mom, often Joey would speak in English and her mom would talk in Chinese. In college Joey took a Chinese class for "heritage" speakers — kids who learned Chinese as a child but mainly spoke English. She and the other students were really good at discussing basic topics such as how to brush their teeth; they had difficulty with expressing the intellectual and emotional nuances of adult life. Joey would never really master the fine points of her mother's language; today she still mainly speaks English when interacting with her mother.

The truth is that when kids are learning to speak, they are not just learning a language — they are also learning their cultural group. Joey had turned into an American athlete and a bit of a party girl. Though she was born in Hong Kong, linguistically and culturally she was American through and through — which is understandable, given that she has lived in the United States from a very young age. All children want to fit in. And what better way to do so than to talk like the other kids?

In my psychology lab, I've studied how young children like Joey are drawn to peers who speak with a native American accent. My former graduate student Jasmine DeJesus and I wanted to learn more about bilingual and bicultural children's thinking about the different languages and accents in their environment. We predicted that a kid like Joey, who spoke one language with her parents at home and English with her friends at school, would like both languages well enough. But what might she not like? Probably English spoken with a non-native accent (even if her immigrant parents spoke English in this way). Kids want to fit in. And if they spoke English with a non-native accent, it would make them feel different from their friends. As it turned out, Jasmine and I were right.

In one study, we tested a group of Korean American families to see how they felt about different languages and accents. The parents in our sample spoke English, but they were much more comfortable in Korean, and culturally, they still felt Korean; they had Korean communities, liked to eat Korean food, and wanted to pass on their native tongue to their children, all of whom were around kindergarten age at the time. And for all intents and purposes, the parents were succeeding at passing on Korean: their children were almost all bilingual in both Korean and English; they spoke English at school and Korean at home.

In our study, children were presented with pairs of unfamiliar people who spoke English with an American accent, Korean, or English with a Korean accent, and then we simply asked them to select whom they liked more. Kids reported that they equally liked new people who spoke in English or Korean. Children spoke both languages and liked new people from either of their two cultural groups. But they didn't like new people who spoke to them in Korean-accented English. Even though that accent was highly familiar to them via exposure from their parents, the kids did not seem to like new people who spoke English with a Korean accent. Kids liked new people who spoke English in the same way that their peers, rather than their parents, did.

Later, we ran the same study with French-English bilingual children and found the same pattern of results — they liked both English and French, but not French-accented English. (And although we did not test it in these particular studies, the French American children would have presumably similarly disliked American-accented French, and the Korean American children would have disliked American-accented Korean.)

These are just two studies, of course, but they reflect a broader pattern of findings: children want to speak in the accent that other children in their local community have. All over the world, children of immigrants typically grow up to sound like their peers, rather than their parents, and this basic social push to prefer new people with a native, local accent may in turn feed into the way that children learn. Language learning is not just about what you hear (since, for instance, Korean American kids had plenty of experiences hearing Korean-accented English) — it is also about what you are socially drawn to. And since language can define identity, kids who want to fit in socially intuit that they need to speak the way that the other kids speak: in the native accent of the local community.

WHO'S AFRAID OF RBG?

The desire to fit in doesn't end with childhood or adolescence. Adults want to fit in too, of course, and our speech reflects even very subtle social bonds, or our yearning for them. When you are in a room with someone else — and especially if you like the person — your voices merge just a bit. You start to speak the same way.

This sort of social mirroring behavior isn't limited to speech. Imagine being on a blind date. You and the other person hit it off well. Your body posture might start to align. Maybe one of you crosses your legs and then the other does too. Or one of you touches your own face and the other — without realizing it — follows suit.

Speech works the same way. When two people come together, and especially when they like each other, they start to sound alike. Linguists have measured subtleties in people's speech, finding that people's voices change to match that of the person they are talking to — when they like them. Talking the same is a measure of social bonding, another oft-unrecognized way that language telegraphs not just who we were, but also who we would like to be.

One subtle feature of your voice that might change according to social circumstance is what linguists call voice onset timing (or VOT) — the tiny pause that occurs between a particular kind of consonant and the vowel that follows it. Say *patio*, for instance, but separate the *p* from the *atio*. You'll hear the *p* come out as a brief burst of air; the *atio* begins as your vocal folds vibrate to make the *a* sound. Put the *p* and the *atio* back together, and you may not notice this gap. But pull them apart ever so slightly, and you'll find that little space between them, with a tiny noisy burst of air. Certain consonants (such as *p*, *t*, and *k*) create this brief "stop" before the vowel sound.

In one study, linguists had people say a bunch of words that have this VOT feature — words like *picky* and *peck*. Next, the participants heard another person tell a story about a blind date; this person said the same words, but the researchers artificially manipulated the speech to allow for just a little extra space between the consonant and the vowel, to make extra-long VOTs. Then the test subjects were asked to say all the same words again. The researchers wanted to see if they would change their speech to match what they just heard. Would they now make slightly longer VOTs, without realizing it?

The researchers found that participants did indeed change their speech to match the other person's — but the participants who said they liked the person who was speaking did it more than the participants who did not like the speaker. Social affinity led people to copy the narrator's increased VOTs, without any knowledge that they were doing so.

This connection between social liking and speech shifting extends beyond one-on-one interactions. How you think about whole groups of speakers also can impact how much you might copy someone's voice. Take the example of English spoken in New Zealand versus that in Australia. They sound very similar — my American ear would have a tough time telling them apart. Yet there are some slight but clear differences in vowel pronunciation that separate Kiwis from Aussies. Fascinatingly, people's private attitudes toward whole groups of people can be subtly observable in their speech, by means of the way in which they mimic others.

A bunch of New Zealanders played a language game similar to the one just described — they said some words, they heard an Australian say them, and then said those words again. The question was whether their vowels would shift to sound ever so slightly more Australian than before. Overall, people's vowels did shift a little bit. But who did it the most? The people who also had implicit pro-Australian attitudes. Though they may not admit it while at a rugby match, some New Zealanders nevertheless had positive attitudes toward Australians, and those were the people whose speech changed to match the Australian vowels.

People in general change their speech to match that of people they like. Recently, linguists asked whether some people do this more than others. For instance, I have an American friend who is especially open to others. She exudes warmth and initiates conversations with cab drivers and fellow passengers on airplanes. And she says that her voice changes to match her surroundings. When in Britain, she starts to sound British.

Linguists have recently discovered that people who are prone to matching their speech to others share some key personality traits. Specifically, on a personality test they tend to score high on openness — being broad-minded and receptive to new experiences. These people change their voices the most to match others'.

To be sure, personality traits may not be the only explanation for mirroring someone else's speech. One group of people is often criticized for imitating a given audience's way of speaking: politicians. If you look up montages of Hillary Clinton or Barack Obama over the years, giving public addresses in different contexts, you will detect different accents emerging — sounding more Northern or Southern, sounding more stereotypically Black or white. The internet is lousy with people mocking these transitions — mash-ups on YouTube with facetious comments: "It's a miracle! A couple of hours

in Alabama can turn an Illinois senator into a Southern gent ...
Obama was not alone. Hillary Clinton also developed a Madonna-
esque transformation of dialect." Similar critiques have been lev-
eled at George W. Bush's degree of "Texas" accent. This linguistic
sway is often interpreted as political maneuvering — sly politicians
trying to gain favor with the local crowd by copying their language.

Such shifts in speech may be purposeful to a degree, but research suggests that mostly it is unintentional and unconscious.
And it may even reveal something favorable about the politicians
or their personalities: if Clinton sounds more Southern while
speaking in Arkansas and more Northern when in New York, her
voice is likely revealing a legitimate feeling of connection with and
affinity for the community she is currently facing. Changes in politicians' voices are not necessarily manipulative, and like anyone
else, these politicians may be responding to particular interlocu-
tors in a particular setting.

Beyond the typical moment-to-moment changes, people's language can alter subtly and consistently over the course of the lifespan, reflecting the social world they are familiar with and, even
more likely, the social world that they aspire to. One famous example comes from none other than the Notorious RBG: Supreme
Court Justice Ruth Bader Ginsburg.

The past half-century of Justice Ginsburg's speech was recently
analyzed by linguists, and the findings are pretty fascinating. But
to understand their significance, you need to know a little bit about
Justice Ginsburg herself.

Ruth Bader was born in 1933 in Brooklyn to a lower-middle-
class family, and as a Jewish girl she faced both anti-Semitism and
sexism. Her life might not have turned out the way it did had she
not grown up with a mother who took her to the library instead
of teaching her to cook, believing that a woman's place was in getting an education and not in the kitchen. Bader went to Cornell
and then Harvard Law School (one of nine women in a class of five
hundred) and became an attorney. She argued before the US Supreme Court, contributing to the very small percentage of argu-

ments made there by women at the time. She made these presenta-
tions, needless to say, to an all-male group of justices. To describe
the experience as tough is surely an understatement, but it apparently sparked something in the young Ruth Bader. In an interview
many years later, she was asked if feelings of "outsiderness" motivated her professional success, and she concurred: "You've got to be
sure you were better than everyone else."

Recently, a group of linguists collected and studied Supreme
Court recordings that featured Justice Ginsburg's voice. They came
from two distinct eras — "Lawyer Ginsburg" from the 1970s, when
she was a trial lawyer living in New York City and making arguments related to six different cases before the highest court, and
"Justice Ginsburg" from 1993 to 2012, during her years on the Supreme Court.

The researchers analyzed two potential features of Ginsburg's
speech that are seen as "typically Brooklyn." First, they observed
whether she dropped the r's at the end of words. (Think of Marissa
Tomei yelling at Joe Pesci in *My Cousin Vinny* to "Imagine you're a
deer," pronouncing the final word as "dee-ah." Or recall that parody
song from the 1960s: "Hello Muddah, hello Fadduh / Here I am
at Camp Granada . . ."). Second, the researchers looked at whether
Ginsburg's speech displayed "thought vowel" raising, a second common feature of New York vernacular. Think of Mike Myers's "caw-
fee tawk" on *Saturday Night Live*. Many New Yorkers are likely to
say the word *caught* in a way that sounds like *cawht* — that's the
"thought vowel." (Classically Brooklyn, Bernie Sanders's speech is
easily identified by linguists — or anyone else — as displaying both
vocal features mentioned here.)

The researchers' findings tell a poignant story about the evolution of Ginsburg's speech. In the first batch of "Lawyer Ginsburg"
recordings, her r's are almost completely enunciated. In one example from 1974 she discusses the law's differential treatment of
men and women, and how in Florida law a woman's husband was
regarded as "her guardian, her superior, not her peer." *Peer* ends
in a perfectly discernible r. In recordings from thirty years later,

Ginsburg sounds distinctly more "New Yorker" than she did in the 1970s. In 2012, when she says *father* and *survivor*, the *r* sound trails off a bit. The pronunciation is not as in-your-face as Marissa Tomei's "dee-ah," but it's there nonetheless, a subtle deletion of the final *r* sound that had been spoken during her younger days.

Why might Ginsburg's accent have fluctuated like this? It isn't that the general population's accent is changing in this direction — if anything, people (even those born and raised in New York) are relatively more likely nowadays to keep the *r* intact and to keep "thought vowels" unraised. And Ginsburg had been living in Washington, D.C., since 1980 (as a circuit court judge before President Bill Clinton appointed her to the Supreme Court, in 1993), where these vocal features aren't as common. Yet there they were, her former New York vocal features, coming through in her years as a justice.

The linguists who conducted this study hypothesize that as a young female lawyer, Ginsburg very understandably had a lot to prove. She may have carefully monitored her accent in an effort to sound as neutral as possible. She would not be the first to put on a "polished" accent — trying to present speech that matches a certain standard.

This jells with other research about how people modulate their accent to fit into new or uncomfortable social situations. A prime example is the important studies conducted by the sociolinguist Bill Labov. Coincidentally, his focus was New York City speech in the 1960s. Labov found that department store workers changed the way they said "fourth floor," inserting the *r*'s more clearly in "fancier" stores, such as Saks Fifth Avenue (as opposed to Macy's or, considered even less classy, Kleins). They would also make this adjustment when they felt that someone might not understand the dropped *r*. As Labov wrote, "In general, New Yorkers show a strong dislike for the sound of New York City speech. Most have tried to change their speech in one way or another, and would be sincerely complimented to be told that they do not sound like New Yorkers."

But not all New Yorkers disliked their way of speaking English as much as others. In different studies, Labov surveyed the speech of four roughly defined economic classes of New Yorkers; he categorized them as Lower Class, Working Class, Lower Middle Class, and Upper Middle Class. Those who felt the most insecure about their speech — who were most sensitive to the differences between "correct" and "incorrect" speech — weren't the people at the very high or very low end of the socioeconomic distribution. Instead, it was the Lower Middle Class — people just like Ginsburg's family, somewhat in the middle — who were most clearly sensitive to the status distinctions in speech. Like Ginsburg, in more formal contexts they tended to keep their *r*'s — even more so than individuals of the Upper Middle Class. Yet despite this effort, in their everyday speech, people of the Lower Middle Class didn't quite produce the higher-status vocal features that they valued; they did so only in formal contexts, when they felt they were being evaluated. This behavior suggests insecurity about how their speech, and the level of sophistication it might indicate, might be judged by others.

As a Supreme Court justice, Ginsburg found the voice of her youth. In these later years, her *r*'s dropped off more across the board, to some extent. The data on her "thought vowel" raising ("caw-fee" for *coffee* and "tawk" for *talk*) show a pretty fascinating pattern, statistically speaking: the pronunciations of the justice years were qualitatively different from those of the lawyer years. *Time* magazine captured this effect in the title and subtitle of an article: "How Ruth Bader Ginsburg Found Her Voice: A New Study of the Supreme Court Justice's Accent Says Something About the Way We All Talk." To say that Ginsburg found her voice implies that she found herself. By speaking comfortably in the accent of her youth, she was revealing her comfort with herself.

Ginsburg is not the only public figure whose speech has been dissected by curious linguists; other studies have found similar shifts in language that signal meaningful social changes related to a person's identity and aspirations. For example, linguists have turned their attention to British royalty and analyzed Elizabeth II's speech, decoding subtle differences in the pronunciation of vowels in her Christmas messages broadcasted from the early 1950s to the late 1980s, a period of more than thirty years. Her fancy, upper-crust "received pronunciation" evolved over the decades, becoming an accent that reflects more elements of middle-class speech. According to the *Telegraph*, in an article titled "Blimey, What Became of the Queen's English?," "In 1952 the Queen might have given a corgi a 'pet' on the head. Today her dogs receive a 'pat.' Similarly the 'grindsman' who mows the lawns of Buckingham Palace has become a 'groundsman.'" The title of an article in the magazine *Nature* summed up this phenomenon bluntly: "The Queen's English Dethroned."

When the linguists analyzed Elizabeth II's vowels in particular, they found changes over time. Vowel sounds thought to be not particularly classy—more like the speech of average younger people—were now emerging from the queen's lips. Over these decades, the boundaries of social class in the United Kingdom had become somewhat less strict, a development reflected in the queen's voice. These changes in speech, whether conscious or not, suggest a sense of openness. They show the queen embracing a new era, in which people from different walks of life may speak in a similar way.

REMEMBERING IN RUSSIAN

In the cases discussed so far, we've looked at how speech can serve as a bellwether of shifting social identity, as people join new social groups or take on new professional roles. But what happens when a person is raised speaking two languages—and thus may have two coexisting social identities to begin with? Does one of these ways of speaking, and its attendant social identity, dominate? Or are speech and identity more fluid? Strangely, the answer to both questions is yes.

Many people—a majority of people in the world, it would seem—speak more than one language. And it turns out that bilingual people can feel very different when communicating in one or the other of their two languages — as if they have two versions of a self. Studies of bilingual people can profoundly deepen our understanding of how a fundamental sense of self — not just our social connections but also our most foundational memories — are tied up in language.

The psychologist Sayuri Hayakawa was a new graduate student at the University of Chicago Department of Psychology, poised to start her research on language and decision making, when I began as a new assistant professor in the same department. Sayuri is half Japanese and half white American. Her interest in how people think in their two different languages blossomed as a result of her personal experience navigating two languages and cultures throughout her childhood. Sayuri recalls that since she was a small child, she felt tremendously different when using each language. She says that when she moves between English and Japanese, it's like flipping a switch. It's not just her language that changes — it's her sense of identity, her feelings of self-assuredness, and her connections with others. Sitting at a table in my office, she demonstrated how her entire posture could quickly shift when she spoke English or Japanese: the way she made eye contact, the way she held her hands, and the way she felt the expressions that passed over her face. She described how her *personality* feels different, as do her emotions. While we conducted our conversation in American English, she looked me in the eye, shoulders back, self-assured. Then she showed me how, when speaking Japanese, she would look down, demure, with a softer expression. The way she felt and the way she expressed herself to others — the basic format of her social interaction — would differ, depending on which language she was speaking.

Research helps explain Sayuri's perception that her experiences of emotion are somehow influenced by a particular language. For some time, the field of psychology defined emotional states, and the expression of them, as basic, meaning that they are universally produced, experienced, and recognized. Researchers such as the psychologist Paul Ekman identified a "basic" set of emotions — happiness, fear, disgust, anger, surprise, and sadness. Ekman could present photos of American facial expressions to people all over the world, and the emotions they expressed were easily recognized. If you are happy in the United States, you are happy in Japan, Brazil, Argentina, or presumably any other place. This emotional state can be felt, recognized, and discussed anywhere, in any language. Babies can understand the feeling and express it — as can blind people, whose physical expressions of emotion are just the same as those of sighted people, though many blind people have never visually observed such displays.

Yet despite the remarkable similarity of emotional expression across cultures, it turns out that some important differences also exist. It seems that cultures vary slightly in the setting of emotional boundaries and the intensity of emotional expression — the way people connect to one another and recognize what they are feeling. These registers of emotion may shift when a person switches from one language to another, just as Sayuri sensed they do. Emotional experience and the behaviors associated with it are entangled with culture and language; your emotions may feel different and show up differently in your gestures and overall demeanor, based on the language you are currently speaking. This has come to be known as the "emotional dialect" theory of emotion.

According to this theory, emotions — just like linguistic dialects — vary slightly across different groups of people. You learn certain emotional signals from your community, typically from speakers of your own language. The way emotion is expressed by your in-group may be a tiny bit easier to parse. The basic ability to detect and decode other people's emotions — to connect with them and know how they are feeling — varies based on language. People who speak the same way are likely to emote the same way. And for bilingual people like Sayuri, the way emotional connections are made and experienced will reflect the language being spoken in a given context.

Like emotion, memory can be tied up in language. This was demonstrated by a famous study in which people who spoke both Russian and English were given tests about their memories — one test in Russian and a separate one in English. Consistently, they remembered different things on the two tests. When questions were posed in English, the test subjects were more likely to recall memories related to their lives as English speakers. Questions in Russian brought up recollections of events that involved speaking Russian, learning in Russian, feeling Russian.

While memories often have to do with people, places, and events outside yourself, they also include more abstract *autobiographical* memories, reflecting whom you want to be and how you see yourself as an actor in your social world. Memories give you a general sense of who you are, as a person with a past. Are you a good person? Conscientious or carefree? Loyal to your family? Experiences that make you feel like *you* are part of your autobiographical memory, which is fundamental to your sense of self. For bilingual people, this sense of self, and the autobiographical memories associated with it, also seems to be deeply enmeshed with language.

It's well accepted that the sense of self is shaped, at least in part, by culture. On average, people in the United States are likely to have a fairly independent sense of self; they see themselves as autonomous and unique. In contrast, people in China often have more of an interdependent sense of self; they think of themselves as part of a group, one node in a network of relationships rather than a "lone self" making their own choices. These differences in identity — people as individuals in the West and as part of a grander whole in the East — have been well documented by cultural psychologists. Two common sayings showcase the difference: "the squeaky wheel gets the grease" and "the nail that sticks out gets hammered down."

It's easy to imagine how a lifetime of memories and experiences amassed in a particular culture might affect how someone sees herself. But psychologists have found that the varying senses of self and related memories are tied up in language. For example, one experiment found that adolescents bilingual in Chinese and English, when speaking in one or the other language, espoused different views of who they are and whom they want to be; they reconstruct relevant memories based on language. When speaking in English, they feel more independent, more self-focused; they remember events that highlight their individuality. They talk about memories of times when they made their own plans, rather than having to ask their parents for guidance. When speaking in Chinese, they talk more about themselves as connected to others. When asked to describe, in Chinese, who they are, they are more likely to state that they are someone's sister, for instance, rather than report their own personality traits or interests (such as "I'm honest" or "I'm an artist"). The kinds of memories they bring up differ too. Even the way that people frame their recollections — starting sentences with the words "We did this" rather than "I did this" — varies according to the language being spoken. Two senses of self, about who they were — and different kinds of memory — are encapsulated in the bilingual adolescents' two languages.

Recently, a student I know, Paola, told me about her experience of learning — very quickly! — a new language, a new identity, a new emotional self, and a new set of memories. Paola's family moved to the United States from Colombia when she was six years old.

Paola cried the whole first week of first grade in an English-speaking classroom. She sobbed at her desk at school and wept at home, feeling alone and scared. The second week she whimpered but started to smile too. After that, she was completely fine. She began to understand more — the gist of things at first, and then more and more detail. Very soon, full sentences in English started to emerge. By the end of the year, she would translate things to her parents that they did not understand. Speaking to Paola today, you would never guess that her first language was not English unless she told you.

Telling this story, Paola noted that she does not actually have any recollection of specific events during this transitional time. She doesn't remember her weeks of tears, or her first few months in the United States, as she gradually learned to communicate with new friends. She remembers snippets of her early childhood in Colombia. She next recalls being a happy, acculturated American grade-schooler, speaking English and helping translate for her parents. It is as though while her identity was changing, her mental computer was rewriting its code; her memory didn't save the file for this transitional period in her life. Her sense of self and identity paused, waiting as her new language developed.

Paola's language and social world shifted dramatically when she moved to a new country. Yet something major is missing from this narrative — the importance and permanence of native tongues. Paola was able to learn English so well because she moved to the United States when she was young. Her mother, in contrast, never felt that she mastered English fully. She forever felt more comfortable in Spanish and wondered whether she really belonged when she spoke in English.

The studies that show linguistic impacts on memory and emotions, along with anecdotal evidence like Paola's and her mother's experiences in learning a new language at different ages, present a powerful paradox. Language is at once a moving target and also in many ways static; our thoughts and emotions are forever tethered to the language or languages we heard as children. Although we may become immersed in a different culture and gain fluency in another tongue, it can be difficult to escape our native language (or languages) and the identity that such a language imparts.

How can both of these things be true? How can language be so malleable, and also so fixed? That is the question we'll turn to next.

2

NATIVE TONGUES

Recently, one of my students told me the story of her grandmother, whom I'll call Gloria. In 1975, while eight months pregnant, Gloria had crossed the border from Mexico to the United States all by herself. She was poor, afraid, and completely alone, save for the kicking company in her large and uncomfortable belly.

Back home, in the care of Gloria's family, was her first child: a four-year-old girl who loved playing ball and eating tamales, who was bursting at the seams with pride at becoming a big sister. Gloria planned to return for her older daughter once she had a foot in the door of a society that was simultaneously foreign, terrifying, and electrifying. It was an English-speaking world, and she spoke only Spanish. Yet, as sad as she was to leave her family, Gloria was leaving a poverty-stricken, dangerous region of Mexico, and she wanted a better future for her daughter and the baby soon to be born.

Gloria's vision of a golden American future did not materialize as she had hoped. Within weeks of giving birth, she was deported and found herself back in Mexico with a newborn in her arms.

Gloria's two girls grew up together in Mexico until they were teenagers, when Gloria made a maternal sacrifice. Surrounded by poverty and violence, she wanted something better for her daughters. "Go without me," she told them. "Go to the United States alone." She thought they would have a better chance of entry on their own. Gloria's second daughter was, after all, a US citizen by birth.

The girls made it across the border, and, in contrast to their mother's experience, they thrived. They learned English, just as Gloria had wanted them to. They grew up and had children of their own. Eventually these grandchildren helped their grandmother Gloria with a petition for legal immigration, and she moved to the United States to join them.

When Gloria arrived in the United States for the second time, she finally met her baby girl's youngest child, and my future student, whom I'll call Eva. She was a lovely kindergartner with the sweetest smile, and she adored school, music, and art. But as Gloria observed her granddaughter, she realized something strange: Eva was American. Thoroughly American. Not just in the legal sense, like her mother. Eva was American in a real, deep, and inexplicable sense.

Eva's first language was English. She understood Spanish, sort of, more or less. But she refused to speak it. Eva's two older siblings spoke much better Spanish than Eva did, but still, they were more comfortable in English. With the passing of time, the family's conversations in Spanish had declined in frequency, and by the time Eva was born, the family spoke more English than Spanish.

Gloria saw the irony. She had wanted her family to come to the United States, and she felt proud of their accomplishments. Nevertheless, she also felt a deep sense of ambivalence and sadness when Eva opened her mouth to produce exclusively American English. It sometimes felt hard for Gloria to accept that this child — Gloria's blood, her genes, her future — would not speak Spanish with her. As she put Eva to bed at night, Gloria longed for her native language to seep into her granddaughter's soul, so that she could feel that they were truly connected.

Although Gloria did not realize it at the time, she had reached Eva at a formative moment. Eva was still young enough for Gloria to impart her native tongue to her granddaughter. There was still time for Eva to learn Spanish with relative ease, but as she got older, this opportunity would grow markedly more difficult.

NABOKOV'S NANNY

Although people are remarkably capable of changing the way they speak, language is not infinitely malleable. People learn languages best as children. Because of this, a native linguistic identity is pretty static. How you sound absolutely reflects your current social world, as well as your social aspirations, but your language also reflects something unchanging about you: the language or languages you heard as a child.

We are relatively bad at picking up new languages when we're older. As anyone who has taken a foreign-language class in college can attest, learning an entirely new language or accent as an adult is extremely challenging — and likely impossible to do well enough for someone to mistake your accent for that of a native speaker. Your speech reflects the linguistic sounds and rhythms of your youth. Fundamental aspects of your language — and hence some fundamental aspects of your social identity — are baked in at a very young age. Despite many people's strong desire to do so, adults simply can't pick up fluency in new languages left and right — nor can American English speakers suddenly snap their fingers and sound British or Australian. Completely changing your native linguistic identity may not be impossible, but it is definitely incredibly difficult.

But wait a moment, you might ask. What about linguistic geniuses? Aren't there people out there who can master a new language at any point in life? Certainly there are some incredible examples of prolific language learners — yet when you closely examine these exemplars, it is easy to discover the native-sounding accent is typically a result of linguistic exposure at a young age. Even people who are tremendously gifted at learning languages may intellectually grasp the fundamental structure and vocabulary of a new language learned as an adult, but they rarely acquire all the nuances to a native-like degree. It is very difficult to completely escape linguistic settings forged early in life.

For example, consider a legendary linguistic talent: the celebrated author Joseph Conrad. Born in Poland when it was part of the Russian Empire, he grew up speaking Polish and later French. Only later, in his twenties, did he become fluent in English, and he went on to write masterpieces of fiction in English. He is heralded as a late-in-life learner — a linguistic genius — yet he nonetheless had a foreign accent. A biography reports that "he talked English with a strong accent, as if he tasted his words in his mouth before pronouncing them; but he talked extremely well, though he had always the talk and manner of a foreigner."

Vladimir Nabokov is another example of someone heralded as a linguistic ace. He grew up in Russia and wrote in Russian before composing novels in English. He became famous for his expertise and facility in both languages. So, could he learn languages perfectly at any time? As an adult, could he pick up a perfect non-native accent? Well, he may have had a head start. If you dig a little deeper, you discover that he was exposed to both French and English early in life. He had an English-speaking governess. And, as he told the *New York Times* about learning English, "It was my first language. I remember my mother taking a Russian book for children and translating it into English." Wasn't that unusual, he was asked, for someone living where he did? "No, not in certain circles in Russia," he said.

There may be other masters of multiple languages you know of, or think you know of. It's fun to look for other examples of apparent linguistic geniuses. I urge you to give it a try. "What about Netanyahu?" my father asked me once. When the Israeli prime minister speaks in English, he sounds just like a regular American guy. I listened to a clip and indeed, he really does sound shockingly American. Is it Israel's relationship with the United States? Does the nations' mutual affinity bring them linguistically closer? Perhaps a crazy hypothesis, but in this case it is probably not accurate. More likely, his linguistic chops came from his years in elementary school when his family lived outside Philadelphia. Linguistically speaking, Netanyahu *is* just like any other regular American guy. He grew up ordering cheesesteaks and talking about the Eagles.

This isn't to say that there aren't savants among us. One of them, I'm proud to say, is my friend and psychology colleague Andrei Cimpian. He came from Romania to the United States as a college student, and after living here for twenty years, he has basically no foreign accent in English. Some people may perceive a very slight hint of a foreign accent, but it is subtle. When I talk with him, I no longer hear a foreign accent at all. Andrei told me that for a long time after he moved to the States, people he met would ask him, "Where are you from?" and he hated this question. He felt as though every time he opened his mouth, he got a message telling him that he didn't belong. Strangers don't ask him this anymore. He takes it as a signal that they perceive him to be American.

I asked Andrei why he is so good at English, because to my mind, his accomplishment violates the rules of language acquisition. He *should*, by all accounts, have a foreign accent. He should sound somewhat like Joseph Conrad did when speaking English.

Maybe Andrei has an ear for languages — he also understands Spanish and Italian pretty well, just from exposure to TV shows in these languages as a child. And he did take some English lessons as a boy, although not enough to make him fluent.

OK, so he is good at learning languages. I accepted the premise that he must be on the talented end of the spectrum of human abilities. But still, this conclusion did not feel very satisfying. Anyone who has moved to another country, or taken a foreign-language class, knows how difficult it is to develop a non-native accent as an adult.

After hedging a bit, Andrei said that maybe the challenges of his social life created a perfect storm that launched his linguistic success. As an adolescent, Andrei thought that he might be gay, but he didn't have the words to express his self-concept and his questions about it. He had no gay role models — no strong, educated gay men in his life. In Romania at the time, homosexuality was illegal. But Andrei's horizons slowly expanded after he moved to the States at the age of eighteen. He eventually came out as gay, found a partner he loved, got married, and found tremendous success in his field. He knew he would never go back to Romania for more than a brief visit, in part because he wasn't sure whether his American husband would be welcome there.

Viewed in this context, Andrei's successful acquisition of English reflects personal need and social necessity. He experienced a nearly complete break with his former life; he counts himself lucky to have learned the language that smoothed this transition.

Yet despite his incredible mastery of English, Andrei says his ostensibly American vowels can slip sometimes, mainly when he is overtired or a bit tipsy. When his mother came to the United States for the first time, nearly twenty years after Andrei had left Romania, Andrei spent the month-long visit translating between Romanian and English. With love (and a slight bit of mocking), his husband told him that during this time, his English vowels were getting wonky. Even Andrei — seemingly a language whiz — can't entirely shake off the influence of the Romanian vowels of his childhood. Some adults are better at language acquisition than others, but all of us — even if you're like Andrei, with your nearly-but-not-entirely-native-sounding English — have an upper limit on how good we can hope to get.

GIVE ME A SIGN

Psychologists and linguists have tried to understand how and why children can learn new languages in a way that adults cannot. Just how early do you need exposure to a language to learn it so well that you understand it easily and also sound just like a native speaker? When is it too late? How much exposure is enough? There is a certain degree of variability — and no hard-and-fast cutoff point in age for all people, in all circumstances. But amid the individual variability lie some general truths about human linguistic nature and our capacity to learn a new tongue.

Young brains are malleable in a way that older brains are not. Young language learners pick up on the language accent of their community seamlessly and easily — whereas older learners muddle through and often don't quite get there.

Babies' brains are great at learning language (among other things) in part because they are miraculously resilient. Here's an illustration of this point. An acquaintance of mine in Chicago left her one-year-old son in her mother's care for the afternoon. The grandma put the baby in the stroller, they went for a walk — and a brick fell off a building at a construction site, crashing into the stroller and fracturing the baby's skull. His life was saved, the doctor said, because it was very sunny out — the umbrella shade pulled over the stroller dampened the force of the brick. This incident was a nightmare for all the adults involved. They worried that the baby had suffered debilitating brain injury and might never learn to talk. Yet several months later the baby was walking and starting to talk. His injury left no perceptible neurological impairments. As the doctor explained, a baby's brain can heal.

Adult brains are not as resilient. This fact was brought home to me when I bumped into a high school acquaintance — we'd played in an orchestra together twenty years earlier. She told me that at the age of thirty-one she'd had a serious skiing accident; she hadn't been wearing a helmet. Managing a traumatic brain injury is now a permanent part of her life. She feels as if she's living with a computer that will overheat if she isn't careful. Her ability with language will never be the same — she has to speak slowly, and it takes a while to find the words she wants to say. She said that this difference in her capacity for communicating has changed her sense of who she is. Yet she is coping and has a remarkably positive spirit.

Indeed, studies show that the young human brain can deal with injury and compensate for language loss early in life in a way that older brains simply cannot. I've provided extreme examples, but they speak to the general rule: younger brains are simply more resilient than older brains and thus more adept at acquiring a new language.

How children acquire language, in practice, is usually straightforward. Most kids are exposed to language early in life, and they learn what they hear. Indeed, it's hard to imagine a different scenario — a situation in which someone receives no language exposure as a child. We simply don't hear of such cases.

But this does not mean that they don't exist.

Sad to say, not all children have the opportunity to acquire language. We have evidence of this, though some is anecdotal — it would of course be terribly unethical to deprive young children of exposure to language in order to study how they cope. And the anecdotal evidence is mercifully rare. But documentation exists for horrific situations of child abuse that included depriving the young of any exposure to language. Two cases of textbook fame are "Isabelle" and "Genie" (code names), children who were rescued from situations of horrendous abuse and neglect. At the age of six, Isabelle was discovered locked in an attic; Genie at the age of thirteen was found tied to a chair in a darkened room; neither had received any language input from their abusive and deranged parents. It's reported that Genie's father barked at her, rather than speaking. But a year after being rescued, Isabelle was speaking English just like other school-age kids. Genie, however, did not rebound as easily. She made huge strides and learned a lot of vocabulary, but she could never master the syntax of English. She produced short phrases — like something a two-year-old would say. Despite extensive therapy, she was never able to progress linguistically to the level of even a typically developing preschooler.

It might be tempting to conclude from Genie's case that we can't learn new languages at the age of thirteen. But one of the many limitations of anecdotal evidence like this is that it is exceedingly difficult to disentangle the subject's linguistic deficit from the social deficit, especially when a situation involves abuse. A child raised by abusive adults who deprive her of language is without a doubt deprived of other forms of typical human contact too, and so it is hard to determine exactly which type of deprivation causes which outcome.

But in some cases, people are not exposed to a language, yet they do not suffer other forms of social deprivation, since they are loved and provided for in caring ways by their parents. Such cases have given us a firmer understanding of how language acquisition works — and how long children have to acquire a native language before the window of opportunity starts to close.

One such story is that of "Chelsea," who was born to loving parents in a small town, where she was misdiagnosed as having a cognitive deficit. In fact, Chelsea was neurologically just fine; she was simply deaf. But because of this misdiagnosis, she was never taught a language (she couldn't hear a spoken language, and she wasn't exposed to a sign language). Finally, when Chelsea was thirty-one, she saw a neurologist who correctly diagnosed her and began to help her. When Chelsea was fitted with hearing aids, she could hear, but although she made impressive gains in many areas of life and learned to speak English to some degree, her new language was made up of short utterances of just a few words in length. They weren't even like a two-year-old's phrases, which might be short but usually reflect a sense of syntax. Chelsea's word order was all over the map. She would say things like "Banana the eat."

Chelsea may be an unusual case, but she is not alone. The psycholinguist Elissa Newport systematically studied deaf children who were born to hearing parents. The children she studied were, at different ages, eventually exposed to a language they were able to learn — American Sign Language or another sign language, which is produced with hand movements and facial expressions rather than with sound. Many became fluent in a sign language, as proficient as children who had been exposed since birth. Others, however, did not — and the difference between these two groups has been instrumental in revealing how age of exposure relates to the ability to acquire language at a native-speaker level.

Now, before I go any further, let me state clearly that the par-

ents of the deaf children who Newport studied were not neglect-
ful. Having a baby who is born deaf—when you are a parent who
hears, and you don't speak a signed language yourself—is incredibly tough. Your baby would not be able to hear the language that
you know how to speak. Only 5–10 percent of deaf babies are born
to parents who are also deaf and who already speak a sign language, so for the remaining 90–95 percent of deaf children, those
who are born to hearing parents, a very tricky language problem
must be overcome.

The psycholinguist Molly Flaherty, who studies the development
of sign languages, told me the most helpful analogy I've heard for
understanding what this might be like for a parent. Molly says to
imagine that you are an English-speaking couple in the United
States. You have a newborn who is completely healthy and typical
in every way, save for one small difference: this baby can learn only
Italian. What do you do? Perhaps you could find a community of
Italian speakers and have them talk to your baby. (Fortunately such
a community exists in the United States — in roughly the same pro-
portion to the English-speaking population as speakers of American Sign Language, hence the analogy.) But even if you found some
Italian speakers to speak to your baby, you wouldn't speak Italian
yourself. Unless you hire a full-time translator, how would you put
your baby to bed, tell her to brush her teeth and not to touch the
stove, and so on? You would have to try to learn Italian. And then
you would find yourself faced with an incredibly difficult task —
picking up a new language as an adult is no small feat.

This analogy is helpful for understanding the experience of hearing parents with babies who are born deaf. These babies are perfectly capable of learning a language (a sign language) — they are
just not capable of learning the language of their parents (a spoken
language). And the parents, unless they previously knew sign language, are not capable of learning their child's "native tongue" as
quickly as the baby can.

This was precisely the group that Elissa Newport selected for her

research: children who were born deaf and — because of the difficulties their parents faced in finding the right linguistic environment for them — were not all exposed to a sign language right away.
The deaf children Newport studied had been exposed to American
Sign Language (ASL) starting (1) in infancy, or (2) around kindergarten age, when they started to attend a school for the deaf and
learned ASL on the playground with their peers, or (3) in adolescence, because they had not been sent to an elementary school that
provided exposure to a sign language.

At the time Newport studied these deaf individuals, they had
all been speaking ASL for a very long time. They were adults, and
mostly middle-aged. Newport tested their language skills to see
how the age at which they had been exposed to ASL mattered in
predicting how well they ended up understanding and produc-
ing it.

She found some very elegant evidence of the importance of
learning a language early in life in order to master it. All the adults
she studied had some mastery of ASL — they generally had the basic word order down correctly, and they all knew a lot of vocabulary. But there was nonetheless a huge difference in ability, based
on the age of first exposure to ASL. The native learners (who had
started learning ASL as infants) were perfectly fluent in their language. The children who were exposed to ASL starting around kindergarten were almost (but not quite) as good as the native signers.
The children who were not exposed until adolescence fared much
more poorly, linguistically. They made lots of errors. When people
speak ASL — just like any language — they use words in a specific
grammatical order. People who started learning ASL in adolescence didn't have the crisp and consistent use of words, and word
order, of a native signer.

Newport's research was revolutionary in part because she was
able to control for length of exposure to ASL, allowing her to pinpoint the age of exposure that signaled a dropping off of language-
learning skills. So, for instance, a thirty-five-year-old who started

learning at age five and a forty-two-year-old who started learning at age twelve had both been communicating in the language for thirty years — but Newport found that the thirty-five-year-old was much more proficient than the forty-two-year-old.

This ASL study has implications for everyone, deaf or not. Linguistic proficiency, Newport showed, is not primarily about the time spent learning the language, or the total amount of language heard. Rather, it is the age you *start* learning a language that really matters. The earlier the better, if you want to sound (or sign) like a native — and by all means before adolescence.

Sign language remains the subject of robust ongoing research. Recently, the creation of a brand-new language — Nicaraguan Sign Language — gave researchers the opportunity to collect further evidence for just how sensitive young minds are to learning languages, but also how language can be created from scratch by new social groups — and, conversely, how the creation of a new language can forge social bonds where none previously existed.

Prior to the 1980s, deaf children in Nicaragua typically lived at home with their families, who (like most families of deaf children in the United States) did not know a sign language. As such, the children were not exposed to a language they could learn themselves. They developed home signing systems — rudimentary forms of language that reflect humans' amazing drive to communicate and the limits of an individual effort to create a language independently.

In the 1970s a school for special education opened in Managua, the capital city of Nicaragua, including classrooms designed specifically for deaf children. Once there, deaf children still were not initially taught a sign language. The language of instruction was Spanish — but of course, the children could not hear the Spanish. Yet the first wave of students — those who entered the school in its first decade — did something pretty amazing together. On the playground, playing and interacting as children do, they scaffolded their own individual sign systems into a shared language. Together these deaf children created a new sign language. In short, the school did not teach the children the language — instead, they created it themselves.

Researchers from other countries came to Nicaragua to study this newly created, evolving language. Among them, the psychologist Ann Senghas and the anthropologist Richard Senghas (who happen to be siblings!) charted the initial development of Nicaraguan Sign Language and the social changes that it has generated. The first group of children created a language that far surpassed what any individual child could express using signing developed as an individual. And the progress of the language didn't stop there. Subsequent groups of young entering students improved on the language. As the language progressed across subsequent generations of young speakers, the signs became more fluid. Signers could more easily and quickly express complex concepts. The new students took the old input and improved on it. As a group, students who entered in 2000 spoke a more complex version of the language than students who entered in 1990, who in turn linguistically surpassed students who had entered in 1980. Language was both learned by and created by young children who came together speaking it.

As was the case in Newport's studies related to American Sign Language, a given child's age of acquisition was impactful. Someone starting to learn Nicaraguan Sign Language as an older child or teenager would never gain the facility of someone who began at age five. Again, early learning was a key to mastery.

The case of Nicaraguan Sign Language also reveals that children — *young* children in particular — can come together to create and expand on a new language. Furthermore, once a group can share a language, its social dynamics change. The anthropologist Richard Senghas has noted that as Nicaraguan Sign Language developed, speakers of the new language developed their own culture and their own social ties. They felt "groupier." And other people would see them as more of a truly established group of people too.

THE WONDER YEARS

Clearly we are much likelier to master our first language when we learn it early in life. But what about second languages? What does current science have to say about when you need to start learning to gain a native-like proficiency? Research has helped us understand how much a person's age affects the ability to master a language — first or second or fourth.

My daughter took a preschool music class from a woman, Anna, who mentioned to me that she moved here from Russia. This surprised me, simply because I had no idea that she hadn't been born in the United States. I had interacted with her casually on a weekly basis — mainly discussing sitting in a circle, going potty, and whether a cheese stick was allowed in class. So these were not terrifically deep conversations. Nonetheless, I had thought of Anna as culturally and linguistically American.

Anna moved here from Russia just prior to her seventh birthday (close to the age of Paola, my student who moved here from Colombia when she was six). Talking to Anna, I could not detect a foreign accent. She says that after twenty-five years of living here, she now feels more American than Russian. She still speaks her native language, but when she goes back to Russia, her family considers her Russian to be just a little "off" — tinged with vowel sounds or a rhythm that somehow sounds a touch American.

Anna is just one example of a person who moved to the United States as a child and now speaks English like a native speaker. It turns out that Anna's linguistic success was no coincidence. It had everything to do with her age.

Elissa Newport, the researcher whose studies of deaf people showed that our language-learning ability drops off considerably in adolescence, has conducted additional research that helps narrow down the exact age range in which this happens. In addition to adult ASL speakers, Newport also studied a group of adults who had moved to the United States as children from East Asian countries. The adults' first language was Chinese or Korean; when they participated in the study, they were all students or faculty at the University of Illinois.

The researchers gave these adults subtle tests of grammatical proficiency in English. The test subjects listened to a bunch of sentences and had to identify the speaker's mistakes. The sentences contained only small errors — you could still understand their meaning — but the errors were of a type that a native speaker would find easy to detect. For instance, "The farmer bought two pig at the market."

Native speakers of English were quite good at this task, unsurprisingly. And so were the Chinese or Korean immigrants who had moved to the United States as young children — the performance of those who moved here from approximately age three to age seven was indistinguishable from that of the native speakers. Those who arrived after age seven, however, tended to miss more errors, a pattern that got more pronounced the later they arrived.

Now, certainly people can still learn a new language after the age of seven, such that they can speak and understand it fluently — I don't want to imply that adults who had lived in the United States for decades could not speak English. They could speak and understand it well enough to live full and productive lives. However, the people who had arrived later didn't have the ear of a native speaker. That voice that native speakers hear in their head, saying "Two pigs," just was not shouting with the same intensity for those who learned English later. The errors, to them, sounded somewhat permissible. And although this study does not report on these test subjects' accents, they would presumably sound like non-native speakers of English, even when their spoken sentences were grammatically correct.

Other studies have added an interesting twist to this "somewhere around age seven" rule of thumb, finding that before this age, we also are adept at *discarding* languages we have already learned. This is strikingly clear, for instance, in studies of international adoptees — children who are adopted across nations and languages. These children must quickly learn a new language, as their survival depends on it. But they often no longer have the means to practice their first language — and thus lose it, very quickly.

Studies of international adoptions show how surprisingly quickly children can erase their first language in favor of the new one, and how social necessity plays a role. In two such studies, psychologists followed children who were adopted from eastern European countries into families in the United States. The researchers wanted to study both how quickly the children learned English and what happened to children's facility in their first language after they stopped speaking it. After a couple of years, children had generally caught up with their age-matched native peers in English language skills. As for the children's first language, parents said that after just a few months, the children were no longer saying any words from it. Social necessity can lead a kid to forget a language fast.

Interestingly, adopted children tend to lose their first language even when they are resettled in sibling pairs. Wouldn't it be easy for the two siblings to keep talking to each other in their first language? That seems logical, but this just isn't what happens. They still lose their first language. The social pressures of their new environment are just too great — children find themselves in a new world where everyone speaks a new language, and they adapt. And they are young enough to completely shift their language.

Some kids may even come to dislike their former linguistic identity. A former colleague of mine adopted a child from Russia who was around a year and a half old. It was amazing how quickly she transitioned from Russian to English. Even more surprising to her parents was how much she started to despise the sound of Russian. Her parents did not speak Russian, except for a few words they had learned to try to help with the transition. They got some Russian music and movies, thinking the familiar language might help their new daughter feel at home. After a few weeks she would start screaming when they played anything in Russian to her, so they soon stopped. To them it seemed as though the linguistic memories of her previous life just did not fit her new reality. At eighteen months, the only way she could express her feelings was by screaming, and the message was clear. In her new social world, full of monolingual English speakers, she wanted to learn English, not Russian.

Scientists have studied international adoptees who have reached adulthood, hoping to understand whether any of their first language remains. The results of measuring their spoken language abilities are consistent. For instance, French adults who were adopted from Korea as children do not speak or understand any Korean at all. If you talk with them, they sound completely French, and when they hear Korean, they have no idea what the words mean. This is the case even for children who were adopted at age seven or so. Their language abilities apparently were completely plastic — replacing Korean with French.

We are so good at learning languages early in life, it seems that we can completely reinvent the wheel — learning a new language and forgetting the old one — provided we start this process early enough.

GHOST IN THE MACHINE

Nonetheless, not *all* traces of these forgotten languages disappear. Early language learning leaves vestiges in the brain that can be detected years down the road, long after other signs of the forgotten tongue have faded.

Studies of international adoptees — such as the Korean children adopted in France, or more recently, Chinese children adopted into French-speaking homes in Canada — find that subtle effects of the first language are still visible in adults' brains. For these adoptees who have reached adulthood, even subtle linguistic tasks will show that they completely lost the first language and gained the second one. From their speech and their listening comprehension, they act just like French speakers — and there is no evidence of facility in

Korean or Chinese. But even when people do not remember any of their first language — even when they have completely switched to a new one — there is some evidence that small signatures of the native language may still be present. You would never know it by talking to them, but the way that these adoptees learned their second language and process it — at a neural level — is just a little different from how someone does it who learned French from birth.

In these studies, neuroscientists simply had the participants lie in an fMRI scanner and passively listen to sentences in French. When an area of the brain is used, blood flows to that region, and fMRI testing can track this flow. For the test subjects, the regions that lit up the most consistently included areas along the left temporal lobe, such as Wernicke's area, and also in part of the frontal lobe, near what is typically known as Broca's area. By using this technology, researchers can assess in real time how the brain is processing information.

The researchers found that native French speakers and international adoptees had very similar areas of activation when processing French — anatomically speaking, in terms of the locations with blood flow, they were the same. Their language abilities are located in the same place. But the *extent* of activation — the amount of change in blood flow — was just a little bit greater for the native French speakers than for the international adoptees.

It seems that even when language is learned and replaces another just a bit later in life — say, if you are adopted as a preschooler — it ends up being processed in the brain just a little differently too. Researchers hypothesize that when the international adoptees first processed French, their brains were working with a neural system that had already been set up to process a different set of sounds, and thus the typical language areas were not initially recruited in quite the same way.

These neuroscience findings are getting support from more traditional behavioral studies suggesting that early language input can impact later adult learning, even if you have completely forgotten the language of your youth. For instance, other research shows the possibility of some savings — even if the Korean was completely forgotten, adults who had at one point spoken Korean would find it easier to learn to hear and differentiate Korean phonological distinctions as an adult. It seems that a tiny remnant of the native language, even for an international adoptee who doesn't speak or remember it at all, could still remain.

These findings also fit with more general studies of the neural representation of first and second languages in the brain, showing that for everyone (not just adoptees), languages that are learned early versus late in life are represented differently. For instance, when native French speakers (who have heard French their whole lives) listen to French, their neural patterns of activation are all pretty similar. When hearing French, most people had tight localizations along a curve in the temporal lobe called the superior temporal sulcus. Their language-processing area was very clearly identifiable, consistent with where language processing is typically thought to be found in the left hemisphere. But when the French participants listened to a language they learned later in life — specifically English, which they learn in school — there was a lot more variability.

At the neural level, it's as if each individual learned a second language in a slightly different way, and each individual's neural activation was generally much more spread out across neighboring areas of the brain. A couple of participants tested in these studies even showed the typical *left* hemispheric dominance for listening to French, but *right* hemispheric dominance for listening to English. In nonscientific terms, processing English as a second language was a little scattershot. It was all over the place.

So we can continue to learn languages into adulthood, but they will never be neurally encoded or spoken in the same way that a native childhood language is. But all is not lost. Before you delete that Duolingo app from your smartphone, remember that you can still learn new languages, and can get very good at them if you work hard — even if you can never get to a level that would be mistaken for native speech.

Of course, learning new languages is much harder for some of us than others. Do all adults have an equally difficult time learning new languages, or are younger adults better at it than older people? Is it better to try to learn, say, German or French as a twenty-something, instead of waiting until you're fifty?

Immigrants are the perfect population to study when exploring the impact of age on language learning at different points in development — including when people start to learn a new language as adults. And the findings from these studies offer hope to anyone who aspires to learn a language later in life. When researchers look at people who moved countries prior to the end of adolescence, there is a linear relationship between age of arrival and resulting linguistic abilities. This fits with an understanding that as children age, their ability to perfectly master a new tongue drops off. Interestingly, though, immigrant adults of different ages are more or less the same at learning a language — at any age. Once people hit adulthood, there is no longer a clear linear relationship between age of starting and ultimate mastery.

To be sure, some adults (like my friend Andrei) are able to learn a new language very well, and others are not. But if you're not one of those lucky people, you might be happy to know that after adolescence, all adults are similarly disadvantaged; or, to put it more positively, all of us can learn a new language to some extent. Sensitive periods in language learning seem to be about neural maturation, not about number of years on the planet.

So, retirees, take heart. Consider my parents, recently retired, who went to try to learn Spanish at a language school in Barcelona. They felt socially out of place because many of the other students were twenty-year-olds on a gap year from college. Learning Spanish was difficult, and my parents felt disappointed by their minimal progress. But linguistically, they were not necessarily more like fish out of water than the twenty-year-olds were; their young adult brains were similarly already too old for them to become the equivalent of native speakers of Spanish. Bad news for the twenty-year-olds but optimistic news for other adults: it may be too late to learn a new language perfectly, but it is not too late to learn it at all.

"I'M JUST NOT AS FUNNY IN ENGLISH!"

Studies of children learning sign languages, being adopted internationally, or learning a new language after moving to a new location show how languages learned early in life are privileged. We learn first languages differently than later languages. Young children are able to learn them in a way that adults cannot. And these native languages are represented in our brains in a way that later-learned languages are not.

It turns out that how you *feel* when using your first language is special too. The way you connect with others, experience emotions, and make moral decisions depends on whether you are speaking in your native tongue.

To get a sense of how emotional reactions can feel more pronounced in your first language, think about which curse words you know in your first language. Now imagine curse words in another language — even if you know exactly what they mean, they probably just don't have the same bite. *"Merde!"* (French for *sh*t*) — eh, I would probably say it in front of a toddler or a grandma. I just googled Spanish curse words (not speaking much Spanish myself). With my non-native grasp of the language, insults aimed at someone's mom just sound silly, not offensive.

Research shows that people are more aroused by curse words in their native language than in a second language, even if they have the translation down pat. This reflects not just people's subjective feelings, but also their physiological state — physical measures of arousal peak more for taboo words in one's native tongue. People get just a little bit sweatier, based on measures of skin conductance. At a physical level they *feel* the effects of the native curse words more.

It's not just curse words in a person's native language that have a special effect. Childhood reprimands and sexual content — anything that may feel provocative or emotionally charged — are extra potent when expressed in a language learned early. Humor may seem just a bit funnier in a native tongue. I had a friend in graduate school who was from Spain (but really good at English — she was in the States for a postdoc). She was fun and outgoing and cheerful, and a bit sarcastic. I would laugh at her jokes, but sometimes she would get frustrated.

She would say, "You don't really know me! You don't know the real Lola! I'm just not as funny in English!"

"What do you mean? You're right in front of me? I just laughed at your joke!"

And she would say, "Yes, but it's not the whole me. It's impossible to really know me when I am speaking in English rather than my native tongue of Spanish."

If you have just one language, you may not realize how much your emotional life depends on it. But people who learn to speak more than one language as adults may discover that they feel different when using one or another of their languages, and the one learned first often has a special potency. Perhaps this is because childhood memories are more accessible in one's first language — for many people, there seems to be something special about the emotions associated with life's earliest years. They are more raw, more intense, more *real*. Maybe you can still hear your grandmother yelling at you in that language. People report feeling less themselves, maybe even a little bit socially "fake," when using a language that they learned later in life. The bilingualism expert Aneta Pavlenko points out that although Nabokov wrote beautifully across languages, he tended to prefer Russian, his first language, for poetry. Since poetry is often about evoking emotion through metaphor and subtle meaning, perhaps the intense emotions associated with the native tongue made it a satisfying medium for this type of expression.

Our native tongue gives us emotional grounding. It allows us to connect to others and to our childhood self. But some counter-intuitive findings show that these native-language emotions can also have surprising consequences. Sometimes they can affect decision making, especially when moral discernment is needed. Do we follow strong gut feelings or carefully use reason when making a difficult decision? Interestingly, according to some studies, that depends on whether you are in a context where you are speaking in your first language, or one you acquired later.

It's not hard to come up with examples of life decisions made when emotions got in the way. Loss aversion is one emotional dynamic that can produce suboptimal results. The psychologists Amos Tversky and Daniel Kahneman made this problem famous. Loss aversion refers to fear of the sting of loss, which can outweigh the thrill of the prospect of gains — and often loss aversion drives people to less-than-rational behavior. Simply put, losing five dollars feels much worse than gaining five dollars feels good. Thus, avoiding the loss is the more emotionally compelling of the two. And because of this, people make choices that run counter to long-term prosperity or happiness, all to avoid the momentary pang caused by fear of loss.

Emotions can also strongly affect us when we need to make extremely difficult decisions that affect others. Here is an example.

Imagine that there is an awful, dangerous new disease that is fatal. 600 people will be exposed, and without a necessary medicine, all will die. Two new medical options are being created, and your job is to pick which one sounds better to deliver to the sick people.

Option A: The sure bet: 200 people will definitely be saved, and 400 people will definitely die. Option B: Roll the die: A third of the time everyone is saved and no one will die; and 2/3 of the time no one is saved and everyone will die.

As you can see, these options present a tough choice — though they are mathematically equivalent, in terms of the overall odds of how many people can be saved. Should you take the sure bet of at least saving two hundred people, or should you roll the die and risk losing everyone in the hope of saving them all?

It turns out that the language used in presenting the problem matters. If you frame the problem as "definitely saving two hundred" versus "definitely losing four hundred" (the same thing, mathematically), people respond very differently. The thought of "definitely saving" sounds a lot better than "definitely losing," which sounds horrible. People are much more likely to pick option A when the problem is framed in this way. It just "feels better."

But there's a linguistic trick operating here. I'm betting that English is your native tongue. The emotional bias I just described to you happens only if you encounter this problem in your first language, as Boaz Keysar, Sayuri Hayakawa, and colleagues have shown. Remember, your first language is emotionally resonant, so that sense of loss, that feeling associated with agreeing to killing four hundred people, sounds awful. When people approach the same problem using a language they learned as an adult, they become much more *rational*. In their second language, they are much more likely to consider the two scenarios equitably — they respond based on the numbers, rather than the emotional tug of avoiding a loss.

Native languages are imbued with emotion; second languages, less so. You feel that "ouch!" of thinking about a loss somewhat less in a second language, and you may be able to make a more cool-headed assessment of pros and cons, losses and gains.

Now imagine the following scenario, typically referred to in philosophy as a "trolley problem" thought experiment.

You are standing on a bridge overlooking a train track. A train is hurtling down the track where five people are standing. It will certainly kill them all. Standing near you is a very large man. You could push the large and heavy man onto the track to stop the train.

This option would sacrifice one to save five. Like the previous scenario, it sounds gruesome but has an additional layer of unpleasantness. It violates an essential moral value: in most any situation, pushing someone to his death is strongly prohibited. To even contemplate the idea can cause a visceral emotional response.

Most people say they would not push the one to save the five. The "right thing to do" is far from obvious — one option feels morally abhorrent, but the other permits the death of five people. Nevertheless, people generally trust emotion more than utilitarian calculation — and thus would refrain from pushing the large man onto the track. That is, unless they are presented with this scenario in a second language. Under those circumstances, people are relatively much more likely to say that they would push the man, and kill one to save five.

So, are we less morally sensitive when weighing a life-and-death decision presented in a foreign tongue? Well, it depends on how you define morality. If, for you, morality is about that gut feeling of right or wrong, that emotional tug toward a certain judgment without needing a logical reason for it, then sure, you might say that second-language decisions are less informed by morality. If, however, morality for you is a matter of figuring out how to do the least amount of harm to the fewest number of people, then second-language speakers would be considered *more* moral. Morality is complex and personal — but however you think of it, our basic moral intuitions feel different when considered in our first language. That native-language morality is emotional, and when speaking a native tongue, our emotions tend to cloud our rational thinking — for better or for worse.

We can see these tendencies in action in the experience of my friend Andrei, when presented with the tests we just discussed. Andrei moved here from Romania at age eighteen and (to my ear at least) his English sounds almost perfectly native, but he is still a bit Romanian at heart. Despite his now thoroughly American life, he is still emotionally connected to his native language. Curse words in Romanian have a stronger bite for him. But like the second-language learners in that study, he too feels a little less loss-averse in English. And, if he were faced with a real-world trolley problem, he thinks that in Romanian, he would be less likely to agree to push the large man off the bridge to save the five.

As we've seen, native language — the language of childhood — is special. Even if as a small child you managed to forget it, traces of your original speech would remain, at a neural level, in your brain. No wonder Gloria wanted her granddaughter Eva to learn Spanish! (In case you are wondering, she did learn Spanish from her grandmother — though she remained much more comfortable in English.)

Up to this point, I've purposely ignored the wider social implications of the incredible deep-rootedness of speech. A native tongue can be a source of positive identity — providing a sense of belonging to a community.

Yet the social inheritance of language can be downright toxic as well. Differences in the way people speak can cause harmful prejudices and sow deep divisions between linguistic groups. The social nature of language runs deep, and it runs in two completely opposite directions — toward deep communion and stark division.

3

HOW LANGUAGE DIVIDES US

Murphy Morobe was a child who loved to read. As he grew into adolescence — reading history and philosophy — he developed an activist streak. A Black teenager in apartheid South Africa in the 1970s, Murphy lived and attended school in Soweto, one of many "townships" — segregated areas where Black South Africans were relocated, after being stripped of their homes and land. He had seen pernicious and deadly acts of racism: his neighbors' homes raided, people arrested and jailed without cause.

Seeking to change this bleak status quo, Murphy threw himself into cultural student groups. He became a member of the inner circle of the South African Student's Movement (SASM), which he saw as working toward unity for the students. For, first and foremost, Murphy wanted to disrupt what he saw as a culture based on a Black "inferiority complex," and the way that Black students were taught, both implicitly and explicitly, that they were inferior to whites.

Black students in South Africa spoke many languages — in Soweto, for instance, students might speak Zulu, Sotho, or Tswana, among others. Most students also spoke English. In Murphy's student group, participants who had different native languages would communicate in English. Afrikaans, in contrast, was seen as the language of the oppressor, the language of apartheid. They absolutely did not want to speak Afrikaans.

In 1975 a policy related to language became the straw that broke the camel's back. The Afrikaan Medium Decree asserted that 50 percent of the school day (and some subjects in their entirety, such as mathematics) must be taught in Afrikaans. English was to be used for the other subjects, and students' native tribal languages were relegated to instruction in religion, music, and physical education.

On June 16, 1976, Murphy and other students took to the streets in peaceful protest. They went on strike from their school, and the demonstration spread to neighboring schools. Thousands of students walked the streets, voicing their objection to the legislation.

The white police force arrived, and — in images shown around the world — opened fire at the masses of unarmed children, killing indiscriminately. It was a tragic, horrific day.

Although he was not physically injured himself, Murphy would always carry the scars of that day with him. Twenty years later (after years spent in jail due to his revolutionary activities), Murphy spoke to South Africa's Truth and Reconciliation Commission, the court-like body that sought restorative justice and a voice for victims of apartheid's atrocities. Murphy explained that he himself wouldn't have been affected by instruction in Afrikaans — after all, he was graduating from high school, so the children younger than him would have faced that insult to their dignity. But for him and his friends, school instruction in Afrikaans represented a racist affront, which had a deeply personal effect on them. Knowing that schoolchildren would be forced to speak a language that represented white domination and oppression was too much for them to bear.

As Murphy learned firsthand, language can act as potent fuel for social conflict. Language is intimate and personal, and oppressing a group's language is powerfully provocative. For Murphy and his friends, the threat that their language would be replaced by that of an oppressor was an incredible personal affront to their identity. They rose up in protest — and their objections were met with bullets.

Though apartheid has ended in South Africa, its lessons are sadly enduring. Language, politics, and identity often go hand in hand, sometimes with disastrous results. Language does not just mark who you are and who you fit in with; it can also create — and be purposely used to create — powerful social divisions. That is a lesson that we would do well to remember, whatever our nationality or our native tongue.

SCARLET LETTERS

When you think of the deepest divisions between humans — those forces that tear neighbor from neighbor and cause violence, warfare, and cruelty — language may not immediately come to mind as a root cause and a blunt instrument. Yet it should.

Language shows you where you fit into the social world, but it also tells you who is *not* like you. Because language is so critical to feelings of identity, when you speak, you let a little bit of yourself out, for the world to interpret. This information includes your current social trajectory and "fixed" aspects of your language, which were set by the people speaking to you when you were a child. The effects can be wonderful: building solidarity among oppressed peoples, for instance, or giving a grandmother a special connection with her distant grandchild. But linguistic identities have a dark side too.

When you hear people speaking a foreign language or with a foreign accent, you can instantly and effortlessly (and perhaps despite your best intentions) place them in these categories: *Not like me. Not from around here. Not from my tribe.* Language tells us who is in and, conversely, who is out: it is the easy and simple signifier of *us* versus *them.*

And of course this evaluation based on a person's speech is a two-way street — you are judging others as belonging to your group or not, while other people are likewise judging you. A person's language and way of speaking are like a badge that identifies his or her

origins. Open your mouth, and reveal your upbringing. Hear someone else do the same, and you can discern remnants of voices that
the person heard during childhood. Based on this, you will likely
draw conclusions as to who someone is, and is not.

Even at a young age, people have an astonishing ability to detect
linguistic differences. I remember my daughter, at about the age of
three, holding her tablet to her ear and making a perplexed face as
she watched a children's show. "His voice!" she said. "What is that?"
The character was speaking English with a non-native accent.

A foreign accent is the easiest to detect. When you hear a non-
native speaker talking in your language, you will recognize within
seconds that the accent is foreign. Adults and children alike can
make this observation effortlessly. For instance, French kids can
immediately pick out a native English speaker who is talking in
French, but they have difficulty differentiating accents from northern versus southern regions of France. Likewise, British kids can
pick out English spoken with a French accent better than English
spoken with an Irish accent. This makes sense, at an acoustic level
— if in some hypothetical linguistic space you lined up all the possible accents in which your language can be spoken, presumably
those spoken by non-native speakers would (at least on average)
stand out as most different from the native speech you are familiar with.

People can also detect smaller differences in accent from
around their own geographic region. Linguists will tell you that
accents and dialects do not have discrete breaks, that language
doesn't split into categories depicting a clear "us" versus a clear
"them." In strictly academic terms, language is a continuum — just
a little bit more "us," and perhaps just a little bit more "them." But
this gentle progression is not what people perceive in such variations in language. Instead, they identify clear group boundaries
between who is in and who is out, based on sometimes subtle differences in accent.

Take a moment to think about it, and you'll appreciate how sensitive you are to the accents you hear. For me, as an American Eng-

lish speaker, subtle distinctions between the various British accents can be hard to differentiate. They all sound kind of the same, although I understand that to a British speaker, "posh" would never be mistaken for "country." But as an American, I can detect without hesitation the difference between Northern and Southern American speech, and tell a New Yorker from a Californian. The instant I hear someone say "aboout" instead of "about," my inner accent detector screams "Canadian!"

Such is our attunement to accents that they are almost impossible to fake successfully, in a way that can fool others. One study demonstrated this by examining whether people could put on a fake accent as a disguise. This is an important area of research, since accent can be a clue used in crime cases that rely on voice identification. Who left that threatening voicemail? Whose shouting voice did a witness hear? Imagine you are committing a crime — would leaving a voicemail in a fake accent help you get away? "It couldn't have been me — that's not my accent!"

Not so fast: it turns out that when American adults from the North were asked to fake a Southern accent, the result couldn't reliably fool others. Actors are better at imitating accents, of course (and some actors are truly great at it). But most people can't just instantaneously and convincingly replicate a non-native accent.

Yet while people are great at detecting accents when hearing people speak in their native tongue, this ability completely falls apart when they attempt to discern differences of accent in a spoken foreign language. Moreover, recognizing a particular individual's voice is much harder when they don't speak like you do. Imagine a "voice lineup" scenario. People have a lot of difficulty telling others apart when they are speaking in a foreign language or with a foreign accent. You may have heard of an "own race" advantage in recognizing people's faces. In a courtroom (or in a psychology experiment), a white adult is generally going to be much better at accurately identifying the face of someone else who is white. Well, it turns out that an "own language" and even an "own accent" advantage exist too. For example, if you speak English, identifying the correct individual's voice in a voice lineup of Spanish speakers would be tremendously difficult.

This research shows that languages and accents have the power to create categories that divide people. In fact, when we've placed someone in the "them" category (for example, "Spanish speakers," if you don't speak Spanish), we have trouble seeing past that label to detect differences between the various accents and people in that out-group. Just one thing stands out — those people are *not like us*.

It makes sense that someone like me can tell American accents apart but struggles to identify different British accents. Think of it as a "close to home" accent advantage. It relates to the importance of figuring out who is inside and who is outside our group and then detecting social divisions within our group. Understandably, we are less concerned about people perceived as outside our group and the subtle differences in their speech patterns, since we don't anticipate interacting with them much, if at all. Yet the amount of exposure we have to various accents may make a difference. In one study, psycholinguists found that American "army brats" who had lived in at least three different states had a better ability to categorize different American dialects than "homebodies" who had grown up exclusively in the American Midwest. The researchers theorized that the children whose parents were part of the army perhaps had a more nuanced and flexible sense of "accent in-groups" since they had lived in more places.

Interestingly, even if your inner voice screams "Not from around here!" when you hear an unfamiliar accent, you most likely will be able to fully understand what is being said. When you first encounter such an accent, you'll likely pay a processing cost — words will be ever-so-slightly harder to identify, and it will take a little longer to understand what someone is saying. (And this may happen for regional dialect differences too — for instance, I once went to Scotland and had some difficulty understanding the tour guide at Edinburgh Castle.) But after just a bit of exposure to the new person's speech, people accommodate. They start to get it. The new speech starts to make sense. It doesn't even take very long — maybe a few sentences for a regional accent that is not extremely different. And even markedly foreign accents can be understood pretty quickly. In one study, researchers played recordings of voices speaking English with a "heavy" Spanish or Chinese accent to adults who were native speakers of English. It took the adults only about a minute to catch on and capably process the speech.

So, categorizing someone as "other" based on her unfamiliar speech is not equivalent to being unable to understand what she is saying. Nevertheless, just because you understand someone, you might still dislike the way they sound. In fact, people sometimes slight others and what they say simply because they are speaking in a non-native accent.

SHIBBOLETH

Picking out other accents may seem harmless enough — a sign, perhaps, of our linguistic sophistication as a species. Yet this ability can be used for different purposes, some of them underhanded.

We've already see how the word *shibboleth* was used to tell *them* from *us:*

> The Gileadites captured the fords of the Jordan and whenever a survivor of Ephraim said, "Let me go over," the men of Gilead asked him, "Are you an Ephraimite?" If he replied, "No," they said, "All right, say 'Shibboleth.'" If he said, "Sibboleth," because he could not pronounce the word correctly, they seized him and killed him at the fords of the Jordan. Forty-two thousand Ephraimites were killed at that time.

This is a bloody example, sure. But ancient and modern shibboleths abound, and history has no shortage of sad examples of what *we* choose to do with *them*. More recently, legend has it that in World War II, Americans would use the code word *lollapalooza* to weed out Japanese spies posing as Filipino or American soldiers, since the Japanese could not pronounce the word correctly.

Linguistic shibboleths are speech markers chosen purposely to reveal a non-native accent. Yet in a broader sense, accent is a shibboleth in and of itself.

A native-sounding accent can be the hardest part of a new language for a late-in-life learner to perfect. An adult may come close to mastering grammar and vocabulary, and yet that pesky non-native accent continues to commandeer their vowels. This is why Joseph Conrad could write perfectly in English yet continued to have a non-native accent. This is why when my friend Andrei is tired or tipsy, he will maintain subject-verb agreement and other grammatical principles of American English while his vowel sounds drift toward Romanian.

People typically wear their language and their accent on their sleeve. You can't miss it. So it can be quite shocking when you have listened to someone's speech, concluded the person is part of your linguistic group, and then discover you got it wrong. It is disorienting, going against our basic intuition that we can size up others based on how they speak. I have had this experience while sitting in a café in Paris. Someone at the neighboring table was speaking French in what sounded like a native French accent (and was, presumably). Then she picked up her cell phone, and I heard her say "Hello" and start to speak in native-accented American English. Here I was, someone who speaks both English and French, and who studies language and social groups — yet I was surprised when someone I had placed in one category (monolingual French speaker) turned out to have a more complex social identity than I realized.

It can similarly be surprising to learn that an actor's onscreen accent does not match their native accent. Think of discovering that *House*'s American-accented Hugh Laurie actually speaks British English. Or learning that *The Americans* actor Matthew Rhys is Welsh, not a Russian pretending to be an American —

which would be a linguistic feat itself! Part of this feeling of surprise may just be awe: this actor is talented enough to sound effectively American, essentially overriding the limits of the critical
language-learning period. But part of the shock is related to the
feeling that you in some sense *know* the actor, at least a little, from
watching him on TV. And then you find out that he is not who
you perceived him to be, and you feel a little jolt. It's as if someone fooled you — you never really knew this actor in the way you
thought you did.

Many stories capitalize on this language-related shock — as in
the unsettling scene in *24* when the supposedly American character Nina reveals herself to be a traitor by speaking Serbian. This
is a fairly common trope in television and film — a stark and effective way to reveal a traitor is a switch in language or accent. We intuitively use spoken language to mark off groups, and so when we
discover that we categorized someone incorrectly, the effect can be
jarring. You think you know who is in and who is out, but you were
wrong.

TOWARD BABEL

The use of language to divide the social world into in-groups and
out-groups isn't just a habit of individuals. It is also foundational to
our notion of culture.

As the United States of America was being formed, the states-
man John Jay argued in the Federalist Papers for the union of
colonies of people who descended from the same people and "together spoke the same language" (though it seems worth noting
that at the time, many settlers in Pennsylvania spoke German).
Around the same time, Noah Webster, of dictionary and spelling-
reformation fame, wrote that "the diversities of languages among
men may be considered as a curse, and certainly one of the greatest evils that commerce, religion and the social interests of men
have to encounter."

To some degree, it's understandable that these early Americans would seek linguistic solidarity. Their nation was just getting off the ground, and its culture was still taking shape. According to the historian Marc Shell, language and national culture are so tightly intertwined that a morphing language reflects a morphing culture, and thus, for individuals in that culture, morphing selves. According to Shell, "Many people maintain that they cannot change their language without ipso facto also changing their gods and themselves."

What's more, there is reason to think that this new "American" English was a product of the nation's independence, not just a token of it. Evolutionary linguistics shows that languages do not just change gradually, nudged along by time and geography. Instead, they shift when new groups form or splinter. It's at these divisive junctures of human civilization that languages split. New social groups give rise to new languages.

This raises questions, ones that John Jay and Noah Webster surely asked themselves: Why don't we all just speak a common language? Why don't all of these minority groups just give up and speak the language they are told to use? Why can't everyone speak English, for instance?

This isn't a new line of inquiry; since early in human history, people have apparently pined for a world in which everyone talked the same. The biblical story of Babel depicts people united by a common language who work together to build a tower so high, it would reach to heaven. As punishment, God confuses their language, so that they no longer understand one another; they scatter all over the globe. The heaven-reaching-tower project is terminated.

The dream of a common tongue may be ancient — but it is not realistic. Languages shift as social groups and allegiances change. It is the nature of human language to morph over time, as groups realign. Insofar as humans exist in different distinct communities, it is simply not possible for everyone to speak the same way.

On a grand scale, languages are always changing — often driven by younger speakers, those adolescent linguistic "movers and shakers." I remember that one of my college roommates could recite a surprising amount of Chaucer on demand. What was interesting to me was not so much the poetry but rather how much Chaucer's Middle English differs from our current language. The beginning lines of *The Canterbury Tales* offers an apt example: "Whan that aprill with his shoures soote / The droghte of march hath perced to the roote." Does this look a little strange? The internet is teeming with help for the flummoxed, at sites such as "Teach yourself Chaucer's English" and "Pronouncing Chaucer's Middle English." This passage, though, was written less than seven hundred years ago. If you time-traveled just a little farther — say, back a thousand years, to Old English — you would feel like a complete foreigner, unable to understand the language.

In one sense, a thousand years go by fast; in another sense, the pace is plodding. Entire languages can form and change in a shorter space of time. The example of Nicaraguan Sign Language, discussed in the previous chapter, shows how a brand-new language can be formed and dramatically evolve over a generation or two; within the same brief time span, many languages face the risk of going extinct.

Furthermore, in modern times, not everyone wants to speak a common language; instead, people within a culture fight to keep their *own* language. This sort of "language loyalty" exists across the globe. In South Africa, in America, and anywhere you look, language marks cultural identity. And when one group wants to oppress another, restricting the use of its language has been frequently used as a tool.

For example, Spain has a longstanding national angst over Catalonia and the speakers of Catalan. For much of the twentieth century, Spain was ruled by the dictator Francisco Franco, who tried to destroy Catalan. The language was forbidden in schools and at some points banned entirely from being spoken in public. Franco died in 1975, and today, Catalan is a co-official language, with Spanish, in northeastern Spain (including the Catalonian capital,

Barcelona). Yet cultural tensions remain. In 2017, in a controversial referendum, Catalonians voted in favor of making their region independent from Spain. Interestingly, this movement was not driven strictly by the older generation, who recall the oppressive years under Franco. Also, many millennials, born well after Franco's death, favored an independent Catalonia. They had been learning and speaking Catalan freely their whole lives. A public opinion poll found that when asked, most people feel a sense of belonging to their linguistic group — they report that they identify as Catalan, rather than Spanish.

Linguistic identities — perhaps even national linguistic identities — can form without direct experience of conflict, and they can form early in life. For evidence of that, we can head across Spain to the Basque country in the north. Here, the Spanish and Basque tongues have co-equal linguistic status today, although during the Franco regime Basque, like Catalan, was outlawed. Adults who speak more Basque in everyday interactions tend to report that they are Basque, and those who use more Spanish do not. Children, it seems, quickly come to share the same feelings.

Depending on which language they heard at home (Basque, Spanish, or both), children, like adults, varied as to how much they felt they were Basque or Spanish. Interestingly, age didn't matter — a six-year-old speaking Basque at home felt more Basque than Spanish, as did a similarly situated fifteen-year-old. Children's home language also predicted how much they said they *liked* new people who spoke in different languages — they liked their own. Again, children of all ages seemed the same here — it doesn't take a whole childhood to figure out where your national group affinities lie. Six-year-olds seemed to know that these identities depend on language.

Creoles are new languages that are created by successive generations of native speakers. This can happen when adult speakers of two different languages come together, and new generations of children create a language based on input from both. This is not necessarily different from the process by which new languages often form more generally; nevertheless, people sometimes view Creoles as less authentic than the languages from which they originated. The Haitian linguist Michel DeGraff has experienced the marginalization of Creole languages both professionally and personally. He grew up speaking Haitian Creole — the language spoken by nearly all people in Haiti — but he was taught that it wasn't a *real* language (though of course it was — Creoles are real languages, just like any others). Haitian Creole emerged about three and a half centuries ago, as a result of contact between French and African languages during the French colonization and the Atlantic slave trade. Since 1987, Creole and French have been the two official languages of Haiti. Yet despite its official status, people often speak pejoratively of Haitian Creole, calling it a "bastard" language. This derogation of the language is surprising, since virtually all Haitians speak Haitian Creole, yet fewer than 10 percent speak French — Haitian Creole linguistically unites the nation. Yet French is considered the primary language of schooling. Most Haitian children are explicitly discouraged from learning in their native language and speaking it in school.

DeGraff describes how people mistakenly think of a Creole language as a simplified version of a "real" language, and thus not worthy of respect. This belief about Creole languages is false — all languages are indeed *real* languages. Haitian Creole is a language like any other, capable of describing all the content of life and the world.

It must be terribly disheartening to grow up while being discouraged from speaking your native language and being told that your language isn't as real or as good as others: not suitable for a classroom environment. As children are taught that their language is subpar, they come to see themselves as subpar too. DeGraff speaks of visiting Haiti now, as an adult linguist, and watching children light up when they are allowed to learn in their native tongue. He recalls how a local teacher summed up the experience: "When we teach in Creole, the students ask more questions."

The United Nations has a policy against language discrimination. According to the UN Human Rights Council's independent expert on minority issues, "Language is a central element and expression of identity and of key importance in the preservation of group identity." Many of the world's constitutions protect (at least in theory) minority language speakers too — from a database of 192 world constitutions compiled by the Constitution Project, 95 include text about the protection of language use. Moreover, article 27 of the International Covenant on Civil and Political Rights explicitly states that "in those States in which ethnic, religious or linguistic minorities exist, persons belonging to such minorities shall not be denied the right, in community with the other members of their group, to enjoy their own culture, to profess and practise their own religion, or to use their own language."

From one perspective, this feels reassuring. Phew, the UN takes a stand to protect speakers of minority languages! Yet from another perspective, rarely do people legislate against a behavior that no one engages in. As any good preschool teacher could tell you, if you have a rule against something, it is a pretty good sign that it's needed.

Nations all over the planet grapple with questions about language policy in schools and how to balance the "local" and the "national," and the situations are indeed diverse: Papua New Guinea (credibly the most linguistically diverse nation in the world), former French and British colonies in Africa, and nations in the Americas, such as Peru, with indigenous language populations, to name a few. Yet maintaining local and indigenous languages — and teaching children in those languages — rather than trying to stamp them out in favor of a single "national language" (often, but not always, English, French, or Spanish), helps children learn and flourish.

Children are capable of learning more than one language, and maintaining both their home language and their school language in concert. Children of all linguistic backgrounds can become thriving and happy multilingual members of their society. This might come as bad news for Noah Webster — but it's good news for the rest of us.

UGLY AMERICANS

Despite the evidence that no language has more inherent value than another, people can be remarkably judgy when it comes to this topic. For instance, in the United States, African American English is sometimes discredited as "bad" English — it may be called pejorative names and considered by some to be less capable of conveying all the content that other dialects can. This simply is not true. African American English is a dialect of English like any other (including Standard American English). No dialect is right or wrong, better or worse, inherently positive or negative.

In the US Constitution, there is no talk of language, nor of protecting minority languages or establishing a majority language. Despite what current political diatribe may at times suggest (or what, perhaps, John Jay may have wished), English is not in fact the national language of the United States. Yet that's not to say that people have not tried to make it so. Several states banned the speaking and teaching of German — the language of the enemy — around the time of World War I. The state of Nebraska took things particularly far with the so-called Siman Act, which outlawed the teaching of any school content in a language other than English. In 1919 the state passed a law forbidding the teaching of any foreign language prior to high school: "Languages, other than the English language, may be taught as languages only after a pupil shall have attained and successfully passed the eighth grade as evidenced by a certificate of graduation issued by the county superintendent of the county in which the child resides."

The "eighth grade" component of this law is striking — and invidious. It was written long before scientific studies demonstrated how the ability to master a language declines as children approach adolescence. Yet the legislators who wrote the Siman Act seemed to intuitively grasp this concept. Believing that national identity is rooted in a common language, they wanted to prevent children from learning a language other than English.

Happily, the Siman Act remained on the books for only a short time before it was challenged. A teacher at a one-room parochial school in rural Nebraska was convicted of teaching a ten-year-old fourth grader to recite some Bible verses in German, in 1920. (The school was part of the Lutheran ministry, which had a number of parishioners who were recent immigrants from Germany; they wanted their children to learn German.) The Nebraska Supreme Court upheld the teacher's conviction, noting the potentially "baneful effects" that might follow when foreigners come to the country and teach their own children their own language. In their opinion, the judges stated not only that they feared foreign-language instruction was "inimical to our own safety"; they also worried that when parents taught their native language to their children, it was to "educate them so that they must always think in that language, and, as a consequence, naturally inculcate in them the ideas and sentiments foreign to the best interests of this country." The Nebraskan judges worried that by learning a foreign language, children would come to *think* like foreigners — and therefore presumably have anti-American thoughts.

This case made its way to the Supreme Court of the United States — *Meyer v. State of Nebraska* — where (fortunately) it was reversed. The US Supreme Court, in short, destroyed its arguments. What *baneful effects* for America? What *safety* could foreign-language instruction possibly threaten? As the opinion of the highest court in the land explained it, no real identifiable emergency had ever arisen from a child learning a language other than English that would warrant infringing upon people's right to teach their children whatever language they pleased. The opinion concluded with a nod to the benefits of language instruction at an early age: "It is well known that proficiency in a foreign language seldom comes to one not instructed at an early age, and experience shows that this is not injurious to the health, morals or understanding of the ordinary child."

Yet just because the Supreme Court struck down attempts to explicitly forbid the teaching of a foreign language, it does not follow that all Americans accept foreign speech or the people who use it. During the 2014 Super Bowl, Coca-Cola launched an ad that included Americans singing "America the Beautiful" in different languages. Xenophobic comments ran wild on Twitter in its wake. In response, *Time* magazine published an article titled "Coca-Cola's 'It's Beautiful' Super Bowl Ad Brings Out Some Ugly Americans." Clearly, we are still grappling with deep-seated mistrust of foreign speech — and it will take more than a historic Supreme Court decision to change that.

ARE PEOPLE NICER IN THE SOUTH?

Language can be divisive, but you don't need stories of violence or warfare or discriminatory laws to see how. Ordinary people are constantly judging and categorizing others based purely on the way they speak. And if you've spent any time on social media, you'll know that people make inferences based on limited information about others and are exceedingly quick to judge them — and they are often wrong.

People often assign particular traits to a whole group of speakers. Thus, a stereotype is born. Although these traits may not characterize any given individual in the group of speakers, people may be tempted to trust the stereotype and feel that they are picking up on something *real*. Maybe you really *can* discern someone's personality based on his or her voice. Maybe beautiful, kind people have beautiful, kind accents. Maybe Italian just *is* more beautiful than German! Maybe people in the South who speak at a slower rate *really* are nicer! Maybe speech that sounds lower in status (remember Labov's studies about dropping *r*'s) indicates that a person who speaks that way is somehow inferior. Or — maybe not.

For instance, Britain has a huge range of posh-to-not-posh accents, although as an American I find it tough to differentiate between them. And I'm not the only one. As a comedic trope, the British comedian and political commentator John Oliver has used his accent to gain the trust of American viewers, despite the fact that his accent wouldn't be considered all that posh to someone in Britain. On his show *Last Week Tonight*, Oliver has talked about being accused of having a fancy accent, because "everyone knows British accents are intellectual." Right? Wrong. As he explains it, "My British accent does not sound intellectual — believe me, I sound like a chimney sweep passing through a wood chipper."

We can all relate. When other people hear us speak, they infer a lot of things about us, which may or may not be true. These are known as *accent attitudes* — preconceived notions based on how a person sounds.

One of the first scientific studies of accent attitudes was conducted in Britain in 1931 by Tom Hatherly Pear; the results were published in his book *Voice and Personality*. Pear wanted to know if people who listened to BBC radio broadcasts could accurately rate the personalities of different radio announcers, based on voice alone. People who participated felt that they could gain insight into someone's personality by merely hearing their voice. And, as they considered the broadcasters' various accents, listeners made very different judgments.

So, were the listeners right? Just by hearing a speaker's accent, could they tell what the person was like on the *inside* — benevolent or vindictive, intelligent or dull? The results of Pear's initial study, as well as decades of further research on this topic, suggest that the answer is no.

Now, it is true that through your speech, a bit of your social self goes on display — vestiges of the people who spoke to you as a child, and the social groups, friends, and loved ones with whom you identify today. Over the course of your life, your speech may shift slightly to match a new sense of who you are and where you are going in the world. So in this sense, when you speak, you reveal something of your social self.

But people often interpret differences in speech — and, in particular, differences in accents — in a way that is neither accurate nor fair. People's personalities are not defined by accent. When peo-

ple judge a person based on an accent, they are not really thinking about the individual person per se—they are thinking about
the stereotypes associated with an accent, and they apply them to
the speaker. And people *believe* that their conclusions are accurate.
Chances are, though, the listener is bringing more stereotypes than
truth to the table.

Since Pear's work in Britain in the 1930s, researchers all over the
globe have studied these accent attitudes. As we have seen, there
are certain things you really can know about a person based on accent. For instance, a person who speaks in British-accented English was very likely exposed to this accent as a child. At the same
time, there are plenty of things you can't know about this person
based on her spoken language—whether she is nice or mean or
if she possesses superior intelligence. People who believe they can
infer the presence of individual qualities like these based on a person's accent are making a serious error.

Many of the seminal studies about accent attitudes were conducted in Montreal in the 1960s by the linguist Wallace Lambert
and his colleagues. Canada had long juggled a sizable group of
speakers of two different languages (English and French). In 1867,
the Constitution Act established that English and French could
both be used in debates in Parliament and in any court, and the Official Languages Act of 1969 recognized the equal status of English
and French throughout the federal administration. Yet during the
1960s, Canada's Royal Commission on Bilingualism and Biculturalism described a country rife with tension across linguistic groups,
verging on a national crisis. Despite ostensible linguistic parity,
English speakers held the lion's share of economic opportunities.

Amidst all the turmoil in Montreal at the time, researchers
stepped in to study what was going on in people's ears and their
minds when they heard English and French. They wanted to deeply
probe what people *really* thought—perhaps revealing opinions
and attitudes about linguistic groups that ran so deep, people did
not even know they held them.

The linguists developed a test—the Matched Guise Technique

— to explore what people thought about speakers of different languages or accents. The test did not involve asking people directly about their opinions. Instead, participants were provided with voice clips of different speakers — ostensibly speakers of different languages or with different accents — and asked to evaluate them based on how they sounded. Yet unbeknownst to the participants, they were actually evaluating a series of "matched guises" — the *same person*, speaking in two different languages or dialects. This method controls for any idiosyncratic features of a particular person's voice and reveals the test subjects' stereotypes and biases about different kinds of speech.

One series of studies tested English-speaking and French-speaking Canadians' views about people who spoke in English versus French. Unsurprisingly, the English-speaking participants preferred the English-speaking "guise" of the person they were listening to. They thought that English speakers sounded smarter and kinder, had a better character, and were more ambitious than the French speakers. They even thought the English speakers sounded taller and better-looking.

Yet not all people preferred their in-group. Evidence suggested that French speakers had internalized the cultural ethos of the time, which relegated French to a lower status than English. Though the French speakers might not openly admit it, they too thought that the English speakers sounded smarter — and also taller and better-looking. The matched guise test surfaced this information. French speakers did, however, judge French speakers as kinder.

The accent attitudes of the French-speaking participants reflect something important about the way we intuitively evaluate others: we tend to assume that people's speech reflects something particular about how *warm* they are and how *competent* they are. As the psychologist Susan Fiske has shown, a person or a group can easily be seen as possessing one characteristic but not the other. This dual perception is a recurring feature of how people evaluate one another — based on speech and other behaviors or traits. Lower-status groups of people — usually including speakers of nonstandard dialects and recent immigrants — are rated more favorably on the warmth side and less so on the competence side. They may be perceived as kind and loving but not particularly effective or intelligent.

In the matched guise tests, the perceived status of the participants predicted their judgments too. In one study, the researchers tested French Canadian adolescents from two different schools: one was a public Catholic school and the other was more elite, a "private college." Among the girls at the elite private school, pro-English biases were more visible and emerged at earlier ages. Perhaps like the "second from the top" group in Labov's studies in New York City, French Canadians at the private school were more sensitive to the status distinctions in their society. When test subjects were sensitive to status, they preferred English speakers.

Someone participating in these studies may not, if asked, tell you outright that they think English speakers are better-looking and smarter than French speakers. Yet these attitudes came to the surface in these tests, revealing what the authors called the subjects' "private" or "uncensored" views.

Why would there be a difference between "public" and "private" accent attitudes? For one thing, most people are socially motivated to conceal prejudice; for another, people may not even be aware of their own attitudes (including seeing their own group as inferior in certain ways) that culture has taught them. Language researchers were prescient in identifying the subtle, hidden attitudes that people might not admit to others (or, at times, to themselves). This split between private and public attitudes (or, in more up-to-date phrasing, implicit and explicit attitudes and bias) has become a major focus of research in social psychology.

One of my undergraduate students, a guy named Tu, grew up in China and told me he joined my lab because he had been so intrigued by language attitudes in his own country. Linguists estimate that there are hundreds of varieties of Chinese dialects, many of which are mutually unintelligible; China also has fifty different ethnic groups, whose members often speak in different dialects. Tu told me that many people in China believe you can tell what someone is like — smart or not, kind or not, and so forth — based on dialect, and his experience is reflected in academic research, which shows that people in China rate speakers of different dialects of Mandarin in dramatically different ways. For instance, they think that speakers of Northeastern Mandarin (NEM) sound lower in status than speakers of Putonghua (which means "common language"). Sometimes called Modern Standard Mandarin, Putonghua is the official language of the People's Republic of China, and its pronunciation is based on the dialect spoken in Beijing. The media depicts NEM speakers as small-town dolts — funny, kind, but unsophisticated, as in shows such as *Country Love*, which is about hapless villagers.

All over the globe, people hold accent attitudes like these. For instance, in the UK, people think of the Received Pronunciation (R.P.) accent as more "proper" or prestigious, though people who speak with other accents may be considered warmer or thought to have other positive attributes. The same thing goes for France, where Parisian French is seen as the standard for competence, despite the fact that speakers of other varieties prefer their own. In Morocco, Algeria, and Tunisia, Fusha, or classical Arabic, is considered the language of the heavens — the most beautiful language, superior to all others. But regular people don't actually speak it. Accents evoke social attitudes and evaluations — including those whereby people devalue their own way of speaking.

LINGUISTIC INSECURITY

Accent attitudes don't just affect how we think about others. They also influence how we treat others, and how we feel about ourselves. When someone doesn't like the way someone else speaks, they usually show it. They may shut down or stop listening. This really does not feel good for the person who is talking, and the experience can have deep, lasting, and sometimes tragic effects.

A professor I know is a non-native speaker of English — his first language is Hebrew — but he has lived in the United States for his entire adult life. His English is nearly perfect — grammatically he sounds like a native speaker to me, and certainly in terms of his word choice, his vocabulary is semantically rich and profound. Nowadays his Hebrew is rusty and somewhat out of date, reflecting the language of his childhood (though Hebrew is likely the language more connected to emotion). Nonetheless, he feels that he cannot shake that pesky foreign accent when he speaks English.

My professor friend is clearly in a privileged position. He is a highly educated man, with fancy degrees and a job at a fancy college. He is respected and loves his career and his life in the United States. Yet despite his impressive résumé, he feels that strangers and students alike take him less seriously because of his non-native accent. He says that when he orders food in a restaurant, sometimes people give him a funny look. The server might pause a little, squinting, making sure that the order makes sense. When my professor friend teaches a first-year writing seminar to college students, some at first act skeptical about him. Could this man with a funny accent actually teach them how to write correctly in English?

Now imagine the discrimination faced by foreigners who are less educated or wealthy. How must they feel when their manner of speech makes others treat them differently? As they try to learn English, perhaps making a heroic effort, they discover that people often glance at them sideways when they attempt to say something in their new language. Sometimes the reaction of listeners is very subtle. A person may take longer to respond, a cloud of doubt passing over their face. Sometimes the response is not subtle at all — the listener may yell "What?" as if the speaker were hard of hearing, or state that they can't understand what is being said.

The experiences of a former student of mine, Jamal, provide a story that exemplifies the biases attached to speech, even among people who simply speak different dialects of the same native language. Jamal was an ambitious student who spent a summer volunteering in my psychology lab. He told me that his high school guidance counselor advised him that as an African American young man, in order to be taken seriously he had to dress perfectly and *speak* perfectly. Jamal would switch back and forth between the dialect that he used at the University of Chicago and the African American English dialect that he used at home, with his mother and his friends from high school. By means of switching dialects he used his voice to help him fit into different social worlds. He told me that if he didn't code-switch — if he did not speak in a way that he felt sounded more "white" when at school — he felt that he was less respected by others. To feel welcome (sadly), Jamal felt that he had to modulate his speech.

People who speak nonstandard dialects, who have non-native accents, or who speak a language considered lower in status, may experience *linguistic insecurity* — they feel that others devalue their speech, and they may even feel discomfort with their own accent. Even when people understand your words just fine, it is still possible to feel bad about the way you sound. A paper by two psycholinguists makes an apt comparison: "Linguistic insecurity may be characterized as a negative or poor 'speech image,' comparable to a poor 'body image,' that is, a bad feeling about the way one talks like a bad feeling about the way one looks." Outwardly good-looking people can have poor body images; people who are quite capable of communicating may dislike the way they sound.

One feature of linguistic insecurity may be caused by taking on cultural attitudes that are prevalent in a particular society (one example would be the French speakers in Montreal who valued English more highly than their own native language). Another contributing factor may be people's own personal experience of being treated poorly because their manner of speech isn't considered *correct* or *classy* or *standard*.

When you speak with a nonstandard accent in a language that is not your native tongue, it can feel nerve-racking to enter some conversations. How can you know whether you will be understood? And if the interchange is awkward, you might feel that it is your fault. But communication is a process that involves two (or more) people. When a listener doesn't understand something, two choices are available. One option is to take steps to help, encourage, and engage the person who is speaking. This invites the speaker to feel more comfortable and thus better able to respond. Or the listener can shut down, project a negative attitude, and ignore the speaker.

One study shows just what happens when a listener brings a negative listening attitude to the table, and the person speaking feels these attitudes being directed toward them. The researcher brought two groups of English-speaking adults into a lab. The individuals in one group had biased attitudes toward English speakers with a Korean accent; the members of the other group did not seem biased. Participants then played a communication game in which the same Korean-accented speaker gave verbal instructions for drawing a particular map. The spoken directions were the only guidance that the test subjects received.

As you might imagine, the accuracy and clarity of the spoken directions could in theory have a large effect on the successful completion of the task. But, as it turned out, in this case the bias that the listener brought to the assignment had a greater impact.

The researchers observed that highly biased people seemed to listen with "avoidance strategies." They shied away from communication. They seemed to shut down, and didn't ask follow-up questions. Sometimes they were able to glean the correct information and draw the map correctly, and sometimes they weren't. But regardless of whether or not they succeeded, the highly biased people thought the interaction did not go well. According to their perception, they thought that they weren't able to communicate successfully with this other person.

The people who did not exhibit bias toward speakers of English with a Korean accent played the very same game with the very same Korean-accented speakers. Unlike the other group, they felt that they had positive interactions. They asked follow-up questions. They engaged with the speaker and did not shut down. Their interactions went well, and they were able to communicate effectively. But for people who brought their bias with them, the conversation was more likely to unravel, suggesting that a lot of communication is affected by what the listener — and not just the speaker — is doing.

One reason why some people are especially prejudiced against accents is that they think that speakers should be able to control their accent. Social psychologists point out that people likely to be biased feel that others should have better self-control. This "perception of controllability" often underlies stigmas related to obesity and mental illness as well, though naturally, obesity and mental health are not just a matter of personal choice.

If you speak with a non-native accent, it may be helpful to know a couple of things. First, you are not lazy, or crazy: a native-sounding accent in a new language is extremely difficult, if not impossible, to learn after a certain point in life. If you feel that someone does not like your speech and is shutting down communication, you may be right, and you are not alone. What's more, your difficulty in communicating effectively with this person is largely not your fault.

And on the flip side, if you feel any bias regarding someone's speech, your attitude is probably no secret. The other person can perceive it, which may spoil what might otherwise be a positive interchange. If you are someone who speaks with what you think is a "standard" accent, take a moment the next time you are interacting with someone who does not. Remember that your choices in the interaction — whether you engage or shut down — can make all the difference in how the conversation goes.

And finally, whether you are evaluating someone's speech or being evaluated yourself, you should know that accent attitudes did not emerge in a vacuum. Across millennia of human development and evolution, people have come to see speech as a significant marker of group membership. To some degree, accent attitudes are a product of this history. By understanding the deep psychological underpinnings of language identity, we can better understand how language and accent function in everyday life, and what we can do about it.

4

DEEP TALK

We are not born as complete blank slates. Instead, like any animal species, we come into the world with at least some of the self already written. Many of our thoughts, reactions, behaviors, and biases have been sculpted over millennia through evolutionary processes. This is true for many things in our cognitive and behavioral repertoire, including the way we learn language.

Our own psychology — and how we evolved to have the minds that we do — can help explain the origins of our tribal feelings about accent and language. These feelings are not just a feature of the modern world. Humans have evolved over millennia to care deeply about the way people talk — and to use this marker as a quick-and-dirty signal of who is *us* and who is *them*.

Becoming familiar with this psychological phenomenon and its evolutionary history can be enlightening, but the fact that we have deep and often unconscious biases in favor of our own group certainly does not excuse the negative behaviors that can sometimes arise from them. The goal of this exploration is wisdom — becoming aware of the inclinations handed down to us as part of our evolutionary heritage, so that when situations related to group identity challenge us, we can respond in a constructive manner.

In short, we are not the sum of our received tendencies as a species; rather, we are sophisticated thinkers who can rise above instinct to create beautiful, uniquely human structures of knowledge and behavior. It is high time we took that attitude toward speech — the taproot of both bias and the urge to create meaningful social bonds.

ORGANISMS OF NATURE

In the nineteenth century, the German linguist August Schleicher charted a family tree of European languages. Newer languages sprouted along branches of trees that represented more ancient ones. The image looked remarkably similar to Darwin's chart of a tree depicting the evolution of species (though Schleicher asserted that he conducted his work prior to reading Darwin's). Compelled to compare his work to Darwin's, Schleicher wrote, "Languages are organisms of nature; they have never been directed by the will of man; they rose, and developed themselves according to definite laws; they grew old, and died out ... The science of language is consequently a natural science." In Schleicher's view, languages are natural biological entities. They arose from their ancestors, lived, and eventually decayed and became extinct — akin to all species of living beings.

We now know that languages are indeed subject to "the will of man," despite what Schleicher may have thought. Languages are created by young children when they come together, which is how Nicaraguan Sign Language got off the ground. And languages divide as social groups fracture — when such splits occur, language changes too. As adolescents interact in social groups, their whims drive generational change in language. In all these senses, the will of people is observed in the way languages change.

At the same time, the way that Schleicher describes languages as natural organisms — each completely different, as one species of animal is different from the next — is helpful when considering many people's intuitive ideas concerning what language is. If we think of different languages as being fundamentally different "organisms," we may arrive at a similar conclusion about speakers of different languages — that they are essentially different kinds of people. Understanding this deep psychology can help us understand where some of our linguistic prejudice comes from, and what we can do about it.

Linguistic anthropologists have observed that people all over the world perceive languages, and speakers of those different languages, as fundamentally different from one another. When people listen to others' speech, they hear discrete categorical boundaries — even when differences in speech exist along a continuum. Our minds, and not just our ears, perceive these differences: we think of language X as being fundamentally different from language Y. From there, it is not a big leap to think of *groups of speakers* as being essentially different from one another — speakers of X are fundamentally different from speakers of Y.

Here's where this perception can get us into big trouble. We also are likely to assume that the language of certain members of a group, such as a particular society, is "pure" — that is, it has a unique characteristic essence — and that some people may be "less pure" group members than others, based on how they speak. In short, people may infer that you can't be an authentic member of a group or a culture without speaking the relevant language in a certain way.

This attitude is known as *essentialism*. It is based on the misconception that particular groups of people are different because of some real, meaningful underlying essence that is present deep in their nature. So if you think that "French speakers" are fundamentally different from "English speakers" due to something about their essential nature — rather than the situational variable of having been exposed to English rather than French — you are using essentialist reasoning. This common but misleading mental habit shapes our thinking in many domains.

What's more, it's not uncommon for people to think that when you learn a new language, you may instantly learn a new set of beliefs, ideas, or customs. The American anthropologist Janet Mc-

Intosh calls this "linguistic transfer" — the idea that by speaking a new language, you — perhaps somewhat mystically — take on the psychic properties of people who speak that language. She has studied this in Kenya, where some people report that language defines their selves, their rights, their land, and their religion — and they say that learning to speak a new language could risk changing any of these.

You don't need to go that far from home to see essentialism in action. Recall *Meyer v. State of Nebraska,* by which the supreme court of Nebraska decided that speaking a foreign language could "naturally inculcate in [citizens] the ideas and sentiments foreign to the best interests of this country." People feared teaching a child a foreign language — it seemed the child's mind might take on "foreign ideas." In East Africa, the American Midwest, or apparently anywhere in the world, this ingrained assumption seems to prevail: what you know — and perhaps the way you feel or think — is somehow embedded in your language. Learning a new one could transfer a set of new ideas into your head.

To put it mildly, people have some funny beliefs about language — imbuing speech with mystical powers that in fact have nothing to do with the way we talk. This peculiarity extends to our beliefs about how languages are acquired — and our assumptions about whether languages are learned through hearing people talk to us or by other means.

If you've read this far, you won't be surprised to hear that humans have the biological faculty to learn and reproduce languages, and children learn languages that they hear in their environment. Yet sometimes people seem to think that the ability to speak a particular language, rather than a different one, is embedded in a person's nature, rather than learned from exposure to it.

To illustrate the absurdity — and long history — of this notion, linguists often retell the ancient story of the Greek historian Herodotus, who in about the fifth century BCE wrote about an ancient psycholinguistics experiment. Allegedly, the Egyptian king Psammetichus wanted to figure out which language was the true first language on earth, the one that most perfectly reflected the human soul: was it Phrygian or Egyptian? According to the story, he separated two babies from their mothers and sent them to be raised by herders. The babies' physical needs were to be met, but no language was to be spoken in their presence. Lo and behold, as toddlers, they were overheard speaking their first words in Phrygian, the true language of humanity!

Presumably, the babies did not learn the Phrygian language on their own. Maybe the herders spoke Phrygian among themselves, didn't follow instructions, and talked to the babies, exposing them to the language. Or maybe the story is made up. Whatever the case, Herodotus's tale reflects our intuition that the ability to speak one language instead of another is somehow rooted in biology, and a child might inherit it.

In the real world, as we've seen, children are born with the remarkable ability to learn languages — but no child is born with the aptitude to speak any one in particular. Logically, speaking English rather than French, Spanish rather than Japanese, could not possibly be codified in your DNA. It is rare to find an absolute truth in just about any field of study, but I will go out on a limb and say that if you are not exposed to French, there is about a zero percent chance that you will learn it.

But that doesn't put the kibosh on the strange intuition that speaking one language over another is somehow written into the genetic code. As Steven Pinker writes in his seminal book *The Language Instinct*, which examines humans' remarkable language-learning abilities, this belief is widespread but utterly false:

> This folk myth is pervasive, like the claim of some French speakers that only those with Gallic blood can truly master the gender system, or the insistence of my Hebrew teacher that the assimilated Jewish students in his college classes innately outperformed their Gentile classmates. As far as the language instinct is concerned, the correlation between genes and languages is a coincidence. People store genes in their gonads and pass them to their

children through their genitals; they store grammars in their brains and pass them to their children through their mouths.

Now, *you* might not need to be convinced that language is passed, as Pinker says, from people's mouths, not their gonads. However, I have observed that even enlightened modern adults, young and old alike, sometimes think of others as defined by and linked to their native tongue, or to the native tongue of their biological forbears.

A colleague of mine is a psychology professor at a large university. In a particular class, she spends a day teaching about language acquisition, typically mentioning research on international adoptions, such as studies of Korean children adopted by French families. She says it does not happen frequently, but every so often, students will express surprise that an ethnically Asian child could learn French so well. When asked to explain their thinking, they offer the opinion that someone who is ethnically Asian would have an easier time learning a "typically Asian" language; French was better suited to white children. In truth, any child can learn any language — it's just a matter of being exposed to it. But some adults hold the mistaken belief that something about your genes specifies *which* language it would be easier for you to learn — even as a baby.

To give another example, a (white, Midwestern-accented) friend of mine recently told me the following story. Her cousin adopted twin African American girls, at age one and a half. The cousin had suffered from infertility for years and desperately wanted a baby; when the opportunity arose to have two at once, she was overjoyed. Fast-forward ahead eleven years, and the girls are becoming adolescents. They are rebelling and finding their own footing, like adolescents everywhere. And their quest for self-definition has extended to their speech.

Recently, the twins' mom shared, her daughters sound different to her. As she struggled to articulate this idea, she mentioned to her cousin (my friend) that she thought they sounded *Black*. Trying to figure out why their speech had suddenly changed, she mused aloud. Perhaps their biological mom (whom she had never met) had spoken a dialect of African American English. Maybe the twins were exposed to this dialect early in life and it stuck, somehow. Or maybe it was transferred in utero, or inherited in their DNA? Could that be why, all of a sudden, it sounded like they were speaking differently?

Of course the answer is that no dialect of English had been handed down in the girls' DNA. Dialects (and all languages) are learned via exposure. The girls are not returning to their "biological linguistic roots." Rather, as adolescents they are seeking new social and linguistic models. After all, as their mom also noted, the girls go to a middle school where everyone else is white. As they have gotten older, the twins have started to feel that people treat them as though they are different, suggesting to them that they don't fit in. As a result, they may be seeking out other role models to provide a feeling of social belonging, which they might find in the media, if not in their local area. Like anyone else, they want to belong, and their modified speech may reflect this desire. For them, as for anyone, a particular language and dialect must be learned.

Studies of children provide some insight into adults' puzzling intuitions about language and where they may come from. Some fascinating evidence suggests that children start out with a pretty naive theory, thinking that learning a specific language (such as French instead of English) comes from biology, not environment. Some adults may hold on to this childhood intuition, even after experience should have debunked it.

In one experiment that nicely demonstrated children's thinking, Susan Gelman and Lawrence Hirschfeld gave Michigan preschoolers a "switched at birth" task. Children learned of two families — the Smiths and the Joneses. One spoke English and the other Portuguese. Now, say the Smiths (the English speakers) have a baby, and the baby immediately goes to live with the Jones family (the Portuguese speakers). When that baby grows up and learns to talk, will she speak English or Portuguese?

You can see how this experiment cleverly pits children's beliefs about nature and language against the concept of nurture and language. Does the hypothetical child grow up to speak the language of her birth parents, which would mean that language is biologically transferred? Or does she instead speak the language of her adoptive parents, which would mean that language is learned from the environment?

Five-year-old children chose the "biological" answer. Hearing these simple vignettes, they concluded that the hypothetical child would grow up to speak the language of her birth parents, though the child lacked exposure to that language. In jumping to this conclusion, these children are following in the footsteps of the Egyptian king in Herodotus's story — the ruler who thought that by rearing children in linguistic isolation, he could determine their "true" language. It seems that some adults may still hold on to this incorrect childhood intuition about where language comes from — and what this intuition represents.

CALLS OF THE WILD

Our propensity to see language as deeply rooted in people's beings — and reflective of something inherent about their social identity — is not new. It has marked human social groups since prehistory, and the groundwork for this phenomenon was likely laid before humans were even, well, human.

Humans are not alone in hearing social meaning in others' vocalizations. In fact, other animal species that engage in vocal communication seem to attach social significance of "accent groups." Songbirds are the classic example of a species with vocal learning capacities that parallel aspects of human speech development. Other species also identify one another based on vocalizations — both to pick out who an individual is and also which social group it belongs to. "Acoustic clans" of killer whales are found off the coast of Alaska, where different pods of whales develop culturally different calls. Learning happens among the young, typically received from mothers or other maternally related individuals. Dolphins too know who is who, based on signature whistles; it seems almost as if, like us, dolphins have names for the individuals they know. Similarly, when baboons hear another baboon's call, they know the identity of the individual, including information about kinship and social status. Horses and crows both recognize the calls of their group members.

But humans are unique in the sheer multiplicity of their vocalizations — our speech has incredible complexity and diversity. This is an unquestionable fact, but how we came to hold this linguistic distinction is a matter of ongoing research. It's hard to find out exactly how linguistic diversity came to be way back in our evolutionary history. Of course, fossil records do not include audio clips. But anthropologists who study the development of culture in humans as long ago as the Middle Stone Age in Africa, or during more recent times in Europe (that would be thirty to forty thousand years ago), have been finding some pretty interesting evidence that the way people speak has varied across human groups for a long time. That evidence comes from beadwork.

Around thirty to forty thousand years ago, a group of Africans arrived at the European continent, traveling on foot, and they slowly spread across the area. These hunter-gatherers lived before the advent of agriculture. To try to grasp what their language might have sounded like, a team of archeologists took a new approach: studying beads, the remnants of ancient people's body ornamentation. These beads were made from long-lasting materials such as shells, stone, ivory, and teeth from a range of species (*eek* — including some from humans). Believe it or not, these artifacts can be interpreted in a way that provides information about how linguistic diversity might have spread across the continent.

The archeologists catalogued the beads found at different sites — 157 total bead types from 98 places, stretching from what is modern-day Germany down to Greece. While the beads varied widely in design, it turns out that they were not spread out randomly. If that had been the case, it would suggest that each little culture had created its own distinct preferences in ornamentation.

But instead, there is a pattern to variability — and it likely reflects linguistic diversity.

The bead patterns seem to cluster in *sets*. Those from geographic sites located far apart had nothing at all in common. The northern European beads found in Germany are entirely different from those in Greece. German beads have a lot of animal teeth, Greek beads more shells. (And four sites in France yielded human teeth used as beads.) You might wonder — are the preferences simply based on the materials available in different geographic regions? But were there no foxes to provide teeth in Greece, no shells available in northern Europe? This "availability" argument did not hold water. First, foxes were everywhere in Europe (not to mention wolves, horses, and other animals that provided teeth — including humans). Next, the Atlantic coast had plenty of the same shells that wash up on the Mediterranean coast, but only the Mediterranean peoples used those shells for ornamentation. Third, and perhaps most interesting, the beads seemed to *travel*. Some beads made from Mediterranean shells were found inland, three hundred kilometers from the sea.

And what about those places in the middle? This is where the research excitement occurs. Here, the preferences mixed and matched. A particular group's beads had something in common with those of its neighbor — but also something a little different. As the groups branched out across Europe, their bead patterns branched out too. Near neighbors had some but not all beads in common; as distances increased between groups, so did the differences between their beads. Groups separated by a great distance had beads with nothing in common.

From this evidence it can be hypothesized that these groups of humans were in dialogue with near neighbors, but not others who were far away. Groups in close proximity could communicate and share customs related to beads. And the similarities and differences between beads provide a pretty good proxy for the likely similarities and differences between languages. Neighboring groups presumably spoke enough of a common tongue to be able to com-

municate (at least to some extent) about beads. And as groups jour-
neyed to distant places and separated from one another, they very
quickly started to speak in different ways.

This has been the case for millennia upon millennia. The beads
nicely illustrate how human speech became differentiated across
various groups for as far back as we are able to study them. In this
manner, language differs dramatically from a much more recent
addition to human social categories: race.

OUT OF AFRICA

Over the course of our species' long evolutionary history, the connections — whether real or imagined — between speech and social
affiliation have become powerful indicators of status and the source
of much misunderstanding.

For many people today, especially those in the United States,
racial prejudice is unfortunately systemic in numerous aspects
of people's lives. Skin color is certainly visible, and in many
countries (including the United States) race has become bound
up with many other social markers, such as class, ethnicity, and
even religion, in ways that are highly complex and freighted
with long histories of oppression and marginalization. People's
modern thinking about race often reflects the impact of historical
and structural patterns of inequality. So you might think that
our proclivity to use race to categorize people is among the
most longstanding aspects of our human psychology in terms
of evolutionary time. This would be a reasonable conclusion. It
would also be wrong.

Although race has tremendous and societally systemic modern-
day significance, it turns out that humans have not been thinking
about race for very long. Differences in skin color across human
groups is relatively recent in terms of evolutionary time, and the
social significance we attach to what we perceive as "racial groups"
is even newer still.

Estimates vary, but it is generally accepted that everyone on the planet today descended from an ancestral group living in sub-Saharan Africa somewhere around 150,000–200,000 years ago. Jumping ahead, about 50,00 years ago, a big wave of migration started. Likely due to changes in the climate, some humans moved out of Africa into Eurasia, Australia, and eventually the Americas. At this point in time, humans probably did not differ very much in terms of skin tone.

Only for a fraction of this time span have different groups of humans varied in terms of what we might today consider race. "Lightness" in skin tone evolved primarily among European settlers, who lived in a northern, not overly sunny climate, starting about eight thousand years ago. In these northern areas, genes for pale skin, which allowed better absorption of UV rays, thus facilitating vitamin D synthesis, were beneficial. What we may think of as race today is — in comparison to the long history of humanity — a surprisingly recent development.

What's more, even after human skin tones began to adapt to northern climates in certain parts of the world, these newly differentiated social groups — groups that differed in "race" as we might say today — were not coming into much contact with one another. Ancient humans certainly migrated and encountered neighboring groups. But those neighbors would not have looked very different in terms of skin color. (Realistically, how far could people travel over the course of a single lifetime, when they were moving primarily on their own two feet? Not that far.) This trajectory contrasts dramatically with the spread of language — the languages of neighboring groups can shift very quickly, over a very short span of time. Separate two groups by a mountain range, and they will quickly evolve different ways of speaking; they will not, however, quickly develop differences in skin tone.

Race therefore would not have been a productive concept for our hunter-gatherer ancestors to ponder. Unlike group differences in the way people sound, which date back as long as humans do (and even earlier, as the different "accents" of animal calls suggest) and can morph quickly, differences in groups' skin color is pretty recent in our evolutionary history. The psychology of race as we think of it today is relatively new to humans.

This is not to say that populations of people who have been separated by time, distance, migration, and mountain ranges don't differ genetically. They do—but these differences don't come down to race. For instance, Icelandic people have long been cut off from the rest of the world, such that most of them are descendants of the same Vikings who lived just over a thousand years ago. Genetic studies of the Icelandic population reveal that their isolation is reflected in their genes; the Icelandic population has a remarkably small amount of genetic diversity. In contrast, the most genetic diversity on the planet is found in Africa. This is because humans have been there the longest, and thus different populations have had time to diversify genetically.

But these genetic differences align poorly with differences in what today we call race. The population of Africans diverged a long time ago from today's current Europeans, certainly. But in the time since, Europeans themselves diverged from Australians and from the Viking-descended population of Iceland. And if you look at the common protein-building genes that scientists have been able to map out, which could in theory predict appearance, you do not find clear race-based patterns. For example, if you looked at the blood types of all the people in the world and sorted them based on who has the recessive O allele in the ABO blood group system, you would (perhaps surprisingly) find Icelandic people clustering with Japanese people, and Ethiopians with Swedes. Populations of people, in short, don't always carry the genes that you might expect.

If race were just about population genetics, then we would talk about the Icelandic race and the many different races of people in Africa. But for the most part, we don't. Genetic differences across populations simply do not enter into our notion of what it means to be Black or white.

This is because the *psychology* of race is categorical in a way that the genetics are not. Patterns of genetic diversity simply do not match up clearly with what we see, psychologically, as modern racial groups. People's psychological perception of human difference doesn't align with the biological reality. This is because the psychology of race isn't about what is *actually* in the genome. The psychology of race is about what people think is real.

Some evolutionary psychologists seeking to explain why we evolved to care about race have come up with a bold answer: in short, we didn't. The psychology of race is not a human necessity. We care about race, psychologically, because of the dramatic consequences it has today for people's lives, and the way it unites and divides people in our current social world. Children learn racist attitudes from a society with systemic racial prejudice. Yet at a deep level the psychology of race is a modern by-product of an ancient adaptation for caring about human groups more generally. This means that if kids were raised in a world in which race were not a big deal, the psychology of race would likely decline, no longer a necessary way of categorizing and dividing other people. We are built to care about groups; race does not necessarily have to be one of them. The fact that it *is* says something important about our societies and their recent history, but not necessarily about our evolutionary lineage.

Throughout human evolution, people have benefited from knowing who was in and who was out: who was in their group and who wasn't; who was friend, and who was foe. Our hunter-gatherer ancestors presumably cared a great deal about group membership long before the concept of race entered the picture. Our psychology, in short, has been honed over millennia to track in-group members and out-group members, signs of friendship and cooperation, signals of defection and deceit.

Our minds are wired to monitor social groups — and our modern society sadly reflects a history of oppression, marginalization, and inequality across racial group lines. But the evolutionary origins of our psychological attention to race are not as ancient as our psychological attention to language, which opens the optimistic possibility that our modern thinking about race may turn out to be somewhat malleable, depending on the social environments in which we find ourselves.

WHO SAID WHAT?

As a thought experiment, consider whether you would put much stock in anyone's racial identity if you were raised in a world that did not correlate race with social group membership. In such a world, race might come to be more like hair color: you would notice it, certainly, but it would not define how you view a person's social identity in the way that it can in our own modern, troubled world. Interestingly, actual experiments bear this out: when you put modern adults in an experimental setting where race is not a good clue to group membership, attention to race wanes. By contrast, attention to language or accent stays strong.

Lots of past studies have found how difficult it is for adults to turn off their awareness of people's racial group. For instance, recall the "new neighbor" anecdote — you can't pick your neighbor out of a lineup, but you remember her gender and her race. A related famous psychology study, called the "who said what" game, dates back to the late 1970s. In this experiment, which has been repeated many times since its debut, adults watch a conversation unfold among adults who differ in gender and race. At the end, they are asked to recall who said what. Onlookers get a lot of the details right, but they also make mistakes. And their mistakes aren't random — the pattern they follow suggests that participants attended to the social-category membership of the people they were watching in addition to the individuals themselves. In a common iteration of the "who said what" game, two Black guys or two white guys are mixed up much more often than two people of distinct racial groups (and both white and Black adults make errors in this same pattern).

It is really hard to turn off this tendency to see people as being part of a racial group. Yet apparently we can do so more easily when social context allows for it. In a clever experiment, a group of evolutionary psychologists demonstrated that when adults are put in a situation where race no longer is relevant to the demarcation of social groups in their local environment, their attention to race wanes. They showed adult participants a group of white men and Black men depicted as being on two rival mixed-race basketball teams — teams that had gotten into a fight in the past season. Team members made various statements about their allegiances, such as "You were the ones who started the fight!" Individuals wore basketball jerseys in colors that identified their team membership. Critically, being Black or white did not predict which team the players were on; both teams had an equal number of individuals of both racial groups. Essentially, the researchers were making team membership — not race — the important category of the day. Participants could see that being on the red team versus the yellow team (rather than being Black versus white) was what mattered for people's social identity in this context.

The researchers found that under these conditions, their test subjects' attention to race diminished. Participants started mixing up the players on a particular team — say, confusing the identities of two guys on the red team — and were much less likely to mix them up based on their race.

Another team of evolutionary psychologists used the same experimental setup, but instead of race, they "crossed" team membership with accent. When accent was presented by itself, people made many more errors mixing up people who speak with the same accent rather than across people who speak in two different accents (in this case, it was American English versus British English). And when the researchers pitted accent against team membership, they found that — unlike race — their adult subjects' attention to accent did not diminish. As in the first experiment, the study participants mixed people up according to their team membership — but this time, they also mixed up two American English speakers with two British English speakers. Participants clearly were attuned to both accent and to team color, but their attention to accent was just a bit stronger. People's awareness of others' accent appears to be harder to "turn off" than their awareness of others' race.

Using an even more subtle variation of "who said what," another group of psychologists found parallel evidence that when we remember others, their accent matters more to us than their looks. These researchers presented German adults with faces of people who were rated by a different group of adults as looking prototypically German versus prototypically Italian (for example, lighter versus darker hair and eyes). The adult participants had no problem categorizing who was who. Next, they added voices in different accents to the mix — some faces spoke in German with a typical native-sounding German accent. Others spoke German with perfect grammar yet with an Italian accent, suggesting, perhaps, that they were recent immigrants. Again, the researchers found that accent won out over appearances. People mixed others up based on whether they *sounded* German or Italian — not whether they looked German or Italian.

This tendency to make the way someone speaks a critical touch point for how you remember them emerges very early in life. Recent studies from the lab of my friend and colleague Kristin Shutts found that differences in the degree of children's awareness of others' race and language are apparent in the preschool years. Shutts and colleagues designed a kid-friendly version of the "who said what" memory-confusion game — a "who saw what" game geared to preschoolers. The researchers paired pictures of kids with pictures of animals — and the researchers described to each test participant that one kid saw a giraffe, another saw a hippo, and so on. Afterward, children were asked to remember which kid saw which animal. They got these pairings right much of the time (zoo animals are pretty interesting for this age set!), but they also made mistakes. By looking at the pattern of their mistakes, it did not seem that the kids encoded race. They mixed up a white girl with a Black girl just as often as they mixed up two white girls or two Black girls.*

When the researchers conducted the same study with language — showing preschool-age children English speakers and Spanish speakers who saw animals at the zoo — their young subjects mixed up two English speakers, or two Spanish speakers, but they were much less likely to mix up an English speaker with a Spanish speaker. This means that young children automatically encoded other people's language in a way that they did not initially encode race.

Now, does this mean that language will trump race or any other social group's importance in any place at any time? It certainly does not. Humans are flexible, and highly susceptible to social influence and to learning from their culture. Their minds easily encode attitudes present in society, and in many modern environments, social groups are stratified by race, and racial prejudice is apparent in people's views and in society's institutions. Biases based on language and race also become intertwined, and linguistic prejudice can become an insidious aspect of systemic racism. But what this research shows is that at a deep psychological level, the way the human mind delineates different social categories is not always the same. Language categories are intuitively psychologically present in childhood, and very difficult to erase among adults. Our minds have evolved to view the way that someone speaks as a fundamental marker of who they are, and this categorization can be persistent, and sometimes even stronger than that of race — even in an unfortunately racist society.

---

* Of course, the children in this study were young, and hadn't yet learned how much race matters in their society (they lived in the United States). When the researchers followed up with a group of eight-year-olds, these older kids encoded race (mixing up two white kids, or two Black kids), just as adults would.

FLURPS AND ZAZZES

Because language as a marker of social groups has such a long history, we attend to speech in making basic moral decisions. We have developed a human moral code with a deep-seated foundation that can, in effect, be boiled down to this: "cooperate with in-group" and "compete with out-group." And what often defines in-group and out-group? Say it with me: language.

Humans divide the world into moral circles, and we feel more morally accountable for people we perceive as in-group members. As psychologists and philosophers have long observed, we humans have a moral compass that allows us to seem discerning about right and wrong; but when we encounter an outsider, suddenly our morality seems to fall apart. You don't have to look far to find sad examples of this. For instance, in 2017, Hurricane Maria devastated Puerto Rico. Yet the American media devoted surprisingly little time to the crisis, and grassroots donations to the relief effort were similarly paltry, especially as compared to the response to the damage caused by hurricanes Harvey and Irma, which made landfall in a similar time period in Texas and Florida. Polling a week after the hurricanes found that people's support of aid to Puerto Rico varied, based on what they *knew* about Puerto Rico. Americans who realized that people in Puerto Rico are US citizens favored sending far more support than people who did not know this. These Americans either had moral circles that included Puerto Ricans, or they didn't.

The psychologist Marjorie Rhodes discovered that these moral circles start early in life — and can hinge on language. In one study, preschool-age kids were introduced to two groups of people — the Flurps, who spoke English, and the Zazzes, who spoke French. First, they heard about the Flurps and the Zazzes working together to build a block tower — they were just characters in normal cartoons, doing some normal cartoony stuff. But then things took a turn for the worse. As the researchers explained to the child participants, "One day, a Zaz teased another Zaz and hurt his feelings."

Or, "One day a Zaz teased a Flurp and hurt his feelings." (How this teasing was supposed to be achieved, in spite of the language barrier, the researchers left to their subjects' imagination.)

At first, kids rated these actions as bad. After all, hurting feelings is not nice, no matter what language you speak! But then the researchers told them that this was actually a special world where new rules apply. "What if there was no rule in their school against teasing? Let's pretend that in the school they go to, the teachers said that the kids could tease each other."

Now what happens? When a Flurp teases a Flurp or a Zaz teases a Zaz, kids say that this is still wrong. Just because some teacher says its OK for one member of a group to do something mean to another member of that group does not make it OK in kids' eyes. But if a Flurp teases a Zaz or a Zaz teases a Flurp, and kids learn that an authority figure says it is OK to not care about this, the kids care much less. They are dramatically more likely to say that this harmful action is permissible when it occurs across group lines. (For readers who are paying attention, the first of these reactions is a microcosm of the US response to hurricanes Harvey and Irma; think of the second as the hurricane Maria condition.)

Recent generations of scholars agree that we have two moralities, a dichotomy that can be seen in kids' intuitions about the moral rules for teasing, which may vary, depending upon who is the object of the teasing. Back in the early days of the Enlightenment, Thomas Hobbes wrote of life as "nasty" and "brutish" — governments are needed to protect people from themselves. Later, Jean-Jacques Rousseau, in contrast, described basic human nature as innately compassionate. But in fact, humans are both at once: we are kind and we are jerks; we are benevolent and bellicose, both selfish and altruistic. Darwin noted this same dichotomy in *The Descent of Man:* he describes humans as undeniably social, collaborative, and intuitively *moral.* At the same time, he notes that these moral tendencies only go so far: "It is no argument against savage man being a social animal, that the tribes inhabiting adjacent districts are almost always at war with each other; for the social instincts never extend to all the individuals of the same species." Darwin describes sympathy as rampant "between members of the same tribe," yet most "are utterly indifferent to the sufferings of strangers, or even delight in witnessing them."

Our evolved linguistic capacities help contribute to — and explain — the double-edged nature of our moralities. As we have seen, we can be moral one day and immoral on the next, depending on context; likewise we are linguistic geniuses and dunces all at once. We are linguistic prodigies as children, yet we muddle through language learning as adults. We are moral with native, less moral with foreign. Someone who speaks in a native way can instantly reveal to others of the same group evidence of potentially similar allegiances, a common upbringing, related cultural knowledge, and consistent moral passions. The typical human response is to treat such a person as a member of a moral in-group. Someone who speaks in an unfamiliar way is seen as having a different past, a foreigner — one with an indecipherable language and perhaps, as a result, an inscrutable spirit. The typical human response is to treat such a person as belonging to a moral out-group. As any Flurp or Zaz could tell you, even the youngest members of our species carry this evolutionary baggage.

Children understand — and care about — linguistic difference in deep and meaningful ways. In part this is because it is a hard-wired part of their evolutionary inheritance as members of our species. But in part, it results from the messages and pressures they are exposed to as they grow up in human society. The former we have little control over; the latter is within our grasp. By understanding how kids develop, think, and navigate their social worlds, we can better understand who we are ourselves, how we came to be this way, and how to foster positive development for the next generation of children, so that their moral circles are as wide as can be. In this, as in so much else, language holds the key.

5

LITTLE BIGOTS?

Have you ever noticed that, until recently, bad guys in many movies had foreign accents and some animals spoke in African American English? This is no accident. Kids' movies —as well as media for adults—feature a disheartening amount of linguistic bias. Studies of movies and television shows find that accents that sound "standard" are overrepresented, and accents that people may perceive as "nonstandard" are often portrayed negatively. People perceived as having less standard accents are frequently depicted as *less than*—less worthy, less good, less complete. In popular culture, as in society at large, language can serve to differentiate "us" from "them" in ways that exploit our evolutionary impulses, weaken the social fabric, and disadvantage those who speak differently.

As a child growing up in a society full of linguistic stereotypes, it can be impossible to tune them out. They are so pervasive that they may seem unsurprising, perhaps even unobjectionable, to the average person. Consider some of the most common examples from American culture:

Northern American English = smart
Southern American English = slow-witted
The Queen's English = educated
Italian = beautiful

German = ugly
Russian = sinister

These stereotypes crop up in our day-to-day lives in myriad ways, and we begin to absorb them starting at a very young age. Children might learn from movies that bad guys speak with a German or Russian accent. They might deduce from TV that people with an Italian accent are sexy or great at cooking. They could learn from a parent or sibling that Americans with a Southern accent are hospitable but not too sharp.

Kids are little sponges, ready to soak up whatever stereotypes — linguistic or otherwise — that society offers them. But that is not to say that they don't have any intuitions of their own about the ways in which speech structures our social lives. Even while absorbing society's linguistic stereotypes, children have preexisting instincts that have been refined across evolutionary time to see language as a marker of social groups. Studying how children respond socially to others' language and accent, therefore, can offer a rich understanding of when and how we come to hold the linguistic attitudes that we do — as well as why language holds such impressive social power over us all.

MOTHER TONGUE

It takes a few years for babies to master a native language, but even newborns emerge from the womb with some pretty impressive knowledge. Because of all the time they spent hearing voices in utero — language that presumably sounded like a speaker broadcast underwater — babies enter the world equipped with a vague sense of what their mother tongue sounds like. They are born with a preference for listening to this native-sounding speech.

The psycholinguist (and noted multilingual) Jacques Mehler started a research program in the 1980s at an infant lab in Paris — where, coincidentally, I conducted research two decades later, when I was a PhD student. Mehler's general finding was that from birth, babies can differentiate the sound of different languages. And they prefer to hear the sound of the native one — the language that their mom speaks.

Of course, it's not easy to figure out what newborn babies do and do not know. For one thing, they are asleep most of the time! For another, they don't display behavior that looks, to a casual observer, like they are processing language in any meaningful way.

But researchers can get around this hurdle by tracking another thing that newborn babies do a lot, apart from sleeping: sucking. Often babies suck for milk, of course, but clever psychologists figured out that they also suck in response to sounds they are interested in. When new babies hear something they are interested in, they become a bit aroused — and therefore suck more. So by changing the sounds that babies hear and measuring the resulting change in sucking, scientists can get a general sense of what babies are learning and thinking when they hear different sounds.

In this way, researchers have shown that babies prefer listening to language that is familiar to them. Play newborn babies a familiar language — say French, if their mom speaks French — and they will suck slightly more than they do when they hear a language that is completely foreign to them (such as Russian, in this case). In these initial studies in the baby lab in Paris, researchers found that French newborn babies, despite having just been introduced to the world, already have a general sense of what their "native" tongue will be.

This sense of what is "native" isn't perfect at the beginning. A newborn baby whose mom spoke French finds that French and Italian sound the same — since the two languages are in fact rhythmically very similar. Likewise, a newborn baby who's heard a lot of English would have a hard time differentiating that language from Dutch — but would be able to tell either one apart from Italian or French. It takes some time to get perfectly calibrated to what is "native" and what is not. Life starts with a rough approximation, and then gets tuned up.

Young babies can even tell the difference between two foreign languages — if the languages are sufficiently different in rhythm. Even so, it seems to be somewhat easier for them to distinguish their own language from another one — for instance, for a French baby to tell French from Russian than English from Italian. The opposite is true for an American baby. In each case, young babies are a little better at picking out a language that they are familiar with. They have a sense of their mother tongue — but only a vague one.

With age, babies get further calibrated to what counts as "native." By five months of age, they get better at noticing some of these contrasts — but only if their own language is part of the equation. English-hearing babies still get confused by the difference between Italian and Spanish (both Romance languages!), but they start to be able to tell that Dutch is different from English. They can even pick out the differences between British and American English (though to a French-hearing baby, Dutch and two variants of English would presumably all sound the same).

Truly, babies seem to enter this world with an ability to distinguish between languages. But their capacity to tell different types of speech apart only goes so far. Seminal research by Janet Werker shows that just as babies are picking out their own language among alternatives, they are also losing something: their ability to easily differentiate subtle sounds in a foreign tongue. For example, different languages have slightly different phonemes — in Hindi, for instance, there are two variants of *d*, retroflex and dental; the difference depends on where the tongue hits the top of the mouth. To a Hindi speaker, these *d*'s sound like different sounds; to an English speaker they are largely indistinguishable. Young babies, whatever language they are used to, can hear the different *d*'s. But with experience, babies exposed to Hindi maintain this ability — and their abilities for hearing native contrasts even sharpens. Babies exposed to English, however, lose the ability. For English-hearing babies, over the first year of life, all the *d*'s become perceptually lumped together.

What this means is that babies are born "citizens of the world," ready to learn any language — but also they are born ready to become accustomed to whatever they hear most frequently, "tuned up" for sounds that are familiar. On the flip side, they are "tuned down" for linguistic differences that are not relevant to their social life. Despite people's essentialist intuition that language is passed down by means of the "gonads" rather than taken in by the ears, babies are universal listeners to begin with, and they need to hear a language in order for it to become their native tongue. But just because they don't know any languages yet doesn't mean babies aren't perfectly capable of using other people's speech to start to make sense of their social environment.

SOCIAL ANIMALS

When I was a new graduate student at Harvard, I discussed this research with my graduate adviser Elizabeth (Liz) Spelke, a leading expert on the origins of human cognitive capacities, and we started musing about what the sociolinguistic lives of young babies might be like. Babies presumably don't really have any deep linguistic identities — at least not in the way adults do. After all, they are not speaking yet and have only just begun the process of learning what their language is. But it nonetheless seemed possible that babies could have some early intuitions about the social function of language. This seemed particularly possible in light of the experimental evidence that from the moment of birth, babies start figuring out what "their" language is, and what is foreign — and they like to listen to speech that sounds native to them.

Liz and I wanted to put these ideas together to ask what babies know about the social relevance of language. Certainly babies don't know anything about the geopolitical plight of warring nations and their subsequently diversifying national languages. But could babies sense something simpler — yet intuitive — about the social significance of language? Without having mastered a language, can babies still intuit that the way people speak matters to their social world?

That fairly simple question launched the next fifteen years of my research in psychology. And in the short term, it led to many others: Do babies start to *like* some people more than others simply based on how they speak? Do babies start to see two people who speak in the same way as sharing a social relationship or having similarities, such as membership in a common social group? If two people speak in different ways, do babies have some sort of rudimentary intuition that they might be *different* from each other in a meaningful social way?

This inquiry led to some interesting discoveries. Just like adults, babies use language to judge and differentiate among groups of people. What's more, they can draw fairly sophisticated conclusions about people's social status from the way they talk. These amazing abilities show us just how deeply the social functions of language are rooted in our brains — and just how ingrained, or how potentially reversible, our tendency to discriminate based on language truly is.

Liz and I began to work from the basic premise that babies were able to *tell apart* two different languages, as shown by Jacques Mehler and colleagues — and that they preferred the sound of their own. We wanted to understand whether this began and ended with an auditory preference. Perhaps babies merely like the *sound* of their native language. Liking and orienting to familiar sounds would make a lot of sense if you are in the business of learning a language — and so certainly this preference for familiar sounds is part of babies' early linguistic capabilities. Additionally, we surmised that these early linguistic preferences could go one step further. We wanted to know if beyond a preference for familiar sounds, babies also started to like the *people in their world* who speak to them in their native tongue.

Our experiment's design was simple. We showed babies who were just over five months of age videos of people speaking in a native language or a foreign language (in this case, English and Spanish), and we measured where babies looked. Babies watched both people intently while they spoke. Next, the two people stopped speaking and were featured side by side, smiling silently at the infant. Where did babies look now? On average, they looked toward the English speaker rather than the Spanish speaker — perhaps as a gesture of interest or an invitation for further communication.

We next did the same study with two people who spoke English — but one spoke with a native American accent and the other in a foreign (in this case, French) accent. We found the same thing. After the two had finished speaking, babies liked to look toward the native-accented person.

Interestingly, there were some limits to our findings. In one study, we had inanimate shapes paired onscreen with the language — a ball and a square that bounced around happily to the sound of native or foreign speech. Here, babies did not preferentially choose to look at the shape that had been paired with their language. Babies are interested in social beings who produce sounds, not simple shapes that are paired with those sounds.

These first studies showed that babies' early preference for native-sounding speech extended beyond an auditory preference. Babies also like to look at the person who had been doing the speaking. But at the same time, determining what exactly this gaze might mean can be challenging. Babies' enhanced looking might mean a lot of things — interest, learning, and liking (and most likely a mix of all of these). We wanted to understand the social thinking of babies in a deeper way.

We worked to develop a measure that would let us test something about babies' early responses to native and foreign speakers that felt a little bit more clearly social. Emmanuel Dupoux, a French psycholinguist working in that same lab in Paris where the original studies of newborn babies' language had been conducted, had been developing such a method. We teamed up to work on understanding babies' early linguistic social preferences.

In this new "social" method, we tested slightly older babies — ten-month-olds — in both the United States and France. By this age they were able to reach for toys. This was important, because the experiment we devised used gross motor skills to measure the babies' interest, in much the same way that earlier experiments had used babies' sucking and visual attention.

All babies saw the same videos of a French speaker and an English speaker, who each talked to the baby onscreen (it was a big, life-sized screen). Next, each person on screen picked up a toy and held it out to the babies. By help of a slight "magic trick" — in reality, some PVC piping that rotated behind a table, attached via Velcro to some stuffed toys — we made it look as though the real toys popped out of the screen, so that babies could reach for one or another. Babies in the United States reached more often for the toy offered by the English speaker, whereas babies in France reached more often for the toy offered by the French speaker. Babies seemed to want to engage with someone who sounded like the people around them.

In another study we found that language influences babies' choices of foods as well as toys. Although many babies like to put any food (or anything, really!) in their mouth, they seem especially interested in eating foods that are "native." After eating two foods, one that an English speaker and one that a French speaker ate, English-hearing babies were given a choice. They tended to reach toward the English speaker's food a second time.

WHEN IN ROME

A few years later, when I became a professor at the University of Chicago, I returned to the question that I had started with as a new graduate student: what do babies think about people who speak the same language versus different languages? I'd been inspired by my time in Croatia, where I had noted that linguistic diversity and social changes go hand in hand. Working with the infant psychology expert Amanda Woodward and our former PhD student Zoe Liberman, I began to study whether babies use language to distinguish between social groups, rather than just as a marker in their interactions with individual adults. Our new studies probed whether babies have an early intuition that language marks social groups more abstractly. Are babies dividing people who speak different languages into some naive version of social groups? As an (admittedly imperfect) analogy, when groups of people speak differently, in some inchoate format, are babies seeing the Croats as different from the Serbs?

To test babies' thinking about how people are grouped together, we used their patterns of looking to get a sense of what they were thinking. In some experimental paradigms, babies' patterns of looking can be used as a measure of their surprise or interest. If you show a baby the same thing several times in a row, their looking time wanes — like anyone, babies can get bored. But if you show babies something new, different, or unexpected, as compared to what they had just been seeing, they look longer.

We first showed babies two people who each spoke on video. For some babies, the two people both spoke English; for some babies, the two people both spoke Spanish; and for some babies, one of them spoke English and the other Spanish. We next showed babies new videos of the two people either being friendly with each other (smiling and waving) or disengaging (turning away in an apparent huff). With this method, we could test which of the two following videos seemed more novel or surprising to them — and thus led babies to look longer.

The results showed that babies do differentiate between linguistic groups. When babies saw the two people speaking the same language, they found the video of them smiling and waving at each other fairly unremarkable. It is as though babies expected that they might be friends. The video of the two people disengaging and appearing to dislike each other, in contrast, surprised the babies — and those who had seen the two people previously speaking the same language spent a long time looking at this video, from which they learned that two speakers of the same language did not in fact like each other. It seemed unexpected to the babies that people who spoke the same language wouldn't get along.

The gaze of babies who saw one person speak in English and one person speak in Spanish looked quite different. These babies seemed unfazed by the video of the two people disengaging, and they instead looked longer when the English speaker and the Spanish speaker were friendly toward each other. It was as if the babies anticipated that speaking different languages licensed a lukewarm (or even hostile) social interaction. Babies probably don't know much about the intricacies of friendship, but their early instincts interpret speaking a common language as one sign of a positive social relationship — and they don't have the same positive expectations of social interactions across language lines.

Building on these findings, we wanted to gain further insight into whether and how babies think that language can structure social groups. One component of social groups is social affiliation, something we had tested already. But when people are members of the same social group, they also tend to do and like the same kinds of things. Do babies also think that two people who speak the same language are similar to each other in other ways? To investigate this in a baby-friendly way, we tested whether babies expect that two people who speak the same language are likely to enjoy eating the same kinds of foods.

In this study, we first showed babies a video of one person who liked to eat one of two foods. We next showed babies a second person — who either liked the same food, or preferred something else. If babies expect two people to generally like to eat the same thing, they would not find a new person coming in and liking the same food very surprising. Instead, they might look longer when the second person showed evidence of liking a different food — since that would be relatively more unexpected.

Indeed, when babies saw two people who both spoke the same language, they expected that they would like the same two foods. But when babies saw two people who spoke two different languages, they had the opposite impression — babies seemed to think that people who speak different languages might also enjoy eating two different things. This added depth to the findings I had observed as a grad student. In my earlier studies we had found that when making their own food choices, babies choose foods eaten first by a native speaker. Now we had found that babies expect the same kind of reaction among two strangers. Their little minds seem to be carving up the world at its linguistic joints and dividing people into rudimentary categories — for instance, dietary preferences — based on how they speak.

As babies grow, they continue to see language as suggestive of many other aspects of people's identities. I saw this firsthand with my own daughter. When she was learning English and French at around the age of three, she went through a phase when she would whisper to me "Is that a French person or an English person?" whenever we met someone new. Her friend from preschool, Lucia, was learning Spanish and English — but because Lucia spoke Spanish at home and was in preschool only part-time, her Spanish was clearly more advanced than her English. (Though Lucia's English soon caught up.) We invited Lucia and her mother over for dinner. My daughter was fixated on making sure we had "Spanish" toys and food, so Lucia would feel at home. I assured her that language did not seem relevant for liking pizza and that Lucia would certainly enjoy playing with all of my daughter's toys. "Oh," my daughter said, "they must have the same pizza and toys in Spanish." My daughter saw speaking Spanish as the category that most strongly defined Lucia.

By preschool age, children see someone speaking an unfamiliar language as suggesting that they are *different* in other meaningful ways — that they more likely wear different clothes or live somewhere unfamiliar. Perhaps they might have a less familiar skin color or look different in some other way. I think of kids' linguistic categories at this stage in life as somewhat fuzzy at the borders, but yet pronounced in understanding what the categories signify. Preschool-age kids presumably do not know anything about what it means to be a speaker of Spanish versus Portuguese versus Russian. If they are monolingual English speakers, they think of speakers of any of these languages as *different*, and therefore likely different from them in other fundamental ways.

The social significance of language also impacts how young children start to learn from others. Babies are interested in learning whatever society has to teach them — and hearing someone speak a familiar language is one way that babies cue into "Hey, learn this now!" even if it may not be clear on the surface why exactly they are learning what they are learning. On the other hand, babies see a *different* person as having less relevant information to share. When babies see someone perform a seemingly bizarre action (such as using their head rather than hand to turn on a light), babies tend to imitate that person — but they do so most when that person speaks in the babies' native language, and less when the person speaks in a foreign language. This makes a lot of sense, since people who speak in a native accent of a baby's native tongue presumably have a lot of culturally relevant things to teach the baby. In short, babies intuitively think of native speakers as particularly good sources of information.

As children grow, they continue to orient themselves to native speakers (and specifically, native-accented speakers) when figuring out how to learn from their social worlds. In another study, Kathleen Corriveau, Paul Harris, and I found that children trust the information provided by native-accented speakers, even for something relatively silly — such as how you move a new object. This makes some sense from a kid's perspective, since again, people with a familiar accent could be a particularly reliable source of *local* information, which children are certainly invested in figuring out. Who cares how an object is used or what it is called on the other side of the planet, or even on the other side of town? When kids learn things, what matters to them is learning from their local social environment. People's accents are seen as a pretty reliable clue as to whether someone is from that environment or not.

Does this mean that kids are born xenophobic, that they're fearful or intolerant of people who speak differently? No — it just means that children's minds are set up to care about language as marking social difference. Children intuit that people who are like each other speak in the same ways, and they orient themselves to familiar-accented people for learning. They think that speaking in different languages or even just different accents is a signal of some other kind of meaningful, broad difference across groups of people. This is a normal function of what it means to be human and predisposed to see the world in categories. In and of itself, this does not need to be bad. Yet when adults taint these early-developing categories with bigotry, children learn to associate languages and the people who speak them with negative, harmful stereotypes. Children are on a journey to figure out who is who and what is what in their social lives — and from day one, language is a tool that they carry on this quest.

"JULIE ISN'T RACIST!"

When children are trying to deduce how their social worlds are organized, they have to sort through a lot of information about people that may or may not denote social difference: for instance, other people's skin color, eye color, ways of dressing, or even ways of walking. Indeed, under the right circumstances, any factor can become meaningful for social grouping. If a group matters to society, kids will eventually become aware of it.

Yet my research, along with other recent research in the field of evolutionary psychology, suggests that not all potential social differences carry equal weight, at least early in child development. It turns out that language (but likely not all social variables) guides infants' earliest social intuitions today.

When I was conducting the studies that showed how powerful accent and language are in guiding children's early social thinking, my collaborators and I wondered how babies' attunement to these social factors compared to their attunement to people's race. In modern times, race has taken on formidable social significance and often reflects societal histories of oppression and inequality; there simply is no disputing the fact that it often matters in people's thinking and frequently divides groups and societies. Furthermore, there is evidence from past studies with infants that they can *see* differences in skin color. Over the first year of life, babies start to look toward faces that are of a familiar racial group membership, and they get better at telling apart faces that are of a familiar race too.

To understand how babies' early thinking about language and about race compare, Liz Spelke and I repeated the experiments in which babies reached for toys offered by a native and a foreign speaker — but this time, we substituted people from different racial backgrounds. I gave white babies a chance to take toys from someone apparently from a familiar racial group (in this case, white) or from someone from a less familiar racial group (in this case, Black). We found that the babies took toys equally from these people, regardless of how they looked. Next, we tried a similar game with children two and a half years old. We gave children a chance to take and receive toys from different people who varied either in race or in language. Our findings mirrored those from the baby studies: when given the choice between a speaker of a native language and a speaker of a foreign language, children selectively interacted with people who spoke their own language. Yet when given a choice between people whose race differed, the color of those people's skin again did not matter to the toddlers that we tested.

Very early in life, it seems, kids may not assign as much weight to racial differences as they do to linguistic differences. But how long does this last? When do societal attitudes about race begin to creep into children's perceptions, changing the relative importance they assign to different categories? This is the question I turned to next.

There is a lot of evidence that by the end of the preschool years, children start to care about race in a more social way. This body of evidence dates back to the 1940s, when, in one infamous study, researchers found that preschool-age children of different racial groups in the United States preferred playing with dolls that appeared to have white skin. Since then, many studies have shown that by the time they enter kindergarten, children have begun to develop preferences for new people based on the color of their skin. Adults' racial attitudes and society's structures of racial inequality, unfortunately, start to seep into children's developing minds.

Yet while children begin to soak up cultural attitudes about race as they grow older, these attitudes remain in nascent — and thus potentially changeable — states for at least some time.

In one study, Kristin Shutts, Jasmine DeJesus, Liz Spelke, and I showed kindergarten-age white English-speaking kids in the United States a series of faces that varied in race; we also played children clips of what their voices allegedly sounded like, in different languages or different accents of English. As in many previous studies, our findings were sad but not unexpected: when children were asked whom they would want to be friends with — based on looking at faces and prior to hearing any voices — the white children chose the faces of other white children. But next, we added a twist. For another group of kindergartners, the white faces were presented as speaking in a foreign accent in English (a French accent, in this case). The Black faces spoke in a native American accent of English. What did the five-year-old white American English-speaking kids do? They picked the native speakers, regardless of the color of their skin. For the kindergartners in this study, accent overshadowed any race-based preferences they might have had.

In another study, my former PhD student Jocelyn Dautel and I asked kindergarten-age kids, as well as an older group of nine- to ten-year-old fourth graders, to respond to a "grow-up task." We showed them one kid and two adults, and asked our little subjects to guess "which adult will this child grow up to be?" We made things purposely tricky for the participants. For instance, imagine a white girl who speaks English — is she more likely to grow up to be a white woman who speaks French or a Black woman who speaks English? Older kids picked the adult who matched the child's race, certainly, and they could even tell you why. Older kids would say something like "Well, people generally look about the same when they grow up." Or, "Maybe she moved and learned a new language." But younger white kids were less likely to see race as stable — they attended more to language. White English-speaking kindergarten-age kids thought that people would always grow up to be someone who spoke the same language, even if it meant transferring to a different racial category. They thought that someone who was white and spoke English was more likely to grow up to be Black than grow up to speak French!

Interestingly, similar to the older (rather than younger) white kids in this study, a group of kindergarten-age African American children also picked the race match as more continuous across development. Likely, African American children are learning more about the current societal significance of race at an earlier age than are white American children.

In another study, led by Jasmine DeJesus, we asked kids from three different cultural backgrounds — monolingual English-speaking American kids, bilingual Korean American kids, and Korean kids in Korea — what it takes to be American versus Korean. Older kids started to think a lot of factors mattered — including race. But five-year-olds across cultural groups all agreed on a common response: they thought that being American means speaking English.

At this young age, children have only a vague or general sense of nationality — and when they think of a meaningful social group, when they think about where they belong or don't belong, language is intuitively part of this equation.

When young white American kids report that someone is likely to grow up and speak the same language forever, or when children of different cultural groups think that language is critical for defining nationality, they are presumably thinking about language as something deep, internal, and stable — something that matters for predicting another person's future self and relationship to a group. They are, in short, adopting an essentialist view of language — one that seems to be more deeply rooted, at least early in development, than their essentialist view of race. (Though, of course, racial essentialism can develop in older children and adults; and in some cultures, racial essentialism becomes incredibly deep and nefarious.)

Seeing kids respond to our research tasks gave me a greater appreciation for how their thinking develops — and also where their social attitudes come from. I remember meeting five-year-old, pigtailed Julie when I was a graduate student. Julie was white and spoke English. She was a little shy, clinging to her mother's leg. Soon my friendly undergraduate research assistant helped her warm up by playing a game of "favorites" — what is something you really love? "Ice cream!" What is something that tastes yucky to you? Julie reported, "Green beans!"

For Julie's testing session, I asked her to play a game in which she picked out faces of kids she thought she would like to play with. She picked out all the white children. Specifically, she picked all white girls. The choices didn't seem to bother her or require a lot of thought. She picked quickly.

I glanced at Julie's mom. A frown appeared on her face, lines deepening. She looked uncomfortable. She fidgeted, her entire body tense.

Next, Julie was presented with a new group of kids, and this time she could both see what they looked like and hear what they sounded like. She heard that the white kids spoke in a foreign accent in English. They said things that Julie understood but with a foreign-sounding lilt to their voices. The Black kids spoke in an American accent — they sounded like any other kid she might encounter in her local playground. They sounded *native*.

This time, Julie picked all the native-accented people, even if they were members of a different racial group.

I looked at Julie's mom again. Her entire posture had changed. Before this, she had been gripping the chair, presumably wanting to jump in and tell Julie that it's not OK to pick some kids over others based on their skin color. Now she had visibly relaxed.

"Phew," she said out loud, after the study was complete. "Julie isn't racist! She is just really good at learning languages."

To be sure, it was great news that Julie was not discriminating on the basis of race after all. But why is it somehow socially permissible for her to like some people more than others based on how they speak?

For Julie's mom, and for many other parents who come into my lab, linguistic bias is completely culturally acceptable in a way that racial bias is not. Many parents feel uncomfortable with any expression of race-based preferences, but when their children express a preference based on the way someone speaks, they are not as concerned. Julie is likely about to grow up in a society where she will learn from adults that it is OK to prefer some people to others based on the way they speak. She will likely encounter a society that talks about people of some linguistic groups as being inferior, or of English (and specifically, some dialects of English) as being better than other languages.

In short, while Julie was doing what all kids do — categorizing people based on how they speak — she also had begun to encounter a society that condones linguistic discrimination. Given how sponge-like children are, and how intuitively they seem to read social significance into the way we speak, it's hard to imagine that Julie will be able to completely escape the linguistic bias and potential xenophobia that will bombard her, with increasing frequency, as she grows up in the United States. What happens when growing minds like hers encounter a world in which language is freighted with status and prejudice? Julie's mind will be ready to receive the message — layering information about linguistic status on top of a preexisting inclination to see language as predicting social difference.

ALADDIN'S ACCENT

Children start out with a preference for "native" ways of speaking, but they don't necessarily know much about the alternatives — they may not really care about the differences between unfamiliar accents or languages to which they have not regularly been exposed. Before long, however, this changes. As they grow older, children figure out that status and prestige are associated with some dialects but not others. Tragically, while they might still like the sound of their own speech, many children also figure out early on that their own dialect is not considered a "high status" way of speaking. This loss of innocence and security related to one's own voice can be profound and devastating — for the children who experience it, and for society at large.

My former PhD student Jasmine DeJesus and I wanted to better understand when and how children in the United States start to think about certain accents as having more status than others. We decided to compare their attitudes toward Northern American and Southern American English, accents that are associated with deep-seated stereotypes; when American adults are asked to draw a map of where different kinds of speech in the United States are found, they consistently draw the South as an area — and claim that they speak the "worst" English there. Even Southerners seem to share knowledge of these stereotypes and often feel insecure about the way they speak. When, we wanted to know, did the children in our study pick up on these attitudes — and did kids in both the North and the South respond similarly or differently to these accents?

We presented kids from Illinois ("the North") and Tennessee ("the South") with voices from both areas and tested them to see which they preferred, and what they thought of each voice. We tested a group of kindergartners (five to six years old) and fourth graders (nine to ten years old), and we found that the responses of the older children (but not yet the younger children) reflected societal attitudes — stereotypes — about the two different accents. Younger kids in kindergarten showed that same relative preference for familiar speech that I discussed above.* But they didn't seem to know anything about the particular voices — what they signified or what stereotypes were attached to them. By age nine, kids in

---

* Kindergarten-age children in Illinois preferred the Northern-accented speakers; children in Tennessee had an equal preference for the two accents, suggesting that they may be familiar with both types of speech.

both places had a firm grasp of the stereotypes that are present in adults' intuitions — they thought that the Northern voices sounded smarter and more in charge; they thought that the Southern voices sounded nicer.

What is striking — and, in a way, saddest — about these studies is that it did not matter where these kids were from; they were all gaining access to the same cultural stereotypes, and by age nine they were all latching on to stereotypes that were both positive and negative about their own group.

Other studies have produced similar findings, helping to sketch out a rough trajectory whereby children go from having no particular value judgments about different languages (outside of preferring what is familiar to them) to saying that some ways of speaking are better than others. They go from preferring native, to incorporating views of status. In one study in Hawaii, children who spoke Hawaiian Creole at the beginning of their schooling expressed positive attitudes toward the way they spoke. But over the course of the first two years in schools, these children started to devalue their native tongue in favor of what they were taught was "standard" American English. Children who speak African American English in the United States may similarly be taught that their dialect is not proper, or not good English, when in fact it is a dialect of English as legitimate as any other.

Judging by our studies with infants, all these kids presumably liked their native tongue when they were babies. They were born with a preference for "native" ways of speaking — that is, the way their family and other people around them spoke — but then over time, society enters. For some children, society can teach that the way they speak — the way that makes them feel most comfortable and most themselves — isn't the *valued* way of speaking. For other kids, society might imply to them that the way they speak is *better* than how other people speak. They may even learn that any kind of foreign languages or speech isn't as good. As I've said, children are cultural sponges, soaking up their society's linguistic — and sometimes xenophobic — attitudes.

Society transmits attitudes to kids in many different ways. Some may be subtle and others more explicit. In the case of children who hear a different dialect of English at home versus at school, children are likely receiving a number of explicit messages from adults in their world: "this is how you should speak here," and perhaps even more influential, "this is not how you should speak here." In this case — particularly if children are explicitly corrected — they may learn that one way of speaking is more valued than another; they may even grow to feel shame over their own speech.

But what about the more subtle stereotypes? When I conducted the research on children's attitudes about Northern- versus Southern-accented speech, what perplexed me the most was how children learned about certain cultural stereotypes. If you are growing up in Chicago (as were all the children I was studying), it seems unlikely that you would encounter many instances of adults explicitly talking about Southern accents, one way or another.

How are stereotypes like this transmitted? One likely vector is the media.

Consider the classic example of Disney's *Aladdin*, the highest-grossing film of 1992. It tells the story of a boy who finds a magical lamp in a fictional Middle Eastern city, and one of its most memorable songs had these lyrics: "Where they cut off your ear if they don't like your face / It's barbaric, but hey, it's home." Following complaints from the American-Arab Anti-Discrimination Committee (ADC), the lyrics were changed in 1993 to this: "Where it's flat and immense and the heat is intense / It's barbaric, but hey, it's home." (I must have seen the movie in its original version, because in my mind and memory, the subsequently deleted lyrics are still playing.) Even after the filmmakers had changed these lyrics, however, negative stereotypes about Arabs endured in the film — and were transmitted to audiences — via the characters' accents.

Aladdin, like so many children's films, relied on stereotypes about accents to convey different characters' moral worth. The good guys don't have accents; the bad guys do. Beyond the content of their dialogue — beyond the question of whether they call some groups of people "barbaric," for instance — films' use of accents can convey social meaning that, whether intentional or not, insults and injures some of the very people they are designed to attract. As the president of the Los Angeles chapter of the ADC said, around the time of *Aladdin*'s release, "While the Aladdin character, Jasmine, and her father speak unaccented, standard Americanized English, all the bad guys speak in foreign accents. The lesson is that anyone with a foreign accent is bad."

This "accent problem" is not limited to *Aladdin*, certainly. The sociolinguist Rosina Lippi-Green has systematically studied accents in children's films, and she found many instances of subtle and not-so-subtle linguistic bias. (She looked specifically at Disney films, though this company is by no means the only culprit.) Other researchers have looked at a wide variety of animated television programs for children, and the results are consistent: speakers of standard and nonstandard dialects and accents are depicted differently.

When you look across American children's media, there are many more characters with a native, Northern American accent than any other. A large majority of these American English–accented characters have positive motives — they are the heroes and heroines, those looking to fight against injustice to save princesses and kingdoms. On the other hand, characters with a foreign or nonstandard accent are relatively more likely to be evil or to have mixed motives. Some characters with nonstandard accents are positive figures, but many others turn out to be either villainous bad guys, or flawed individuals who turn out to be OK in the end. Some foreign accents, such as Eastern European accents, are particularly likely to be portrayed negatively, as are certain native dialects of American English — such as African American English and Southern American English — which are often culturally devalued in their home country. (Outrageously, as Lippi-Green observes, film characters speaking African American English historically have been more typically portrayed as animals than humans. Think of the crows in *Dumbo*, the hyenas in the animated version of *The Lion King*, or the orangutan king in *The Jungle Book*.)

Just think about this for a minute. In film, speakers of Standard American English often are depicted as expressing the full range of diversity of human states and emotions. Most have positive intentions, but some do not. Most are heroes, but some are flawed. This means that they are *human,* with all the complexities that come with that designation. On the other hand, characters who speak in a foreign or nonstandard accent (and yes, also characters who are women, on average) portray a much smaller range of human character and emotion. They play particular limited roles, which are, relatively speaking, more likely to be negative, and they are depicted in line with (often erroneous) cultural stereotypes about their group.

These observations of devalued accents and characters fit with a classic observation in social psychology called dehumanization — the tendency for people to perceive a lower-status out-group as being more "animal" and less "human." People think of lower-status others as missing high-level cognitive experiences and rich emotional lives — ranking low, perhaps, on emotions like pride and shame and awe. We easily are able to see some people as having a more complicated humanity than others, and this is communicated to our children through the use of accents in children's media.

Of course, it doesn't end with movies for children. Lippi-Green notes that even *Schindler's List* — winner of seven Academy Awards and often heralded as one of the greatest films of all time — nonetheless depicts some linguistic cues to group bias. (The more attractive the woman, the less likely she is to have a German accent. The more nefarious the guard, the more likely he *is.*) Other researchers have looked at prime-time television shows geared to adults, finding that speakers with standard accents are dramatically overrepresented — limiting viewers' access to people who speak in the full range of voices. And when speakers of non-native or nonstandard accents are featured on these TV shows, they are likely depicted as lower in status and less desirable.

These correlations between certain accents and certain attributes in TV and film are averages, not absolutes. *Sometimes* good guys speak with a foreign accent and bad guys speak with a native accent — so it is not to say that bias is reflected in all cases at all times. And certainly the media landscape is less biased now than it was a generation ago. But as kids (and adults) consume media, these trends can add up.

In this way, the media — much like society as a whole — is effectively bombarding children with negative biases about different ways of speaking. This is one route by which prejudice can seep into children's absorbent, developing minds. They are not born with any particular form of prejudice or xenophobia, but they *are* set up with the cognitive underpinnings to see language as something that unites and divides groups in the world in general — and society fills in the blanks, teaching kids that some ways of speaking are better than others.

Society can communicate bias in myriad ways, of course, and the media is just one. Indeed, accent-based discrimination is everywhere, though you may not have noticed it. In fact, you may inadvertently have engaged in it yourself; well-meaning people do so all the time. Most American adults will tell you that racial discrimination is wrong (even if they don't always act in accordance with these ideals), but those same people are comfortable with perpetuating negative stereotypes of nonstandard accents without a second thought. Not only is this ignorance easy to find — it also is easy to pass on to kids.

But once you recognize how prevalent this sort of bias is, it's impossible to overlook. At least, that is my hope. Speech discrimination is one of the few remaining frontiers of permissible discrimination in my country and too many others. It's time we changed that.

6

ON THE BASIS OF SPEECH

Trayvon Martin, a seventeen-year-old African American kid, was unarmed when he was fatally shot nearby his relative's home in their gated community in Florida. The shooter was George Zimmerman, coordinator of a neighborhood watch. After Zimmerman called the police to report Martin walking in the neighborhood, the two had an altercation, and Zimmerman shot Martin. Zimmerman was charged with murder for Martin's death, yet after a highly publicized trial in which Zimmerman claimed self-defense, he was acquitted.

In the moments leading up to his death, Martin was on the phone with Rachel Jeantel, who heard the horrifying final moments of her friend's life. She described how over the phone, Martin said that Zimmerman was "creepy" and was following him. According to Jeantel, Martin was trying to get away, not trying to assault Zimmerman.

Jeantel's testimony indicated that Zimmerman's claim of self-defense may have been meritless, and that he may indeed have murdered her friend. She should have been the prosecution's star witness — providing the most compelling evidence against the defendant — and yet her nearly six hours of testimony were completely overlooked. Neutralized. Why didn't it make a difference in the outcome of the case? The reason may have had something to do with the way she spoke.

Jeantel spoke in a dialect of African American English — a native dialect of American English, certainly, but one that was different from the dialect spoken by the jurors, and critically, one that is often stigmatized. Clips of the way she talked were mocked on social media. One juror reported later that the jury did not take her testimony into account during their sixteen hours of final deliberations. Talking later on CNN about the trial, another juror explained why: she just seemed "hard to understand" and "not credible."

This is a clear-cut example of accent bias. The jurors were treating Jeantel as less worthy — and less trustworthy — simply because of the way her words sounded. The linguists John Rickford and Sharese King point out that there was not a single African American individual on the jury; because of this, Jeantel's dialect was less familiar to all the jurors and therefore potentially harder for them to understand. Crucially, though, the juror's reactions were not the result of a simple miscomprehension, which could be easily resolved with a translation — Jeantel's dialect also evoked stigmatizing stereotypes, which led people to think of her as less intelligent and less credible, independent of what she said. Just like any dialect of any language, African American English has its own rule-governed grammar and accent, and is often a part of the cultural fabric of its community of speakers. Yet, African American English has a long history of being unfairly devalued in the US. Because of these cultural biases against her language, Jeantel did not have a fighting chance as a witness — and neither, in this case, did justice.

Sadly, the investigation into Trayvon Martin's death is hardly the only example of people with nonstandard dialects being misunderstood or marginalized by courts. Rickford has documented similar cases all over the globe, involving Aboriginal English speakers in Australia, Viennese working-class speakers in Austria, and Jamaican Creole speakers in the UK. Researchers also have reproduced this observational evidence in laboratory settings: when people hear mock eyewitness testimony, they *believe* the witness who speaks in a standard accent. People tend to perceive accents that sound higher in status as also sounding less guilty, a finding that tells you a bit about the tremendous real-world consequences that biases toward speech can have.

Yet people are not typically aware of the consequences of accent discrimination. People — and institutions, such as our legal system — are not aware of how much it can impact people's lives. When people discriminate against others based on their speech, they may not realize they are doing it. And when they witness other people being discriminatory in this way, they may not understand how problematic it is. Indeed, linguistic bias still seems *permissible* in a way that other forms of bias no longer are among enlightened, progressive people who seek to treat others equally, without regard to their looks or creed.

Part of this may be about the fact that — as I mentioned in Chapter 3 — people misperceive language as more controllable than it is. Some of the harshest forms of social stigma are aimed at those thought to be (often erroneously) capable of changing their speech, their obesity, or their mental health, for example. People mistakenly view others as having a sense of control that they may not indeed possess — and language falls into this category.

Linguistic bias may also remain culturally permissible because some listeners feel they are *justified* in feeling biased. They think that the other person is simply a bad communicator. People think — "Hey, I'm not being a prejudiced jerk — I just did not understand this person with the different accent! So, it's not my fault." An even more subtle version: "Well, maybe I can understand them OK — but I doubt other people can. So, out of concern for *others*, I will disregard this person and what they have to say."

The problem isn't just that linguistic discrimination is still considered basically OK in many arenas, even in situations where it reflects and informs racism and other cultural prejudices. From a broader cultural and legal perspective, in America as well as in many other places, language-based discrimination has become *routinized*. This means that linguistic bias is part of our basic cultural fabric. It is so ubiquitous that we don't even think about it. It's sanctioned by the law, it's allowed by culture, and it is practiced so frequently that people do not even realize when it is happening. Linguistic discrimination is seen as normal and typical, and because of this, it flies beneath the radar. It has become so common and so ingrained that most people do not question it.

But we need to start questioning it, and each other, and more important, to start questioning ourselves — particularly those of us who speak in a way that conveys linguistic privilege. If you speak in Standard American English or with a high-status British accent, you may not be fully aware of the challenges routinely faced by people who speak in a way that is considered less standard. But of course communication is two-sided, and when we inadvertently harbor linguistic bias toward someone else, it actually makes *us* worse communicators.

Linguistic bias actually hurts real people, and it hurts some people more than others. Beyond criminal trials, for instance, the American legal system neglects to appropriately protect people from language and accent discrimination. Employment law, for example, fails to adequately protect against employment discrimination affecting people who speak in nonstandard ways, despite some fairly straightforward fixes that could be made.

But the problem isn't limited to the law. At a broader level, our society fails to comprehend the critical social significance of language and the role it plays in people's lives. My hope is that once we understand it better, we can reconceptualize our relationship to speech, address the many downsides of this ancient and deep-rooted feature of human life, and wherever possible, harness the power of language for the good.

"THEY CAN'T EVEN SPEAK ENGLISH"

It's a common misperception that everyone who speaks differently from you has an accent, but that you yourself do not have one. But — as probably has occurred to you already, if you've stopped to think about this — that can't possibly be true. Everyone who speaks any language has an accent. No one is accent-free; it just is not possible. Even people who know sign languages have manners of signing (which seem to be akin to manners of pronunciation) that vary. Every person has an accent.

A second misperception is to think everyone hears every accent the same way that you do. When you hear a person's speech, you might think "Aha, a strong accent!" or "Eh, that's just a little accent," or "Wow, no one could ever understand that accent!" It is easy to assume that everyone else in the world hears that voice the same way that you do. But a lot of speech perception is subjective — one person could hear a "heavy" accent, while another might disagree.

A third misperception is that when you hear someone talk, you always know what you do and do not understand. If you are like the average listener, when you hear an unfamiliar accent, you are more likely to underestimate your comprehension (thinking you can't understand someone), rather than overestimate it. People tend to self-handicap when they hear an accent that isn't familiar — they think they can't understand when in fact they can (and some people do this more than others). This hurts those who speak in a non-standard way; they are often pegged as poor communicators even when it might be more accurate to say that they were talking to a poor listener.

Imagine listening to a speech delivered by a person with a foreign accent. How well could you reflect on what you heard? It turns out that actually understanding something — and thinking you understand something — can be two different things. Science shows just how much we misconstrue accent. We do not realize the extent to which the perception of accent is subjective and comes to life in the ear of the listener; it may not accurately reflect what is projected through the voice of the speaker. An accent to one person does not always sound the same as an accent to another. And we are not always consciously aware of what we can and cannot understand.

To demonstrate how subjective the detection of accent can be, in one study, linguists presented English speakers with voice clips of people who spoke English with a Chinese accent. People were remarkably good at understanding and transcribing even speech that they perceived as having a heavy accent. The interesting part was what happened when people were asked to reflect on the experience. When they were asked questions such as "How heavy is this accent?" or "How much did you understand?" people's responses varied a lot.

Some people actually understood, and realized that they understood. But for other listeners, actually understanding — and *thinking they could understand* — did not come together in a tidy little package. Some people were able to transcribe the content of the speech perfectly, yet reported that the "very heavy" accent kept them from understanding it.

Interestingly, people did not even agree on what it meant to have an accent to begin with. There was also a huge range of judgments about how "heavy" any particular accent was.

It seems that the accent put out there in the world is not necessarily the same as the accent received by people's minds. People's feelings related to what they can and can't understand don't always map onto evidence of their actual, objective comprehension. Language is not a perfect and clear signal sent out to listeners, ready to be understood. Subjective and objective assessments of communication do not always match.

As a result, people who speak with a foreign accent often worry that even if their grammar is perfect and their vocabulary extensive, a listener may deem their communication incomprehensible. They may feel stigmatized even when speaking correctly.

The difference between subjective and objective measures of comprehension can be clearly seen — and have potentially big real-world impacts — in the domain of education. On a college campus with an international population of graduate students, it is not uncommon to hear undergraduate students complain about their teaching assistants' accents. In some cases, perhaps communication really is difficult. Yet in others, students' grievances are completely fabricated — allegedly "incomprehensible" accents are a figment of students' linguistic imagination.

Some students are aware of the impact of accent-based discrimination on campus. At Stanford University, the student-run newspaper, the *Stanford Daily*, made the following report: "'They can't even speak English.'" This blanket statement is often thrown around by college students to describe professors with even the slightest of accents. At Stanford, where students profess to being anti-bigoted, we would expect them to think twice before making inflammatory statements on others' quality of English. Instead, however, it still remains acceptable to castigate foreign-born professors and TAs for their supposed inability to communicate in English — an issue that has both racial and cultural implications.

How exaggerated are these student reports, really? Are the students complaining unnecessarily, or are the teachers really bad at communicating? And how can we know the difference?

One way to figure out whether real bias is occurring when students complain is through controlled laboratory studies. In a series of studies with college students, the sociolinguist Don Rubin tested whether student complaints about their teachers' accents seem to be a result of the students' biased listening, rather than the teachers' inadequate communication. As Rubin's studies show, a lot of accent bias is based on the ear of the listener — and sometimes a student who claims to hear a "foreign" accent is wrong.

In one study, Rubin presented undergraduates at the University of Georgia with mock lectures recorded by native speakers of Chinese, speaking in English. A Chinese-accented English speaker spoke either in his typical way (with a slight accent, but he was very good at English) or with an exaggerated, "thicker" accent.

Again, all participants did not hear the accents in the same way. Some people thought the second accent sounded heavy, but others did not. And this perception mattered — students who thought the teacher had a heavy accent also were more likely to conclude that he was a bad teacher.

In the next study, Rubin explored whether students might sometimes invent the presence of a foreign accent altogether. What if students mistook a native accent for a foreign one — would they stop listening, thinking that they couldn't understand this incorrectly identified foreign person?

To test this possibility, Rubin had American students listen to a recorded lecture. They were told that the speaker was a TA; in fact, the lecturer was a native speaker of English who grew up in central Ohio. Half of the students heard this voice accompanied by a photo of a white person, and they presumably thought this TA had grown up in America and spoke "native" English. Half of the students heard this same Ohioan's voice, but this time it was accompanied by a face that looked Asian. Rubin thought that this group of students might think that the Asian-looking TA was foreign — perhaps one of those maligned foreign teaching assistants that many complained about. Could merely thinking about someone as being Asian lead people to hear a foreign accent where none exists?

Indeed, when the students thought the TA was Asian rather than white, they imagined a foreign accent that did not exist. Their ears transformed this Ohioan accent into a foreign one, which they reported was more difficult to understand. And when students report that an instructor has an accent, they are more likely to give that instructor a poor evaluation.

Another linguist wanted to see how perceptions of accent were reflected in students' evaluations of their teachers on a broader scale, using real data from classrooms across the nation. He delved into the vast database of Ratemyprofessors.com — the online site where undergraduates can rate their instructors.

The huge data set included student reviews of professors with surnames typical of white Americans and surnames typical of Chinese Americans and Korean Americans. Focusing on math and statistics classes, he studied what the students had to say about these professors.

Here are the top five words that regularly appeared in the students' comments about the Asian instructors, but not about the white instructors: "Barrier," "accent," "thick," "English," and "language." (You can be sure that I didn't cherry-pick, relaying only the top five, because number six is "speak"!) When talking about the Asian professors, students focused on language.

The computer was also asked to pick out common phrases. You might expect words like "accent" or "understand" to be imbedded in a phrase like "she has an accent," or "she is hard to understand." Indeed, this happened sometimes.

But a closer look at the data revealed that many students commented on a teacher's accent even when they perfectly understood what the instructor said and had no complaint about their ability to speak English. In many of the comments, the phrase "hard to understand" was actually part of the statement "she was not that hard to understand." "She does have an accent" became "she does have an accent, *but.*" So, even when students thought that an instructor's accent was completely unremarkable, they still brought it up. As the researcher says, it's as though the students "feel compelled to comment on 'Asian' instructors' language even when they have nothing noteworthy to say about it."

The broad permissibility and routinization of accent bias makes students feel comfortable, and even obligated, to think about and comment on teachers' accents. Imagine students writing "She may be of [XX race], but . . ." or "She may have a disability, but . . ." Such statements would be seen as a horrific demonstration of bias. Yet "She may have an accent, but . . ." remains a typical, everyday feature of teacher assessments. Such comments are considered fine, even when the foreign accent does not affect comprehension and when the accent may not even be real, but imagined.

IN TALK WE TRUST

Educational settings are useful for evaluating how one person's assessment of another person's accent can affect the willingness to learn from that person — in essence, to *trust* them, and to trust that they are imparting accurate information. Yet people learn and retain information in many different environments — not just the classroom. And researchers have found that, whatever the setting, people's perceptions of a strong accent — real or imagined — have an impact on their basic feelings of trust.

In general, we seem to trust native-accented speech more than foreign-accented speech. Shiri Lev-Ari and Boaz Keysar demonstrated this in an experiment. They presented English-speaking adults with pieces of information that might be true or false; the topics were quite obscure, and few participants would be familiar with them (they included how long a bear sleeps and how much water a particular animal consumes each day). The participants simply had to guess whether each statement of "fact" was true or false. When people heard the statement about a bear's sleep played in a native-accented voice, they were more likely to say it was true; when they heard that same information spoken in a foreign accent, they were relatively more likely to guess that it was false. You may not know how long a bear sleeps — but if someone gives you an estimate in a native accent, it is more likely to sound correct to you.

This study can be thought of as a very stripped-down example of accent credibility. The adults were in a lab, and the stakes were low. But in real-life situations, the stakes can be higher. What happens when someone presents crucial facts in an accent that is considered stigmatized or devalued? It is not hard to imagine cases in which doctors might disagree over a medical case, or witnesses might clash over the facts in a courtroom. But assigning less credibility to facts presented in a particular kind of voice — just by nature of how it sounds — can have big consequences in critical situations. And yet we are not usually aware of this tendency in ourselves.

Some people may be especially susceptible to mistrusting foreign-accented speech. The social psychologists Karolina Hansen and John Dovidio found that people's thinking about inequality in society was related to their ability to understand accented speech.

Social Dominance Orientation (SDO) is a measure of people's thinking about whether inequality in society is the way it is *supposed to be*. People who agree with statements such as 'It's probably a good thing that certain groups are at the top and other groups are at the bottom" or "Inferior groups should stay in their place" are considered high in SDO. You can think of SDO as a proxy for social prejudice.

A group of native English speakers — some who were measured to be high in SDO and some who were not — listened to a voice clip of a person speaking in English with a Hispanic accent. The speaker was supposedly applying for a "lower management position" — nothing fancy, and he sounded reasonably qualified. He described a bunch of mundane details about himself — for how long he held his previous job and what his professional skills were.

The people who were higher in SDO gave the speaker a lower rating as a communicator. When given a subjective measure of comprehension (How much did they *feel* that they understood him? In their view, how easy would it be for others to understand him too?) they thought he was a poor communicator. Yet when the test subjects were given a more *objective* measure — recalling details about what he said — it was clear that all of them had actually understood the speech just fine. This experiment shows how easily biases can come into play.

As I've already noted, biases against accented speech feel permissible, and many people speak of them with no fear of censure. The antidiscrimination legal scholar Mari Matsuda describes how candidly people tell her about their linguistic bias — they don't think there is any reason to be less than open about it: "Listening to these and other stories, I have found that accent discrimination is commonplace, natural, and socially acceptable. People who know of my strong commitment to civil rights felt no hesitation in telling me things like 'I couldn't have someone who sounds like that represent our law school' or 'People who talk like that sound so dumb' or 'My business could not survive if I had to hire people with foreign accents.'"

Why does this routinization of accent bias matter? Because it means that many societies today are overlooking a major source of discrimination. And this has huge consequences, affecting not only the people our children grow up to be, but also the ability of parents and families to care for and support them. The way we talk may signal who we are — but for all too many people, it also *determines* who they are, and are not, allowed to be.

LIVING; WAGE

Among other essentials, people's access to housing can be dramatically affected by accent bias; so too can their housing budget, thanks to the depressing effect that linguistic bias can have on the earnings of people with nonstandard accents.

A person's ability to rent or purchase a home should not be affected by the way they speak, but it often is. The housing market is not free of linguistic bias — but unlike other forms of discrimination, many of which are (at least technically) illegal in the United States today, speech-based housing discrimination can fly under the radar.

Since 1968, the Fair Housing Act has prohibited discrimination in housing — if you are selling or renting your home, you cannot take into account a potential tenant's or purchaser's race, ethnicity, religion, or national origin. More recently, families with children and people with disabilities were added to this protected list. Nevertheless, social scientists have found that landlords do not always live up to the ideals set out in the law — and enforcement of this statute is sporadic at best.

As a method to assess subtle discrimination in housing, researchers use an approach that relies on "paired testing." They start with a whole bunch of ads for housing. Then they assign a pair of people to separately attempt to purchase a particular home, and see whether one kind of person is more successful than the other. The pairs are closely matched on all dimensions except for the one variable of study, and in this way they can ascertain information about potential bias based on this variable. The results of these paired tests are grimly consistent.

Imagine a pair of one Black and one white individual who respond to the same housing ad. Each such team would be matched as closely as possible on other dimensions: the same gender, age, education, marital status, finances, and so on. For any given pair, it might be difficult to know for sure that the white guy got the apartment instead of the Black guy *because of* his race or due to some other idiosyncratic difference. Yet if you look at a lot of the pairs and their results together, you can see race-based differences emerging systematically in a given housing market.

One such large-scale housing study sent pairs of Black and white individuals, and also pairs of Hispanic and non-Hispanic white individuals, to talk to housing brokers about buying a home. Sad but not unexpected, the white individuals got much better treatment than the Black individuals when discussing a down payment or being offered financing, and this reveals racial bias. The results also showed that housing brokers favored white buyers a little bit over Hispanic buyers, but this discrimination was not as clear-cut as it was in testing pairs of Black and white individuals. All Hispanic homebuyers were not treated equally, however. What predicted whether they faced discrimination was the degree of Spanish *accent* in their spoken English.

Housing is not the only market in which accent bias is present. Accent is an important, and overlooked, factor in the amount of money that people earn in the United States. It probably won't surprise you to hear that there are demographic gaps in earnings in our country. On average, men make more than equivalently qualified women; white people make more than Black people. What may be more surprising is how much of what you earn depends on how you *sound* — and how sometimes your speech can overshadow your other characteristics when it comes to determining your wages.

The economist Jeffrey Grogger found that sometimes when the labor market seems to show that differences in earnings are based on race, the actual situation may be much more subtle — and involve a consideration of accent.

Grogger used data from a big government study that monitored young adults' success as they grew. This data set — the National Longitudinal Survey of Youth — shows that Black individuals' wages are about 10 percent less than those of white people studied. After the main interviews and surveys of this study had been completed, a subset of the population interviewed got a "validation interview" — someone called them to check that everything had been administered properly. It turns out that these interviews had been recorded, so Grogger could use them to check on the interviewees' accents.

Then he put together a study. First, he chose a group of recordings and pared down each interview to a few snippets — nothing that would tell you anything of substance about the individual who was talking. Next, each brief recording of speech was played to a group of listeners, who then were asked a simple question — does the person sound Black or white?

It turns out that this accent variable — how someone sounds — was hugely predictive of the wages that the person made. That "Blacks earn 10 percent less than whites" finding was not the whole story. Looking closer at the data, Grogger found what he calls two different subgroups of Black workers. One group had voices that were distinctly identified by the listeners as Black. Those individuals actually faced much more of a deficit in wages than the average of 10 percent — they made 19 percent less in wages than comparably skilled whites. The other group, with voices that were not clearly identifiable as Black, made basically the same amount as white workers. It seems that the amount of money people made was highly predicted by how they sounded to others.

This is not to say that racism does not exist apart from accent discrimination. Certainly it does. But a major part of what seems, on the surface, to be race-based discrimination may in fact also involve linguistic discrimination in the mix.

One way to think about the impact of accent in employment concerns the amount of money that people earn, as in Grogger's study. But another way to think about employment is who gets a job in the first place — and who gets promoted. Thanks to Title VII of the 1964 Civil Rights Act, which protects against employment discrimination based on myriad social factors such as race, religion, sex, and national origin, employers can't fire someone (or not hire them in the first place, or not promote them if they are deserving) because they don't like the person's race or national origin, or because they think their customers won't like the person's protected social group either. But what about discriminating against a potential employee based on language or accent? Here, the law is much fuzzier. If an employer feels that they cannot understand someone's accent, or that their clients won't be able to understand the person and communicate with them effectively, it often can be considered legal to deny them a job or turn them down for a promotion based solely on this "'communication' factor." Through this gap in civil rights law, there is plenty of room for accent bias to seep into employment decisions.

COMMUNICATION SKILLS

In the early 1980s, a sixty-six-year-old Filipino American named Manuel Fragante was looking for a job. Fragante, an army veteran living in Hawaii, was hoping to work at the Department of Motor Vehicles (DMV). That simple desire would set him on a collision course with the US government, and — in time — set a startling legal precedent for the ways in which accent can be used in hiring decisions by American employers.

Fragante grew up in the Philippines, where he spoke multiple languages — including English, which he had spoken his whole life and which was the language of his schooling. He was valedictorian of his class at his (English-speaking) high school, and then he got a bachelor's of law (also in English). He had served with the US Army during World War II, with several training tours in the States.

As a naturalized US citizen, Fragante studied and took a civil service examination to qualify for an entry-level job at the DMV. Of the seven hundred people who took the written exam with him, he received the highest score. With this achievement in hand, he was ranked first, on paper, for the job he desired: DMV clerk.

Yet despite the DMV's initial interest in hiring him, Fragante was rejected after a brief in-person interview. This meeting took approximately ten to fifteen minutes. The questions asked were not written or standardized—just a casual conversation with two DMV supervisors. His Filipino accent, he was told, made him just not the right fit for the position.

Fragante filed a discrimination suit against the city of Honolulu, alleging that the DMV had discriminated against him because he was Filipino. No, the city argued—this decision was not because he was Filipino. It was about his *accent* (which isn't in and of itself a protected category). Their concern was his "inability to orally communicate to the point of being understood." They also argued that other city clerks had Filipino ancestry, so clearly it was not the case that they were biased.

The written records prepared by the DMV about his interview included comments about Fragante, including these: "He has 37 years of experience in management administration ... However, because of his accent, I would not recommend him for this position." "Very pronounced accent, difficult to understand." "Heavy Filipino accent."

The district court ruled in favor of the city: Fragante had not faced discrimination; rather, he was simply not a good communicator.

Fragante filed an appeal. This time the legal scholar Mari Matsuda, an expert on discrimination law and accent, worked pro bono on his team. As she describes it, witnesses on behalf of the DMV noted frequently during the trial that they were concerned other people would not understand Fragante. Yet there was no evidence that anyone had actually misunderstood anything he said, either during the initial interview or during the court case:

Attorneys for both sides suffered lapses in grammar and sentence structure, as did the judge. Mr. Fragante's English, a review of the transcript confirmed, was more nearly perfect in standard grammar and syntax than any other speaker in the courtroom. Mr. Fragante testified for two days, under the stress of both direct and cross-examination. The judge and the examiners spoke to Fragante in English and understood his answers. A court reporter understood and took down his words verbatim. In the functional context of the trial, everyone understood Manuel Fragante's speech. Yet, the defendant's interviewers continued to claim Fragante could not be understood well enough to serve as a DMV clerk.

During the trial, a linguist was called in to testify and offer an expert opinion. The linguist testified that communication was a two-way street — and the evaluators likely "turned off" and disregarded what Fragante said, despite his otherwise perfect English. But this case occurred prior to the most compelling scientific studies showing that bias can cause someone to stop trying to listen. It was prior to the studies showing that sometimes people understand perfectly well, yet they have the subjective experience that they can't understand someone. This linguist, though, had a level of understanding that was ahead of the times.

The city said that the linguist "failed to produce any documentary or scientific evidence." We can now see that the evidence is in, and the linguist was right — though one has to wonder if this would have actually made any difference in this trial.

Despite all the compelling facts of the case — a guy who was overqualified, competent, and the perfect applicant in every other way — the appellate court sided with the city, saying that the city was within its rights to conclude that Fragante was not qualified for the job due to his poor communication skills. According to the court, the DMV had not discriminated against him.

The Fragante case is unsettling because it seems so obvious that accent discrimination occurred. It also illustrates a problem with employment law: accent, in and of itself, is not a protected category. Insofar as accent or language is used as a *proxy* for national origin, people are protected from discrimination on the basis of their speech. But employment discrimination based on someone's (alleged) "inability to communicate" — for instance, based purely on the person's accent, if the accent is deemed not sufficiently comprehensible — can be permissible under US law.

Imagine an employer who has a history of hiring Mexican American or Chinese American employees. Yet it turns out that the employer hires people who are "clear communicators" (read: no foreign accent) and does not tend to hire applicants with foreign accents (due to their alleged lack of communication skills). Here the employer would have a plausible defense against claims of discrimination based on national origin, since other individuals who shared the same national origin had received job offers. It would be accurate to describe the bias in such a case as being about accent in its own right, not national origin.

Furthermore, current laws do not protect against accent bias directed toward particular "native" American accents. The United States, after all, is not just one undifferentiated group of people with one homogeneous linguistic origin. There are lots of different American accents, and many are stigmatized yet are not expressly protected from discrimination. For instance, if an employer is prejudiced against accents from the Southern United States, an employee or job candidate with a Southern accent would not be protected against the employer's linguistic discrimination by the national origin laws. Likewise, if an employer has a good track record for hiring African Americans in general, yet refrained from hiring someone who spoke in African American English because the employer determined they were "a poor communicator," the job applicant would be out of luck.

To be sure, some jobs really do require communication abilities that some applicants don't have, so we cannot disallow all employment decisions based on communication skill. And when trying to figure out if national origin discrimination has occurred, the government agency that enforces employment laws (the Equal Employment Opportunity Commission, or EEOC) tries to grapple with accent, but only insofar as it is considered a signal of national origin. The EEOC says that an employer may legitimately base an employment decision on accent if the employer can show that (1) effective communication is required for the job, *and* (2) someone's accent *materially interferes* with their ability to communicate in English. Yet the law could be much more reflective of, and responsive to, the fact that — as common sense tells us, and ample research confirms — communication is a two-way street. People's biases can obscure their judgment concerning someone's accent and their ability to communicate, and people can shut down when they don't want to listen. Moreover, not all accent discrimination can be reduced to national origin discrimination.

Claims based on national origin discrimination that have an accent component seem more likely to succeed when the national origin and accent discrimination is completely egregious — the sort of huge violation that hits a lay reader over the head and couldn't possibly be missed. Additionally, the person generally must present evidence of being an exceptionally good communicator or argue that the job does not actually require much talking. Otherwise, these claims may be dismissed at summary judgment, meaning that the judge dismisses the case prior to trial.

One example of how courts have acknowledged claims of accent bias as part of national origin discrimination comes from the state of Georgia. Adesuwa Albert-Aluya, a Nigerian American working at a Burlington Coat Factory store in Georgia, was good at her job. Because she was so effective, she was promoted to a new management position. Nevertheless, her new boss kept complaining about her accent — "speak like an American," he would tell her. When he ultimately fired her, she was told that because of her "thick African accent," she just didn't fit in. The appellate court said that Albert-Aluya could go forward with her case based on national origin discrimination — both because she had evidence that the bias was explicit and because she claimed evidence of a track record of being good at her job.

Another example is a case from 2010, in which the EEOC filed a discrimination suit on behalf of sixty-nine Filipino American hospital workers (mostly nurses) against the hospital where they worked, in California. The nurses described constant harassment about their language and nationality, which created a hostile work environment. Other hospital staff members berated them for their language and accent, telling them to speak English — sometimes even when they *were* speaking English, albeit with a Filipino accent. In one particularly upsetting instance, a nurse said someone sprayed air freshener in her food, saying she hated Filipino food. The hospital settled and paid almost a million dollars on their claims of national origin discrimination. Again, here the bias was over the top, and there was not clear evidence that the nurses' language had any bearing on their professional success.

In short, to win a claim based on national origin discrimination involving accent, the bias must have been very explicitly articulated, and it must be pretty clear that the person indeed faced discrimination because of where they were from. In these cases, employers' claims of "communication difficulties" are interpreted as national origin discrimination in disguise.

Yet much of the time, when the bias isn't blatantly obvious — or when a plaintiff can't prove that they are overqualified, with impeccable speech and proven skill (as in the Fragante case) — it is easy for national origin discrimination cases to be dismissed at summary judgment.

It has also been very difficult for college professors to prove accent discrimination. One example is the case of Yili Tseng, a Taiwanese academic who wanted a tenure-track job at Florida A&M University. He thought he was a competitive candidate, but a woman from China got the job, in part, he was told, because of her better accent and communication skills.

Having been on faculty hiring committees myself, I can say that these decisions come down to a million different factors, and it is often very difficult to prove who exactly is the most qualified candidate. Nevertheless, in light of all the scientific studies showing that students exaggerate their teachers' accents, or even fabricate them altogether, courts should at least consider the possibility that accent bias occurred, and try to discover whether or not it did. As for Yili Tseng, the federal district court that evaluated his case missed the chance to consider the nuance of the matter. The court simply argued that given the link between effective communication and teaching skills, if a teacher communicates in a manner that is hard to understand, this could be a legitimate reason not to hire them, or in fact to fire them. Courts are generally not aware of the relevant research; as a result, they are not asking the right questions.

A simple change to employment law would guide courts to ask more nuanced questions. Critically, the law could make a distinction between accent and national origin. Sometimes accent is an aspect of national origin discrimination, but sometimes it is not.

To make things simpler, accent could be added as a protected category under civil rights law — just like race, gender, religion, and nationality (and like disability, which is covered under a different statute, the Americans with Disabilities Act). This change would, among other things, give people vocabulary to use in identifying and describing instances of linguistic discrimination, and to differentiate between accent discrimination and discrimination involving other protected categories.

This would, for instance, effectively protect an African American woman or a Chinese American man who faces discrimination because of their accent (but not necessarily their race or national origin). It would even leave open the door to protect a white Southern American who is discriminated against due to his or her accent. It would allow courts to more carefully consider where "communication" ends and "accent bias" begins.

In changing the law in this way, we could acknowledge that accent often overlaps with other protected categories in complex and sensitive ways. Imagine a nasty comment made to an African American woman — was it because she was Black or because she was a woman? Possibly both. Or what about a Black woman who is from Africa? She might feel discriminated against because of her race, sex, and her national origin. The law acknowledges "multiple protected bases" — meaning that a person could face *double* or even *triple* (or more) discrimination. If accent were its own protected class, it could easily fit into this preexisting legal rubric.

Once accent becomes a specific protected category, the next step would be to establish a set of best practices to fairly determine what it means to communicate effectively enough for a given job and how this could be evaluated fairly.

As a rough start, as Matsuda describes it, these best practices might include asking employers to clearly delineate (1) the level of communication skill that is actually needed for the job, (2) how a candidate's communication skills can be fairly evaluated, and (3) how the communication skills can be evaluated with an *unprejudiced listener* in mind.

Defining the level of communication skill required for a job is the place to start. This would differentiate a job like 911 operator (where quick, effective communication may be a matter of life or death) from a job as a clerk with the DMV, where verbal communication may be required, but problems could be resolved by asking a question, repeating an explanation, or pointing to written text. Simply put, no one dies if a customer at the DMV has to ask a follow-up question. Moreover, the questions likely to arise on the job (Can I renew this? Do I need a new photo?) are presumably fairly routine, predictable, and uncomplicated.

Once the necessary degree of communication skill is decided, employers could identify how an applicant's communication abilities can be fairly evaluated — in particular, with a nonprejudiced listener in mind. One possibility is administering some sort of standardized test. These kinds of tests exist and are used all the time, particularly in educational contexts. Another way to test communication skill would be to set up a tryout, with a scenario drawing upon actual job requirements, to see how the person does. Any concern that an applicant cannot communicate well might be dismissed by actual on-the-ground evidence that they in fact can.

Those involved in the evaluation of communication skills should be aware of the fact that some languages and accents are more likely to evoke prejudice. A posh accent might be evaluated differently than one that is associated with a lower socioeconomic group, or a group that may be economically, politically, or socially marginalized. When evaluating a claim of accent discrimination, courts might carefully scrutinize rationales for discriminatory behavior based on the idea that that people with potentially stigmatized accents lack communication ability. Any fair evaluation must likewise throw out the idea of catering to the potential prejudice of other people. The claim that "people just won't understand this person" needs to be discarded, just as "customers won't like this Black person or this woman" has been.

These guidelines could be used by courts. They might also become part of a set of cultural "best practices" that help employers understand where bias could be getting the best of them. Such an evaluation system could help employers sort out when poor communication is truly impeding performance, and when bias is the problem.

It may happen, of course, that an otherwise promising candidate could fail an impartial and fair assessment of communication skills. One likely outcome is that the person will not be hired. But there is another possibility. In some situations, the employer may consider making a reasonable accommodation. Tweaking the job description to make it work for a given applicant could be an approach an employer might consider taking, even without any laws requiring it. Perhaps a change in the work environment — something as straightforward as clearly worded signage at the DMV — or minor changes to a job description could make the difference between a candidate's being hired and performing a job well and a potentially excellent candidate being disqualified prematurely. This approach has the potential to benefit both employer and employee. Take Fragante as an example — a guy who was intelligent, kind, and patient, with the highest score on the civil servant exam. Isn't this just the kind of employee that the DMV should *want* dealing with their sometimes cranky customers?

This proposal for changing employment discrimination law is somewhat straightforward — make accent its own category; set up clearer guidelines for evaluating communication. And it hopefully would lay the groundwork for the larger shift we need to make as a society. These details, however, should not obscure the fundamental point: we need to rethink linguistic discrimination and policies related to language, and to change how the law conceptualizes linguistic discrimination more generally. Only by starting at the foundations of society, after all, can we hope to someday change it.

SPEAK TRUTH

Legal systems do not exist solely to punish people who violate the law. Some argue that they also engage in *norm setting* — signaling to people how we should treat one another. And where language is concerned, there are places where the US legal system is sending a bad message. At the moment, the American legal system does not adequately signal that language matters for our social lives — for our identities, for our interactions with one another, and for our humanity.

To be fair, in some instances laws about language have been on target. For instance, English-only policies at a place of work — without a very important reason to implement them — are generally not allowed. Federal laws have prohibited such policies since at least 1980, acknowledging that prohibiting people from speaking their native tongue can result in an "atmosphere of inferiority, isolation and intimidation." (This does not mean that there can never be an English-only rule in a workplace; for instance, a hospital can require that everyone working in an operating room during operation time must speak English, to help avoid miscommunication in a high-stakes environment. But this same hospital should not require nurses or housekeepers to speak English to one another when engaging in other contexts, such as the hall or break rooms.)

Another place where employment law generally gets it right is in allowing preferential hiring of bilingual employees. For instance, what if you *need* a bilingual speaker who can communicate with different groups of people? Some employers recognize the benefits of bilingualism — and if they feel that a bilingual employee would be better equipped to do a job than a monolingual employee, the law allows them to hire the bilingual person for that reason alone. For example, a school district in Texas was looking for a supervisor of their custodial team — and then went with a bilingual Hispanic woman over a man who spoke English but not Spanish. As the court says, "An employer's preference for employees who are bilingual is not a violation of Title VII of the 1964 Civil Rights Act."

Yet employment law still has a lot of room for improvement in acknowledging the impact of linguistic bias. And this need for a broader rethinking is seen in other areas of the law too. As an example, bilingual employees may be treated fairly, but bilingual jurors may not be.

Dionisio Hernandez was on trial for attempted murder in 1986, after firing his gun on the street in Brooklyn and hitting one intended person and two other people sitting at a nearby restaurant. Everyone survived. Several key witnesses in the case spoke Spanish — so they were going to be questioned in Spanish, with a translator translating their words into English. Two of the potential jury members were bilingual speakers of English and Spanish. During the process of voir dire (which, in Old French, translates to something like "speak truth"), the attorneys on both sides have the chance to question and dismiss potential jurors — and the prosecutor dismissed these two bilingual people from the jury without cause, simply because they spoke two languages.

What is the problem with being bilingual and a juror, you might ask? You might imagine that these jurors would actually be better qualified to understand the proceedings of the trial; unlike monolingual jurors, they understood both languages. Yet this increased level of comprehension was exactly what the prosecution was worried about. The prosecutor wanted jurors to focus on the translation (in English) and disregard the actual testimony (in Spanish). The prosecution argued that these bilingual jurors might have trouble disregarding the person's actual words and favoring someone else's translation.

It is kind of a bizarre argument, if you think about it. If the goal is truth seeking, wouldn't having a subset of jurors who can actually understand the Spanish-language testimony be helpful? Apparently the US justice system doesn't think so — because the prosecution's argument was subjected to, and withstood, a considerable legal challenge.

In the Hernandez case, which eventually made its way to the US Supreme Court, the Court said that it was permissible to dismiss the jurors simply because they also spoke Spanish. As the opinion read, "It is a harsh paradox that one may become proficient enough in English to participate in a trial, only to encounter disqualification because he knows a second language as well." Yet despite recognizing the irony of its decision, the Court allowed the dismissal of the bilingual jurors all the same.

The Hernandez case points to a mistrust of multilingualism in the courtroom; other examples point to a mistrust of speech that is considered nonstandard in the legal system as a whole. As Rachel Jeantel discovered when she turned to the legal system, seeking justice for her friend Trayvon Martin, nonstandard accents can be stigmatized in the courtroom. This demonstrable and routinized form of bias can have tremendous implications as to whose truth is ultimately heard, who benefits from the law, and who is ground down by it.

The solutions to linguistic bias in the courtroom are not obvious. Some have proposed offering translators to all speakers of nonstandard dialects, but some people may find this idea demeaning; after all, they are speaking a perfectly legitimate dialect of English, so why would they need a translator?

But while addressing speech bias in the courtroom won't necessarily be easy, it should be done — and in grappling with the problem, courts and citizens will be making important progress toward solving it.

Linguistic discrimination should be part of our national and judicial consciousness, and we should make an effort to curb it in our legal system and our minds. Think about all the ways in which you do, or might, interface with your government or legal system. Think of how you seek education, or how you rely on other public institutions, such as hospitals or the police. Now imagine being in a court to fight for custody of your kids or to stand accused of a crime. If you have a non-native or stigmatized accent, you will likely be offered less protection and help than what is given to someone who speaks in a standard way. An influential person who feels that they don't understand you or don't care to understand you could make the difference in a decision that might completely upend your life.

Now, if you instead have an accent that is standard — which makes you sound privileged and credible — then you will much more likely be believed, trusted, and heard. It would probably never occur to you that you start out ahead of the game, simply through the way your words sound.

That such a wide gulf exists between these two extremes — these two different ways of experiencing language — is unacceptable. We need to shift our cultural thinking about language and change our legal system to better support people as they make use of the basic services that should allow everyone to live, work, and be free. If we become better aware of how much language matters, we may be able to do something about this.

7

A LINGUISTICS REVOLUTION

Miraculously, although speech is the cause of so much strife and prejudice, it also can be used to overcome them.

The solution starts, as it often does, with children. Their amazingly capable brains allow them to learn more than one language at once, and they have yet to be exposed to society's xenophobia. Raising children in an environment that values multilingualism can expand their horizons, broaden their linguistic circles, and may create a world in which mutual understanding allows people to unite across borders. By embracing — and exploiting — humans' miraculous ability to learn more than one language early in life, we can help children build a brighter tomorrow.

In the process, we also can help brighten today. By changing how we think about, and value, multilingualism and linguistic diversity, we can make strides toward improving the lives of people with nonstandard speech by making our systems of law and education more equitable and just. This will make our society healthier and more vibrant.

THE MONOLINGUAL MYTH

Despite humans' amazing linguistic potential, skepticism about bilingualism abounds. Well beyond the courtroom and the workplace, lots of us wonder whether speaking just one language (particularly when it is English, which you might assume is the lingua franca of the twenty-first century) might not actually be preferable to speaking many. People may (incorrectly) intuit that our brains can "normally" process one language, but that two or more languages may somehow exceed our mind's capacities. Think of this as the "monolingual myth" — the understandable but mistaken assumption that we are better off — and more neurally capable of — learning just one language instead of two or more.

Some skeptics are parents weighing the pros and cons of bilingual education. Will bilingual children be confused and mix the two languages together, unable to separate one from the other? Will learning an additional language burden the native tongue, such that children's linguistic development — or perhaps even their cognitive development more generally — is delayed? Plus, think of the headache of it all! What happens if the exposure isn't perfect? What if a child doesn't have the right amount of linguistic input in each language? What if you try to raise a bilingual child, and instead find yourself with a linguistically confused child who can't even speak one language properly?

Many parents seem to view the human brain as a limited vessel, with the capacity for only a single language. Is there any truth to this? When a second language is introduced, might it crowd out the other one — or get in the way of a child's otherwise orderly process of cognitive development? The short answer is no — although that hasn't stopped people from worrying about this. Fear about bilingualism, you see, has a very long history.

Scientists used to think that bilingualism was bad for children. Prior to the 1960s language researchers argued that bilingualism should be avoided. They claimed that the second language interfered with children's learning of the first — it made children slower and less efficient learners. Learning two languages also (allegedly) led children to be less intelligent overall. Researchers gave intelligence tests to children in different places and generally reported an intelligence handicap among bilingual children. Rural children in Wales who were learning both Welsh and English (compared to those who learned just English), American children of foreign-born immigrants (compared to children of parents who were native speakers of English), children of indigenous populations in Canada (compared to white, monolingual English-speaking children) — all of these groups allegedly faced an intelligence handicap as a result of their bilingualism.

In modern times, these claims about the drawbacks of bilingualism have all been squashed (presumably they were socially biased against marginalized groups to begin with). It turns out that these largely faulty studies did not account for other factors across the groups (for example, socioeconomic status) and often involved translated versions of intelligence tests that may not have been valid to begin with. There is no convincing modern evidence that bilingual children suffer any sort of a cognitive deficit.

That doesn't prevent otherwise reasonable people from believing the monolingual myth. For instance, a good friend of mine was a math whiz growing up. She is now a tax attorney who has always prized math, order, and calculations. She wanted her son to learn Spanish and English and to reap the future benefits of speaking both languages. Part of her motivation was practical: speaking Spanish might help his employment prospects down the road. But part of her motivation was personal: wouldn't it be wonderful for him to have the ability to communicate with a whole different world of speakers?

My friend even went so far as to hire a nanny who was a native speaker of Spanish — but then she chickened out. She asked the nanny to speak to her baby in English, with the exception of half an hour a day of "Spanish time."

Somewhat chagrined, my friend admitted to me that she just felt too nervous about Spanish. What she wanted most of all was for her kid to be good at math. Math was her own strength, and she wanted to encourage mathematical thinking in her child. She believed me, at a logical level, when I said that a child could learn two languages and math all at once. But at a more emotional level she just felt too nervous to make it happen. What if learning Spanish somehow got in the way of learning other things? Happily, I was finally able to explain to my friend that there's no support for the notion of a "bilingual handicap."

But parents aren't the only ones with apprehensions related to the monolingual myth. It is not hard to find remnants of mistrust of bilingualism among child development professionals. I encountered it myself when I had my first child.

My daughter was born prematurely, but fortunately healthy. At one point, my husband and I spoke with a pediatrician and a speech-language pathologist to see if there was anything we could do to help facilitate her language development.

Here is what they said: First, my daughter's language would get there (and it did, of course). For babies born early, the onset of their speech is often delayed. We should just keep doing what we were doing, they said. Babbling, talking, and eventually negotiating would all come.

This was good advice. The other recommendation they gave us, however, wasn't: they told us we should consider stopping our daughter's exposure to two languages, and just focus on one.

At the time, we had a French au pair living with us. She was speaking in French to my daughter. The doctors made us question our resolve to raise our daughter in a bilingual environment. They cautioned that it may be better to hedge your bets and just focus on one language.

There is something uncomfortably intuitive about this advice. After all, if you want to focus on helping your child to learn one language, wouldn't it seem that adding a second one might tax the system too much?

The problem is that this intuitive-sounding advice is wrong. There actually is no good evidence that bilingualism taxes the early cognitive system, even for children who are at risk of facing linguistic or cognitive delays. Studies of children with Down syndrome, autism, and even Specific Language Impairment (a developmental language disorder that can run in families) show that these kids can safely be exposed to a second language, and potentially more, without negative consequences for their first language or other aspects of their development. Children with many different kinds of abilities can be exposed to more than one language without risk of setbacks in other areas of life.

Fortunately, I disregarded the advice from the doctor and speech pathologist, and continued exposing my daughter to two languages. She now speaks English just as well as any other kid her age. Her negotiation skills give me a run for my money. And she is starting to become bilingual, with French as her second language.

It turns out that the medical professionals we saw were not alone in cautiously recommending linguistic simplicity. While writing this book, I spoke with the bilingualism expert François Grosjean. He confirmed that the advice I got was misguided — yet he said that he hears some version of it all the time. This idea — a manifestation of the monolingual myth — is pervasive. Researchers empirically demonstrated its reach, and its lamentable effects, when they surveyed teachers and speech-language pathologists who worked with children with developmental delays across several nations (the United States, Canada, the UK, and the Netherlands). These professionals uniformly reported that children who speak a minority language at home and have language delays often received poor access to services to support second-language learning in school. It is as if the system is set up against these kids, likely due to people's erroneous intuitions about the false danger of teaching them more than one language.

For many parents, the consequences of this faulty advice can be grave. In my case, bilingualism for my daughter was optional (albeit something we desired). For parents who speak minority languages at home, this bad advice can have bigger consequences. Children can be deprived of their parents' native language, which may impart critical social and cultural connections. Parents of children with developmental disabilities may be forced to make difficult choices that they actually need not face. This is tragic, because being exposed to multiple languages is completely normal; in fact, in much of the world it is not the exception, but the rule.

WHAT LANGUAGE DO YOU USE TO BRUSH YOUR TEETH?

From the American (or British, or French) vantage point, monolingualism may feel normal and comfortable. But most the world's children grow up in environments where more than one language is spoken. Even in the United States, the number of multilingual kids is increasing. The world is globalizing, and people who speak more than one language can take part in new conversations and new opportunities.

Despite all the myths, bilingualism is completely natural and not unusual. Through some fortunate twist of evolution, we have an amazing language-learning opportunity early in life. The human mind is not only built to learn language; it is also set up with the capacity to learn multiple languages. Children in multilingual environments are capable of learning more than one language with ease. Their brains seamlessly process and keep straight multiple linguistic inputs.

Modern science has set the record straight. Scientists have carefully tracked language acquisition across monolingual and bilingual children, finding that when exposed equally to two languages early in life, children can learn both of them. Their overall linguistic milestones are remarkably similar. Bilingual babies start babbling at the same time as monolingual babies. They speak their first words at the same time (at around a year of age), and they grow up to be fully proficient speakers, having mastered the syntax and phonology of more than one language.

Parents may note that a bilingual child's initial progress in each language seems a little slower to get off the ground than that of a monolingual child — but this is completely normal (especially since they are mastering two languages — not just one!) and should not be a cause for concern. The bilingual "disadvantage" that has been most consistently documented concerns growth and size of vocabulary. Parents of bilingual children may discover that their kids know a particular word in one language, but not the other; or the kids may substitute a word from one language for a word from the other, ostensibly to fill in a gap in their vocabulary. Indeed, researchers who study language development find that in each language, a bilingual child tends to have a smaller vocabulary than a monolingual kid would.

But when you stop to think about it, the size of a kid's vocabulary in each language they speak may not be the fairest measure of their overall vocabulary. First of all, bilingual kids need to learn many of the same words two times over; if a speaker of Spanish and English learns both *cat* and *gato*, this counts as only one word. Then too, because kids tend to learn languages in different contexts, with different people, for different purposes, their vocabularies across languages are rarely the same. This is what Grosjean calls the linguistics *complementarity principle*. Imagine that our same hypothetical Spanish-and-English speaker uses Spanish at home. He probably has all the "home words" down: words for night-night routines, words for brushing teeth, and so on. But if he speaks English in school, he probably has a very different vocabulary in that language: one that might contain specialized terms for concepts in math, or music, or technology, which he encounters at school but not at home. One study shows that bilingual kids and monolingual kids know the same "school words" in school — where they differ is in the "home words" also available in their school language.

Bilingual people of all ages, not just children, "distribute" their vocabulary across the languages they speak. My friend who learned Chinese as a baby (and speaks it with her parents) says she sounds like a kid in Chinese — and sometimes she worries that she sounds a bit stiff and formal in English, because she learned English in school. In some topics, people can even become more fluent in a language they learned as an adult. Imagine a scientist who learned all the jargon in English — she may not know the words to describe her research in her native language.

Anyone raising a bilingual kid can tell you that their kid is unlikely to be perfectly linguistically balanced. Sometimes people have a "dominant" language; and sometimes people just have languages that cover different domains. We learn the words that we need. Bilingual kids are not behind; their vocabularies are just diversified, reflecting the words they need in different contexts.

What's more, bilingual kids' *conceptual vocabulary* size — the total number of words they know across languages — is just as large as that of monolingual kids. And I would add that if you double-counted words they learned twice — words like *cat* and *gato*, bilingual kids' vocabularies are likely even greater.

Young kids who are exposed to more than one language learn words in more flexible ways. When monolingual kids learn a word for an object, they are hesitant to learn a second label. Synonyms take a while to develop. This word-learning bias is functional in that it helps kids orient to first learning one word for everything, but it is also limiting. Bilingual children, in contrast, are more linguistically flexible in that they are open to learning that the same object has two different words from two different languages attached to it.

It's true that, in general, the more hours a child spends exposed to a particular language, the better their proficiency gets. At the same time, it is not clear that there is a "magic" percentage of time needed. Hearing a language 1 percent of the time is not likely to result in meaningful proficiency. Yet the difference between hearing a language 50 percent of the time (imagining a perfectly balanced bilingual child, who splits her time across two languages) and 100 percent of the time (imagining a monolingual speaker) is much more negligible. So, percentage of time is not always a perfect proxy for resulting proficiency, and this shows that language learning is not all about quantity of exposure. The quality and complexity of the language children hear also predict their learning. Children's vocabulary does not depend on just the total amount of speech they have heard. It also matters what those words are and how the words are put together. When parents use a diverse vocabulary, when their phrasing includes grammatical complexity, and when they consider concepts that are abstract rather than exclusively concrete, their linguistic input influences their child to learn and use richer language.

Children's language mastery may also depend (to some degree) on who is speaking to them. Input from a native speaker can be more effective than input from a non-native speaker. This may simply be because it is often easier for adults to provide this high-quality input in their first language. And, with a similar logic, children learn languages better when they hear multiple speakers (likely providing slightly different personal takes on the same language) than just one. This is another reason for parents to feel comfortable speaking their native tongue to their kids, even if it is not society's majority language.

For any parents who are wondering, there's no "best" way to expose a child to more than one language, and people's practice of raising bilingual children varies widely. In some communities, bilingualism is inescapable, in that everyone speaks more than one language, and so children will necessarily pick up both. In others — particularly where parents speak a language that their broader community does not — parents are left with a choice. They may choose to expose their children to more than one language; there are several ways to do this. Some people recommend a "one language, one person" rule; Mom might speak English and Dad, Spanish. Others recommend a "one language, one context" plan — for instance, Spanish at home and English outside the home. Or a home language and a school language (for example, Spanish at home and English at school). Or just a free-flowing mix of the two languages, with everyone code-switching back and forth, letting words fly as they do. Just as there is no single *right* way to learn or use one language, there is no right way to learn or use two of them. All of the strategies I've mentioned can work to teach kids more than one language, and parents should pick whatever arrangement feels most comfortable for their own family and community context.

In all language-learning environments, kids are adept at learning whatever language is socially necessary for them. Children like my daughter, who are exposed to a second language (in my daughter's case, French) but who are immersed in a social world where everyone around her (including the French speakers) understands English, often don't produce much of the second language (though they comprehend it). My daughter understands French just fine, but — likely without conscious awareness — she realizes at some level that she does not need to produce French to be understood by others and to socially engage with them. I'm confident that if she finds herself in a social environment where she needs to speak French, she will.

Some people who are attempting to raise bilingual children may be proficient in both languages and therefore able to provide kids with varied and complex vocabulary and grammar in both. But some people may be less proficient or non-native speakers of a language they want to speak with their children — which is fine too, because children are remarkably flexible learners. When given slightly imperfect linguistic input (for example, from a speaker who makes occasional grammatical errors), children standardize the speech in their minds, and they do not tend to repeat the occasional errors. So, parents shouldn't feel nervous about exposing children to their languages — all of them. They should just talk to their kids.

Today the monolingual myth is in the process of being overturned — once and for all, I hope — by new research showing that speaking multiple languages has no deleterious effect on children. Not only that, but the evidence suggests that multilingualism has potential benefits. Even just being *exposed* to a second language can make us better problem solvers and better at social understanding. It might even hold part of the key to stopping bias — linguistic or otherwise — in its tracks.

THE BILINGUAL BONUS

Bilingualism has a clear benefit in that it enables children to speak more than one language. But that's not its only advantage. In the process of debunking the myth that bilingual people suffer "lower intelligence," researchers have not only found no differences in general cognitive functioning between monolingual and bilingual people — they have also found some evidence that speakers of more than one language may experience some cognitive *advantages* over people who speak only one language.

Representing more than one language in the mind requires daily mental gymnastics. Bilingual speakers are generally very good at separating their languages in their interactions with the world — even young children speak the correct language to the correct person. It can look effortless (and it may even feel effortless to the speaker). Nevertheless, if you look "underneath the hood," you find that although people who speak more than one language seem to do so with ease, their attention systems — the cognitive machinery that allows us to attend to some incoming information while suppressing attention to other information — are busy selecting the correct language from competing options. Bilingual speakers have attention systems that have become adept at stopping one task and starting another, at switching among ideas flexibly, and at thinking about problems from different angles. By toggling between linguistic systems, people may gain practice in cognitive switching more generally.

This toggling between different kinds of information — and being able to select the appropriate focus in order to achieve a chosen goal — is generally called executive control, and there is some evidence that people who speak more than one language may grow to develop better executive control than those who are monolingual.

Throughout childhood, people with greater executive control tend to do better academically, and the benefits of enhanced executive control don't end at adulthood. In fact, decline in executive control is a hallmark of old age, and some people face more age-related decline than others; it is not always clear why. By giving children practice in attending to and switching among different languages, bilingualism may help these little people develop and maintain executive control.

To be fair, evidence of potential advantages of bilingualism has been mixed; some studies find that bilingual speakers enjoy cognitive advantages over monolingual peers, whereas other studies find no clear differences between the groups. This continues to be a heated area of ongoing research and debate. The most consistently observed differences seem to be among young children and among older adults — perhaps because between childhood and old age, people are generally at the peak of their executive control, so bilingual and monolingual people alike get pretty good scores for this ability. Children and older adults tend to have the most variance in executive function (and more variability overall makes it easier to observe difference across groups), and differences in cognitive flexibility can be observed as early as infancy.

Some recent evidence from the lab of the bilingualism expert Ellen Bialystok even suggests that bilingualism may serve as a protection against the onset of symptoms of dementia and Alzheimer's disease — again because that control of attention is on overdrive for bilingual people, and so their daily cognitive tasks are keeping their minds sharp until late in life. New studies are taking this promising (albeit debated) finding to a global level — preliminary reports indicate that in countries where people experience longer life expectancy, the incidence of Alzheimer's is slightly lower for those who speak on average two or more languages (rather than one).

The bottom line is that bilingual people may potentially enjoy cognitive advantages that last throughout life, and they certainly do not experience cognitive detriments, as was once believed. This is reason enough for many parents — myself included — to pursue a bilingual education for their children.

For me, as a scientist and a parent, this tantalizing evidence about a "bilingual bonus" motivated me to dive deeper into the potential benefits of bilingualism.

POLYGLOTS PREFERRED

Around the time that I had my daughter, I began thinking about the potential benefits of bilingualism in a personal rather than an academic way. Like any parent, I wanted what I felt was the best for my tiny human. I felt convinced by the evidence that bilingual people enjoy a number of advantages, ranging from broader cultural exposure to cognitive flexibility. But I also started thinking a lot about the *social* dividends of bilingualism — a topic that was starting to emerge in the scientific literature at the time.

For many families, bilingualism is a social imperative because kids simply need more than one language to communicate with everyone who is close to them. Among bilingual and bicultural families, sharing a linguistic past can be a good thing. If you look at immigrant families in the United States, adolescents who know their parents' first language have closer relationships with their parents. Interestingly, this closeness occurs even when the kids just know the parents' first language but speak mostly in English. The knowledge alone seems to build a connection and a feeling of shared identity.

When my daughter was born, I already knew French fluently, and I wanted my daughter to learn it as well. It wasn't culturally imperative that she do so; we were raising her in the United States, and both her parents and all four of her grandparents speak English. In some sense a second language was "optional." But I thought that it would bring her personal and intellectual enrichment down the road.

For any kid, bilingualism opens up opportunities for new and interesting social experiences. By being exposed to more than one language, kids encounter social worlds that monolingual kids simply do not: they watch people engage in different languages with different people in different contexts, and they learn to navigate those interactions. Kids who are raised in an environment where multiple languages are spoken gain practice in linguistic perspective-taking. They think about where and when language A is spoken and where and when language B is spoken, and who speaks what language to whom. They may think about who understands which language, and who does not.

Even by the time she was a toddler, my daughter exhibited some adept perspective-taking of her own. She quickly figured out that her au pair spoke French, and that I understood it but her dad didn't. I would speak French with the au pair at home, but if we were out with other English speakers, we would switch to English. She learned that the au pair would speak French with her own family, and when they visited, the French family could talk to me but not others. As my daughter got older, she wondered out loud which language our dog understood (final conclusion: "Actually, I think he only speaks dog").

As I watched my daughter make sense of the different linguistic perspectives of the people around her, it got me thinking about all of the ways in which children might go through a similar experience. After all, there are endless ways in which children are exposed to more than one language. There are families that have a home language and a school language, multiple home languages, or different dialects of the same language, which may map onto class or religion or race or any other variable that divides groups. Bilingual children take for granted these social and linguistic variants since they are very proficient at navigating linguistic complexity and responding correctly. When a new situation arises, they quickly assess its linguistic dynamics and how they should respond. I started to wonder whether all this practice with linguistic perspective-taking makes multilingual children more adept at taking people's perspectives more generally.

Perspective-taking is important for communication. This is because language can sometimes be ambiguous. When someone speaks, you might interpret just the literal content of the words. Alternatively, if you are taking their perspective, you might think about what they see and know, to infer their intended meaning. This approach could lead to better interpersonal connection and understanding.

The children's book character Amelia Bedelia is the incarnation of someone who interprets all language literally, without any perspective-taking. As a result, she has a comically hard time understanding what other people intend to convey. When she is asked to make a "chicken dinner" she makes a dinner that chickens would enjoy; when she is asked to "dust the furniture" she adds (rather than removes) the dust; a sponge cake is made with actual sponges.

Amelia Bedelia is a far-fetched example of the perils of literal-mindedness (and that's why she is funny). But little errors and achievements in perspective-taking happen all the time — and they can lead to communication breakdown or success. Thinking about what someone else sees or knows can help you understand what they are talking about. And ignoring this information can lead to misunderstanding.

My colleague Boaz Keysar and our former graduate students Zoe Liberman and Samantha Fan and I decided to test whether bilingual kids' regular practice with taking the linguistic perspective of others contributed to a more general ability to put themselves in someone else's shoes.

In our study, children of ages four through six sat across from an experimenter, with some toys placed between them. The toys sat on a grid of squares, like little window shelves. Yet there was a simple trick involved. Some of the window shelves were open windows — visible from both sides. And some were closed on one side, so that a child could see the toy but could also observe that the adult could not view it. For instance, the child could see three toy cars — a small car, a medium-sized car, and a large car. Because the small car was blocked from the adult's view, the adult could only see two cars: what was the medium car according to the child's perspec-

tive, and what was the large car according to the child's perspective, the largest one.

After the children got settled, the adult experimenter said, "Oh, I
see a small car! Can you move that small car for me?"

What is the child to do? If the child takes the Amelia Bedelia
approach, she should take the exact literal meaning of the adult's
speech and move the small car. But if the child considers the perspective of the person uttering the words, then she should move
the medium-sized car. Children who are better at perspective-
taking, we hypothesized, would think, "Well, the adult can see
only the medium-sized car and the large one, so when she says
'the small car,' she is probably referring to that medium-sized
one."

What we found was pretty striking: the bilingual kids in our
study were much more likely than the monolingual kids to move
the medium car, successfully adapting to the experimenter's point
of view. What's more, even when monolingual kids reached for the
medium car, they often glanced at the small car first (we measured
where kids looked before they reached). These monolingual kids'
own perspective apparently got in the way, preventing them from
taking the experimenter's perspective as easily as the bilingual kids
did — they were more likely to spontaneously look to the medium
car. It is as though perspective-taking came more naturally to the
multilingual kids than to the monolingual ones.

Bilingual children were not the only kids who were good at taking other people's perspectives. We also tested a group of "exposure" kids — children who had a nanny or grandparent who spoke
to them in another language at times. These kids did not speak a
language other than English themselves. On average, they were just
as good as bilingual kids (who had a much more equal degree of exposure across their two languages) at taking someone else's perspective — even though they had heard much less of a second language, and didn't speak it themselves. Clearly, children who hear
different languages — even if they don't hear them enough to be-

come proficient bilingual speakers — are still getting a lot of practice in linguistic perspective-taking.

In a follow-up study, we found that the benefits of exposure to more than one language are emerging even among babies who are a little over a year in age. The study's design was simpler — each baby sat across from my former PhD student Zoe Liberman and saw two toys (say, two cars again). The baby could see both, but Zoe could see only one (and if the baby was paying attention, the baby could see that Zoe could see only one). Zoe would say, "Ooh! A car! I see the car! Can you give me the car?" If you were taking Zoe's perspective, you would reach for the car that she could see. Again, we found that babies living in bilingual homes were more likely to pick the car that Zoe could see.

None of the babies Zoe tested were talking very much yet — they were on average fifteen months old. We asked the parents of the babies from bilingual homes to evaluate how much time the babies spent hearing each of their two different languages. "Balanced exposure" would mean hearing each language 50 percent of the time. Some babies, by contrast, might hear English 90 or 95 percent of the time and just a little bit of the second language.

As was the case for the older kids, it did not seem to matter whether the babies heard the two languages equally, or heard primarily English and only a small amount of another language. Even a little bit of exposure to another language was sufficient. Just being in an environment where more than one language was regularly spoken seemed to make babies perform better in a perspective-taking task. Although they were hardly talking yet, kids who experienced multilingual environments were able to better understand someone else's intended meaning, thereby showing signs of effective communication ability at an early age.

Bilingual kids' adept communication skills show up in other subtle but noteworthy ways. For instance, they attend carefully to the way that other people communicate with them. Bilingual kids more easily point out inconstancies, redundancies, and non sequiturs in other people's speech. The psychologists Quin Yow and Ellen Markman have found that bilingual preschoolers, more than monolingual ones, are better able to use the emotional tone of someone's voice to interpret their words. If you say "I'm fine!" (chipper voice) or "I'm fine" (passive aggressive "I'm not really fine" voice), adults know the difference — and bilingual kids start to pick up on this too. They also excel at correctly integrating verbal and nonverbal channels of communication — such as the direction of someone's gaze or use of pointing gestures — to help interpret what the person is talking about. Again, just a little bit of exposure to a second language may achieve results — one study found that even monolingual kids become better at interpreting nonverbal cues after experiencing only a brief time in a bilingual environment.

It seems clear, given all of this evidence, that bilingual kids' experiences with multiple languages can make them successful communicators. One way to think about this — and some researchers have — is to posit that bilingual kids are particularly good at understanding others' *mental states* — thinking carefully about what other people know and don't know. This is a hallmark of effective communication and interpersonal relationships, and evidence suggests that young bilingual children are especially proficient at it.

New research shows that people's abilities in visual perspective-taking are related to their degree of empathizing with others. People who are able to picture the world through someone else's eyes are also better able to imagine the emotions that the person may be experiencing. When someone tunes in to another person's perspective by means of visual cues, they also become more likely to take into account their thoughts and feelings. By simply developing skills in perspective-taking, bilingual children may grow into more open-minded, more flexible, and potentially more tolerant people.

At the same time, for a kid in a multilingual environment, life is not all about seamless perspective-taking and communication. Inevitably they will find themselves in situations where not everyone speaks the same language, and this may also lead to miscommunication and misunderstanding. And to be fair, just like monolingual kids, bilingual kids prefer new people who speak a familiar language or with a familiar accent; bilingualism is by no means a panacea. Even ostensible breakdowns in communication, though, provide opportunities for growth. Experiencing some failure — and then learning how to repair a miscommunication — provides an additional pathway for bilingual kids to hone their communication skills. They practice using nonverbal communication and look to others for feedback. They tinker with word choice until they get it right.

These findings give me hope that parents (including myself!) can feel less pressure to achieve some "perfect" form of bilingualism and instead make it part of their lives, in whatever way it works for them and their children. Any multilingual exposure for children — even when limited by the practicalities of daily life — can be valuable.

Bilingualism breaks down social boundaries and may open a path to social openness and tolerance. This is vital for developing children, because in many ways, understanding others — taking their perspective, empathizing with their feelings, and imagining their mental life — cuts to the heart of what it means to have a human interaction. By enhancing our ability to understand others, multilingualism may offer a small step toward human togetherness — one that counts.

IT'S ELEMENTARY

The benefits of bilingualism may be clear, but what if you're a parent who speaks only one language — and you don't have close friends or family members who are bilingual, or have the luxury of hiring a nanny who speaks a different language? It might be hard to imagine how you too can raise a bilingual child.

But the most miraculous thing happens as children grow up — they start to attend school. They go off to kindergarten (or, if they're able, to preschool), at which point their little minds are still comfortably within the critical period for language acquisition.

Education policy could certainly do more to support all children, whatever their background, in learning more than one language; increase awareness and tolerance of linguistic diversity, in all its forms; and build a greater understanding of cultural biases, raising children in such a way that they will grow up to fight them. At the moment, we're falling short in all of these areas, with a sad result: school should be a safe place, but for children who do not speak a standard language or with a standard accent, it can feel threatening.

Ruth Bader Ginsburg may have felt that she needed to mask her Brooklyn accent when she went to law school, but one of her colleagues began to feel insecure about his language at a younger age: Supreme Court Justice Clarence Thomas. He is known for many things, and among those is his silence during oral argument — the time when justices have the opportunity to ask questions of the attorneys presenting a case. When he asked a question of a lawyer in 2016, it apparently drew gasps from the audience — not because the question was so interesting, but because it was the first time in ten years that he had asked a question of a presenting lawyer. Many people assume this silence is simply a reflection of Thomas's temperament. But when asked about it in an interview with a group of teenagers, he gave a startlingly personal reason: "When I was 16, I was sitting as the only Black kid in my class, and I had grown up speaking a kind of a dialect. It's called Geechee. Some people call it Gullah now, and people praise it now. But they used to make fun of us back then. It's not standard English. When I transferred to an all-white school at your age, I was self-conscious, like we all are. It's like if we get pimples at 16, or we grow six inches and we're taller than everybody else, or our feet grow or something; we get self-conscious. And the problem was that I would correct myself midsentence. I was trying to speak standard English."

Based on his response, it seems that his silence reflects, at least in part, his former feelings of linguistic insecurity. As the linguist John Baugh explains, Thomas was part of an American educational system that "made African American students of his generation feel a sense of linguistic inferiority and, by extension, a sense of linguistic shame." Sadly, Thomas's experience is not unique.

Linguistic biases do not exist just in the adult world of interviewing for a job or applying to rent an apartment. Children too can be subjected to them constantly — and not just on the playground. Even well-intended teachers can be biased against children who speak in a dialect they consider to be nonstandard. One study finds that teachers can't turn off their reliance on the sound of a student's voice as they make inferences about the child's intelligence and capability — even when objective evidence of their ability, such as their compositions and drawings, is available. Being negatively evaluated can subtly but surely make school an uncomfortable place for children whose speech is considered nonstandard, and this experience can diminish their chance of achieving academic success.

If parents and elected leaders demanded it, our schools could become a starting point for a linguistic revolution. Not only should children who attend school have an opportunity — and be encouraged — to learn more than one language, but children of all languages also should be taught that linguistic diversity (including all the languages or dialects they speak) is an asset, not something that they need to hide. In language, as in so many other aspects of public life, schools can and should be leading the way.

Certainly, many of our leaders profess to be interested in the benefits of language learning. In 2014, a bipartisan group of eight US senators and representatives (half of them Democrats and half Republicans) wrote to the American Academy of Arts and Sciences, requesting information on bilingualism and "the relationship between language learning and the nation's strength, competitiveness, and well-being," noting that the myriad challenges of our time require international understanding and cooperation. They feared that an English-only nation might suffer a disadvantage in the global arena. The academy's response explained that, yes, the United States is falling behind. Compared to other countries — including European nations and China — this country is far more monolingual. As the report argues, this could change: "It is critical that we work together at this moment in history, when there is so much to gain by participating in a multilingual world, and so much to lose if we remain stubbornly monolingual."

Some lucky families already follow the academy's advice and have found a way to introduce a second language into their children's lives. Many after-school programs offer language lessons, although these may strain a family's budget or schedule. Dual-language and immersion programs also can be extremely effective at teaching more than one language, and many families with the opportunity or the means to send their children to such institutions gladly sign them up. But not all schools offer language classes, let alone a full-immersion environment.

I believe we have a responsibility to change that. Elementary schools should, in my opinion, offer a second language to students as early as possible. Waiting until middle school to teach children a second language risks missing the time in life when children are most able to learn languages, hobbling even the hardest-working students. And that's assuming that language classes are even an option at this late stage; lamentably, many American school systems do not even teach foreign languages in middle school, and the number that do has been declining in recent years.

Adding second-language instruction to elementary school curriculum would require resources — particularly for increasing the number of language teachers and making it possible for them to move to underserved areas. This budgetary necessity might be more palatable, and fit within a broader structure of educational planning, if we viewed language learning as a critical goal of education. Children do not need to learn only math and reading; they should also learn languages. Being proficient in more than one language should not just be icing on the cake — a rare treat for an occasional monolingual parent who invests in after-school language classes or for kids whose parents can afford private school. It should instead be seen as a basic right, and a life-broadening experience, for any child. American children should be prepared to interact with other peoples and cultures, to enjoy increased opportunities for employment in different sectors, and to strengthen their skills in executive control, perspective-taking, and communication by means of this relatively simple shift in educational priorities. Our society as a whole would benefit.

There is tremendous value to be gained by educating all children, including children from different linguistic backgrounds. Although the United States lags behind most other nations in percentage of bilingual citizens, America's linguistic diversity is nonetheless growing. Around 20 percent of American families speak a language other than English. Nearly 10 percent of American schoolchildren are "English language learners"— children who do not yet know much English when they start school. Many schools have programs in English as a second language, yet their quality is variable, and some schools may not have the expertise and resources needed to run these programs effectively.

Teaching a class full of children who speak different languages is challenging, certainly. To do it well takes time and money. But it can be done. Many other nations have thought carefully about language in their curricula and how best to educate diverse groups of speakers.

Some places in the world have no choice but to tackle linguistic diversity in the classroom. In, for example, Papua New Guinea — likely the most linguistically diverse country in the world — the educators needed to figure out a way to effectively teach children in their local language yet also build bilingualism. The national education system provides schooling in 430 languages, with a pathway toward bilingualism in English. Other nations too are facing the challenge of educating children in both their native tongue and other languages. Some countries are concerned about endangered or dying languages. In Wales, for example, children are taught both Welsh and English.

In Brunei, bilingual Malay-English classrooms switch between the two languages. The teachers and learners decide together which languages are most appropriate for different subjects and time periods. The United States too has some promising examples of dual-language classrooms. Some schools in New York, California, Utah, Delaware, and Louisiana have had great successes in teaching children in dual-immersion classrooms in English and Spanish, English and Chinese, and English and French. States and cities can experiment with programs that both teach English-speaking kids a new language and teach "English language learners" English in addition to their first language.

Creative language policies require careful planning and need teachers with particular expertise, but these examples show that it can be done. Reframing the debate and changing the cultural perception of diverse language experiences to be seen as an asset, rather than a liability, will help more schools and parents become invested in getting programs up and running. We owe it to future generations to make the effort, because the alternative — sticking with our current blinkered approach — is limiting to students. Instead, we could open the door to the vast opportunities that multilingual education can provide.

I was recently talking to a seventy-year-old woman whose parents immigrated to the United States from Italy when she was six. She didn't speak English at the time. No one really knew what to do with her at school, since the family lived in a rural area without many immigrants, and no one at school was prepared to teach English as a second language. Wanting her to assimilate, her parents stopped speaking Italian to her. She remembers crying and crying — feeling that she did not have a language. Forever marked by this experience, she grew up to pursue a career in teaching English as a second language.

She said that she is personally wary of bilingualism because it was such a challenging and lonely path for her. But her experience highlights exactly the kind of situation that we can protect against. Her parents should have never had to make this difficult choice for their daughter, and schools should be capable of teaching a child who is learning more than one language. Indeed, bilingualism was not the enemy here — this young immigrant needed to know both languages in order to adapt to her new environment and remain close to her family. What her family lacked was proper educational resources. As our nation diversifies, more and more families find themselves in this predicament.

This ESL teacher — as well as Clarence Thomas, Ruth Bader Ginsburg, David Thorpe, and countless others — learned the hard way that speech is a double-edged sword. On the one hand, the way we talk signals group differences, laying the groundwork for terrible prejudice. On the other hand, speech can give us a strong sense of belonging, helping us find ourselves and our cultural identity, while preparing us to thrive. Learning to speak in more than one language appears to make us more socially perceptive and more cognitively flexible, potentially keeping our minds sharp later in life.

Speech, in short, can be the problem and also the solution. By changing our relationship to language — becoming aware of how much it matters to our social lives, opening up to linguistic diversity in its many forms, and implementing changes to improve our educational, legal, and civic institutions — we can harness the power of speech for the good. The time for this revolution is now.

AFTERWORD

IT'S ~~NOT~~ WHAT YOU SAY

In this book, I've focused on *how* we talk, rather than the content of speech: not what we say, but how we say it. That's because language, dialect, accent, and other ways of speaking all play a huge but overlooked role in our lives and deserve increased attention — and decisive action. But I cannot end this book without acknowledging the power of the *content* of speech.

The words we use, just like the ways in which we say them, have a social impact that most of us don't fully understand. When we think about the myriad social groups that currently exist, or which are coming into being, related to race, gender, religion, nationality (any group, really, that becomes salient as a basis of social divisions), we may not realize that our language helped create and define these groups in the first place.

Our speech can be used to reify already familiar groups and to create new groups as well. When we are trying to navigate a new social landscape and figure out which social groups have meaning and why, it is often via language that new groups come into focus. Language can make a new social category feel real, essential, and important, and it is not a far leap to instill it with bias and prejudice. Left unchecked, our speech can take on a tremendously consequential — and sometimes even dangerous — social function.

A classic example of how quick we are to create new social groups, and to imbue them with hostility, is the famous "blue eyes brown eyes" experiment in an elementary school classroom. The day after the assassination of Martin Luther King Jr., Jane Elliott, an elementary school teacher and subsequent activist, launched a research project to study the roots of prejudice. Specifically, she wanted to understand how prejudice could develop in children who seemed entirely innocent.

To examine this big question, Elliott focused on the narrow topic of how quickly children could become prejudiced against a brand-new group — one that the children knew nothing about, one that did not matter *at all* until that very moment. Could it all of a sudden become a subject of prejudice? (Elliott's motivations were not purely academic. As a teacher, she was guided by the hope that if students experienced prejudice for themselves, they might grow up to be less prejudiced citizens.)

On the first day of the experiment, Elliott told the students that the color of their eyes — whether blue or brown — mattered. And it mattered a lot. She told kids that the blue-eyed children were on top — they were better than and smarter than the brown-eyed children and therefore deserved more trust and privileges in the classroom. This created the perfect storm. Over a matter of hours, the blue-eyed children had accepted their new position of privilege and were expressing the bias they had only just acquired. On subsequent days, their teacher flipped the power differential. By the end, all students had experienced what it was like to have high status — and to experience active discrimination.

The third time that Elliott ran her classroom exercise, in 1970, it was filmed and made into a documentary, *The Eye of the Storm.* Years later, footage of her experiment with the children was juxtaposed with video of these same students coming back for a high school reunion and reflecting on the classroom experience. This became the 1985 PBS documentary *A Class Divided.*

As you watch the documentary, it is shocking to see how quickly the children picked up on the new social order — only a matter of minutes. The blue-eyed and brown-eyed children start to get into fights at recess. The blue-eyed students mockingly called the others "brown-eyes." One blue-eyed child suggested that Elliott keep the yardstick on her desk in case the "brown-eyed people get out of hand." (When I play this documentary in an introductory psychology class, students gasp out loud at this line every time.) Reporting later on the experience, Elliott said, "I watched what had been marvelous, cooperative, wonderful, thoughtful children turn into nasty, vicious, discriminating little third-graders in a space of fifteen minutes."

This new social order impacted children's academic success too. For example, Elliott had the groups participate in a timed group phonics game. The group "on top" completed the game much faster than the group "on the bottom," though there was no reason for this outcome. And when, on a subsequent day when the other group was "on top," the higher-status group again performed better, though the same children had previously fared poorly.

This experiment impressively illustrated what psychologists call *stereotype threat*. When people feel that their group isn't as good as another, this sense of inferiority can affect their performance. People buckle under the weight of the stereotypes that the rest of the world has burdened them with. One classic social psychology study shows that Asian women perform better on a math test when they check the box identifying them as "Asian" rather than the one signaling that they are "female." Even this subtle suggestion of group membership, and the baggage that comes with it, can impact people's academic success. Here Elliott created meaningful groups — and differential academic performance across groups — in just a single day. Imagine what happens after a lifetime of feeling as if you are a member of a disadvantaged group.

What was it about Elliott's speech and the setup of her experiment that was so effective at creating prejudice? What hit kids designated as lower status at a *personal* level, such that they felt bad about their group and felt as if the teacher was taking their "best friends away"? Why did their new groups start to feel "real" to children? How did they form so quickly, and why did they matter so much?

Here's the key: Elliott deployed language strategically and effectively. Though not trained as a psychologist, somehow she implicitly knew what to say. In fact, it's only recently that the field of psychology has started to uncover the secrets of why language matters so much in the creation of new social groups.

Elliott talked about children not as individuals who each had a particular eye color. She did not say, "Laurie who has brown eyes." She instead referred to Laurie as a member of this new group of people called "the brown-eyed children," or for short, "a brown-eye."

Using speech to refer to whole groups of people can take a category that was unknown, or perhaps known only a little, and make it stand out. Language can in effect *make categories real.* Recent studies show that when people use language to discuss groups of people (rather than individuals), they can cause social categories to emerge. Through their words, adults can create newly meaningful social groups for children to latch onto. If there is a new social category that adults want to make salient for their world and their children, they can use language to do so.

Jane Elliot's language about groups was notably negative. She explicitly taught kids prejudice. But mere "groupy" language itself, used to refer to sets of people, can subtly set the stage for prejudice.

Knowing that language can make new categories become real, Marjorie Rhodes (the researcher who conducted the "Flurps and Zazzes" experiment described in Chapter 4) wanted to understand exactly *how* speech works to imbue new categories with social meaning.

In one study, Rhodes tested how very simple differences in an adult's language — referring to individuals rather than an entire group of people — could affect how children thought about a completely new social category. She taught children about a fictional world in a storybook. Each picture featured a new cartoon creature (from a group she called Zarpies) who was doing something silly, such as being scared of ladybugs or eating flowers. To some children, an adult read the storybook focusing on the actions of *individuals* — "This Zarpie is scared of ladybugs!" To others, the adult described the same actions as representative of the *whole group* —

"Zarpies are scared of ladybugs!" This type of phrasing — generalizing across a whole group — is called generic language.

This subtle turn of phrase made a huge difference in what children ultimately learned. Children exposed to generic language identifying the Zarpies as a group started to think of them as belonging to a biologically and culturally real category, an *essentialized* group who were basically all the same.

The researchers also tested the kids' parents and found that when parents were led to believe that the Zarpies were a distinct group with biological and cultural traits that set them apart from others, they were more likely to use generic language about the Zarpies with their children. You can see a feedback loop between language and social thinking occurring in real time. The more you think of a group as truly distinct based on biology and culture, the more you produce generic language to describe individuals in the group. And the more you produce generic language about individuals in the group, the more others hear your speech and come to believe that the group is culturally and biologically distinct.

Here is the most shocking part of this research, in my opinion. When parents thought of the Zarpies as a biologically and culturally distinct group, parents also liked them less. Parents were more likely to say negative things about the Zarpie eating a flower ("That's yucky"). They conveyed their opinion to their children, adding a bit of negative flavor.

Subtle but consistent language about groups can make intergroup animosity spread. Think about how the news can bombard us with statements about certain people: "Mexicans are . . ." or "Muslims want . . ." This way of talking generically about a group of people makes them seem like one unified entity. It probably doesn't even matter that much whether the completed statements say something neutral or even positive: "Mexicans like tacos" or "Muslims want peace." Talking about a class of people generically teaches kids to pay attention to it as a monolithic entity. And just by nature of *thinking* that a group is real and different, it often becomes natural to cast it in a negative light.

The next time you hear the news and talk to your children about it, pay attention to this generic language about groups. The best remedy is not to actively disagree: "That is wrong. Mexicans are nice." The most positive effects come from talking about group members as individual people — some may be mean and some may be nice. Most important, all humans are individuals and not mere faceless members of one particular group.

We often hear generic language about gender. Kids learn a lot about gender early on, so the generic language a preschooler hears about it is not creating a category from whole cloth, the way that language about a new category like the Zarpies could. Nevertheless, "groupy" language about gender can have big negative effects, and teachers and parents are often unaware of how much their talk about gender matters to children.

At first blush, gendered language seems pretty harmless. If you go into any preschool classroom in America, you are very likely to hear it: "Good morning, boys and girls!" It's so familiar, it just rolls off the tongue. And it sounds harmless enough; "Girls and boys, let's stop playing and line up now!" But when children hear adults constantly referring to gender — or any other social category — they can't help but intuit that these categories must be extremely important socially, and that they should *care* about these categories. Gender stereotypes get off the ground through this type of language.

One classroom study by the psychologist Rebecca Bigler manipulated the ways in which gender was discussed in elementary-school classrooms. She wanted to test how subtle differences in speech about gender impacts children's thinking. When teachers speak to children in a way that makes a big deal about gender, do children all of a sudden start to care about it more than they did before?

In Bigler's studies, classroom teachers were given one of two sets of instructions. Some classes went along with business as usual. Other teachers were instructed to focus more on gender than they typically would. They were, however, told to treat girls and boys equally and positively — not to introduce any bias, per se. This test

was not a re-creation of the "blue eyes/brown eyes" experiment —
but as it turns out, the findings had some parallels.

Teachers in this second group of classrooms were merely supposed to highlight the idea that gender was significant. Children
would be labeled as "boys" and "girls" wherever possible. Some of
this talk was positive — "What smart girls, you finished on time!"
And some might be neutral, such as instructions for boys or girls to
hang their art on the wall, or for boys or girls to line up first.

The teachers' language suggested to children that gender was
real, and something that mattered a lot. But the teachers did not
impart anything explicit about gender stereotypes to the children.
Nothing negative was ever said about anyone, as a matter of fact.
The teacher wasn't instilling any particular knowledge — she was
just "marking" a social category that children already had access to.
It was a subtle difference, yet it turned out to be a meaningful one.

Bigler wanted to see what children thought about gender after a
few weeks of being in a classroom where teachers marked it. Would
they think that gender mattered more? And if so, in what ways? Before and after the experiment, Bigler assessed how much the students endorsed stereotypical beliefs about gender. Who should be a
scientist — boys, girls, or both? Who should be a nurse?

As it turned out, after just a few weeks of being in a classroom
where gender was marked in this way, children started to endorse
society's stereotypes about gender. They became more likely to
think that boys, but not girls, should become scientists, and only
girls should be nurses.

Where did kids learn these stereotypes? Teachers never mentioned scientists or nurses. But they did subject them to a lot of
gender talk — language that, over time, had apparently shaped the
way the children thought about boys and girls.

You can imagine the wheels turning in a child's mind: *My teacher
keeps talking about this — therefore it must be really important!
What could it mean? How could boys and girls be significantly and
fundamentally different? Hmm . . . where can I find these gender
differences?* It seems that merely talking about gender as a category

at all led the children to look out into the world and try to figure out *why* this category was significant. They picked up on cultural stereotypes about the category and used them to fill in the blanks.

When children look to cultural stereotypes for guidance about social groups, things can turn ugly fast. Sadly, many gender stereotypes are not positive for little girls. Children may assume that these incredibly important differences between boys and girls that everyone is always talking about have something to do with the stereotypes that they observe in the world — for instance, boys, but not girls, are good at science or math. In short, children may tune in to sexist cultural stereotypes simply because of the seemingly benign categorical language about gender that they have been exposed to. When you linguistically mark groups and use the related labels all the time, children pick up on it.

So if a child hears gendered comments that are seemingly benign, such as "Oh, you are the only girl cousin! All your cousins are boys!" the speakers are not likely intending to convey anything very meaningful. But when a child hears this constant talk about gender, how can she help but think something along these lines: *OK . . . everyone around me is commenting on the fact that I'm a girl. There must be something super-duper meaningful about this distinction. I have absolutely no idea what it is. So, I'll look out into the world to figure it out.*

I don't mean to argue that no longer talking about boys and girls as "boys and girls" would fix all our woes related to gender. Certainly it would not. But by using our speech to tag gender as a meaningful group in the presence of children, we may be opening the door to gender stereotypes.

Stereotypes and prejudice about race, too, can spread through language. Language that describes racial groups in generic, essentialized ways can easily encourage stereotypes and prejudice to grow. The more people psychologically think of racial groups as being essentialized, meaningfully different kinds of people, the more likely they are to express racial biases.

But it's also important to understand and appreciate the social complexity around discussions about race and to know that simply avoiding talking about race with kids is not the answer, either.

Research with white American parents shows a common tendency of "colorblind" approaches to parenting, where parents often treat discussion of race as taboo and may even avoid talking about it at all. For many parents, this may be motivated by thinking that if you don't talk about racism, kids won't learn racist attitudes—but unfortunately, this doesn't work.

As we've seen, children are cultural sponges who pick up on the stereotypes and prejudice that society offers. When parents or other adults in children's lives avoid discussions about race, children can sense that a topic is taboo. They are then left to their own devices to parse the social world and any aspects of racism and inequalities across groups that they observe. This leaves unjust narratives of racism — such as the legitimacy of racial hierarchies in society — out there to be internalized.

Parents of underrepresented groups are much more likely to talk about race, including discussions that help protect their children in a world where they may experience discrimination. Discussions with all groups of children can be most effective when they acknowledge racism (rather than brushing it under the rug), explaining historical and structural inequalities in a way that highlights the injustices in society, rather than any intrinsic or essentialist differences in groups of people.

Language marks groups and makes them real. The way we use language can also — subtly — teach us positive things about some groups and negative things about others. Imagine seeing someone (person A) hit someone else (person B). A whole range of inferences might be drawn from this scenario. If A is someone like you — your race, your nationality, your friend — you will be more likely to describe just the action and nothing more: "A hit B." (Or, if you were being magnanimous, you might consider B's feelings and add some interpretation to the facts: "A hurt B.") If, on the other hand, person A is *not* like you — a member of a group you do not like much, say, or even just someone of a different race or someone who speaks with a different accent — you will be likelier to conclude that "A doesn't like B." Or you might go farther, drawing a broader conclusion about A's behavior and temperament. Maybe A always acts like this. Maybe "A is aggressive." Maybe "A is a criminal."

Not coincidentally, the words I've used to describe this hypothetical event — *hitting, hurting, disliking, aggressive* — follow a concrete-to-abstract trajectory. The more you use abstract terms about someone, the more your speech conveys of a permanent, rather than transient, aspect of that person.

Psychological research on this phenomenon — known as *linguistic intergroup bias* — shows that the ways people talk about in-groups and out-groups are subtly but significantly different. Positive actions taken by an in-group are often communicated to others in abstract terms, whereas negative in-group actions are communicated more concretely. The opposite is true when people talk about out-groups. In this way, people's speech can communicate to others what they think about a particular group.

These linguistic differences are subtle, but they matter. This biased, subtle-to-abstract continuum of language reflects how people talk — and also how they listen. Speech conveys our subtle feelings about others, which other people are able to discern. We may think that we are simply reporting the facts, but based on the level of abstraction that we use in our language, we provide another completely different set of information to the person listening.

From the categories we choose to talk about to the words we use to describe them, the social potency of language resides not just in the way we sound but also in the words we use. The way we sound divides groups; the words we use create new groups that people and especially children can learn about; and we frequently characterize those groups in ways that are demeaning to people who are not like us. This often happens without our intention or awareness. My hope is that by becoming alert to the many ways in which our speech affects those around us, as well as ourselves, we can better match our language to our personal ideals. Because at the end of the day, your social world is a reflection of both what you say, and how you say it.

ACKNOWLEDGMENTS

I am indebted to the researchers and individuals whose work and stories I've included in this book. Many were willing to provide helpful feedback on their science and their experiences. I particularly appreciated their response when I had to ask for feedback on a short deadline, over the holiday season. Thank you to all of them: Molly Babel, Mahzarin Banaji, Martyn Barrett, John Baugh, Ellen Bialystok, Krista Byers-Heinlein, Aaron Cargile, Andrei Cimpian, Cynthia Clopper, Emma Cohen, Leda Cosmides, Michel DeGraff, Jean-Marc Dewaele, Julie Dobrow, Marko Dragojevic, Penelope Eckert, Susan Gal, Fred Genesee, Jeffrey Grogger, François Grosjean, Karolina Hansen, Sayuri Hayakawa, Lola de Hevia, Molly Flaherty, Caroline Floccia, Agata Gluszek, Erika Hoff, Stephanie Lindemann, Judith Irvine, Paola Ocampo, Boaz Keysar, Sharese King, Joey Lee, Sarah London, Janet McIntosh, Salikoko Mufwene, Benjamin Munson, Elissa Newport, Sylvia Perry, David Pietraszewski, Tamara Rakic, Marjorie Rhodes, John Rickford, Steven Roberts, Donald Rubin, Ann Senghas, Robert Seyfarth, Allison Shapp, Nicholas Subtirelu, David Thorpe, Barbara Trudell, Tu Tu, Laura Wagner, Janet Werker, Alan Yu, and Quin Yow.

I am also grateful to other colleagues and students who took the time to read and comment on drafts at different stages. I am thankful for the insights of Janet Connor, Rebecca Frausel, Grace

Hwang, Hannah Kim, Sanghee Kim, Alex Shaw, Elan Shpigel, and Anna-Marie Sprenger.

I am lucky to have some amazing friends. A special thanks to a few in particular who read earlier versions or parts of the book — despite busy schedules — and provided extremely useful big-picture feedback: Daniel Casasanto, Laura Casasanto, Sital Kalantry, Kate Oakes, Kristina Olson, Emily Oster, Jane Risen, and Jessica Weiss. Thanks to Kristin Shutts, who has been an amazing reader and intellectual partner and collaborator over the past fifteen years. I am also grateful to Melissa Ferguson and Sian Beilock for moral support when I needed it, and to Dave Nussbaum, who encouraged my early interest in writing for a general audience.

My former PhD students Jasmine DeJesus and Zoe Liberman have been tremendous partners in my research program, and I am grateful for the feedback they gave as I wrote. Thanks to Isobel Heck and Radhika Santhanagopalan, who provided thoughtful comments and who are taking the research forward. Thanks to Rachel King for her impressive effort at helping me fact-check the research on a tight deadline. A huge thanks to Molly Gibian, a leader in my laboratory group who offered extraordinary support, research assistance, and editorial feedback on this book. I could not have finished it without her, and I am so grateful for her contribution.

Many mentors along the way have supported my research and academic development. My graduate adviser Elizabeth Spelke provided inspirational guidance as I began my career. Thanks to Karen Wynn, my undergraduate mentor, who fostered my initial interest in psychology research, and to Susan Carey, Steven Pinker, and Paul Harris, who offered exceptional mentorship as members of my dissertation committee. Thanks to Paul Bloom, who encouraged me to start writing, and to Tom Gilovich, who encouraged me to continue. I have been fortunate to spend my career so far at the University of Chicago and the Cornell University Departments of Psychology; I am grateful to colleagues and students in each program, who were sounding boards along the way. A special thanks to

Susan Goldin-Meadow, Susan Levine, and Amanda Woodward, my dedicated colleagues and mentors.

I am grateful to my agent Katinka Matson, a fierce ally who encouraged me to think bigger. Thanks to Olivia Bartz for extremely wise initial edits, helping me cut down my first draft. Thanks to Susanna Brougham for judicious and lively copyediting, which helped the book's flow and tone. Thanks to the whole team at HMH as well. I greatly appreciate Rachel Kamins's thoughtful attention to detail in getting the book's endnotes in order. A big thanks to James Ryerson, who helped me to think through the initial structure of the book and to feel confident that its ideas were compelling.

A most sincere thanks to my editor, Alexander Littlefield, who has invested remarkable time and energy in this project. Alex's excitement about it and dedication to it were palpable from our first meeting and right through the final edits. Alex pushed me to think carefully, to write clearly, and to trust myself. I am grateful for our collaboration and Alex's keen insights, from which I learned so much.

I am indebted to my family. My parents, Carol Kinzler and Tom Kinzler, are my first and most enthusiastic supporters and readers. Thanks especially for their help in getting my book over the finish line with both edits and time spent with their grandchildren.

My heartfelt thanks to my amazing daughter, Taylor, who offers me thoughtful, unwavering support. She reassured me that "it's not your fault that you are late to hand in your book, Mom. You have a newborn baby and that is really hard!" And a resounding welcome to baby Nate, who arrived just in time for this book's copyediting review.

And most of all, my utmost thanks to my husband, Zach Clopton, my incredible partner through every journey. He inspires me every day: he is my bedrock, my sounding board and editor, and my best friend in the world. I could not have written this book without his love and support.

NOTES

INTRODUCTION: IT'S NOT WHAT YOU SAY

page

xii   *The Hebrew Bible contains:* Judges 12:5–6, in *The Holy Bible, New International Version.* (1984). Grand Rapids, MI: Zondervan.

"ear of corn": Translation from *Oxford English Dictionary.* shibboleth, n. (2019). *Oxford English Dictionary Online* (2nd ed.). Oxford University Press. Retrieved from OED Online Database https://www.oed.com/view/Entry/178050?redirectedFrom=shibboleth&

xiii   *Croatian or Serbian:*   For information on Croatian, Serbian, and Bosnian languages, see Browne, W. "Serbo-Croatian language," *Encyclopedia Britannica,* retrieved at: https://www.britannica.com/topic/Serbo-Croatian-language; Vezenkov, A. (2013). *Introduction to section two: Languages and language policies in the Balkans.* In Daskalov, R. & Marinov, T. (Eds.), *Entangled Histories of the Balkans, Volume One: National Ideologies and Language Policies,* Koninkijke Brill Nv, Leiden, The Netherlands.

1. HOW YOU SPEAK IS WHO YOU ARE

1   *David Thorpe:* Thanks to David Thorpe for providing comments on this section of the book.

turned his camera on himself: Gertler, H., & Thorpe, D. (Producers) & Thorpe, D. (Director). (2014). *Do I sound gay?* [Motion picture]. United States: IFC Films/Sundance Selects.

2   *as the linguists have shown:* Pierrehumbert, J. B., Bent, T., Munson, B., Bradlow, A. R., & Bailey, J. M. (2004). The influence of sexual orientation on vowel production (L). *Journal of the Acoustical Society of America, 116*(4), 1905–8. https://doi.org/10.1121/1.1788729; Smyth, R., & Rog-

ers, H. (2002). Phonetics, gender, and sexual orientation. *Proceedings of the Annual Meeting of the Canadian Linguistics Association*, 299–311.

"sounding gay" to others: For additional insight into the vocal features that listeners use to guess whether someone's voice sounds "gay" or "straight," see Smyth, R., Jacobs, G., & Rogers, H. (2003). Male voices and perceived sexual orientation: An experimental and theoretical Approach. *Language in Society, 32*(3), 329–50.

continued scientific research: Ganna, A., Verweij, K. J. H., Nivard, M. G., Maier, R., Wedow, R., Busch, A. S., . . . & Zietsch, B. P. (2019). Large-scale GWAS reveals insights into the genetic architecture of same-sex sexual behavior. *Science, 365*(6456), eeat7693.

do not differ in overall pitch: Pierrehumbert et al., The influence of sexual orientation on vowel production (L); Smyth & Rogers, Phonetics, gender, and sexual orientation.

an explosion of research: Munson, D. (2011). Lavender lessons learned; Or, what sexuality can teach us about phonetic variation. *American Speech, 86*, 14–31.

3   *Social group membership:* Fiske, S. T. (1998). Stereotyping, prejudice, and discrimination. In D. T. Gilbert, S. T. Fiske, & G. Lindzey (Eds.), *The handbook of social psychology* (4th ed.) (vols. 1-2, pp. 357–411); Fiske, S. T., & Neuberg, S. L. (1990). A continuum of impression formation, from category-based to individuating processes: Influences of information and motivation on attention and interpretation. In M. P. Zanna (Ed.), *Advances in experimental social psychology* (vol. 23, pp. 1–74). New York: Academic Press; Stangor, C., Lynch, L., Duan, C., & Glas, B. (1992). Categorization of individuals on the basis of multiple social features. *Journal of Personality and Social Psychology, 62*(2), 207–18; Messick, D. M., & Mackie, D. M. (1989). Intergroup relations. *Annual Review of Psychology, 40*, 45–81.

4   *the prism of categories:* Murphy, G. L., & Medin, D. L. (1985). The role of theories in conceptual coherence. *Psychological Review, 92*(3), 289–316; Medin, D., & Rips, L. J. (2005). Concepts and categories: Memory, meaning, and metaphysics. In K. Holyoak & B. Morrison (Eds.), *The Cambridge handbook of thinking and reasoning* (pp. 37–72). Cambridge, UK: Cambridge University Press.

stereotypes and prejudices: Devine, P. G. (1989). Stereotypes and prejudice: Their automatic and controlled components. *Journal of Personality and Social Psychology, 56*(1), 5–18; Gelman, S. A. (2003). *The essential child: Origins of essentialism in everyday thought.* Oxford, UK: Oxford University Press; Bodenhausen, G. V., Kang, S. K., & Peery, D. (2012). Social categorization and the perception of social groups. In S. Fiske & C. N. Macrae (Eds.), *The SAGE handbook of social cognition* (pp. 311–29). Los Angeles: SAGE.

5   *indicator of social identity:* For evidence that hearing someone's voice

triggers perceptions of them as more human and mentally capable, see Schroeder, J., Kardas, M., & Epley, N. (2017). The humanizing voice: Speech reveals, and text conceals, a more thoughtful mind in the midst of disagreement. *Psychological Science, 28*, 1745–62.

7   *seminal linguistics studies:* Deckert, S. K., & Vickers, C. H. (2011). *An introduction to sociolinguistics: Society and identity.* New York: Bloomsbury; Gordon, M. J. (2012). *Labov: A guide for the perplexed.* New York: Bloomsbury Publishing; Labov, W. (1963). The social motivation of a sound change. *WORD, 19*(3), 273–309. doi:10.1080/00437956.1963 .11659799; Labov, W. (2001). *Principles of linguistic change, Volume 2: Social factors.* Malden, MA: Blackwell Publishers.

9   *"linguistic movers and shakers":* Eckert, P. (2004). Adolescent language. In E. Finegan & J. Rickford (Eds.), *Language in the USA: Themes for the twenty-first century* (pp. 361–74). Cambridge, UK: Cambridge University Press. doi:10.1017/CBO9780511809880.021
     "As people age": Pinker, S. (2015). *The sense of style: The thinking person's guide to writing in the 21st century.* New York: Penguin Books.
     the way they spoke: Eckert, P. (1989). *Jocks and burnouts: Social categories and identity in the high school.* New York: Teachers College Press; Eckert, P. (2003). Language and adolescent peer groups. *Journal of Language and Social Psychology, 22*(1), 112–18. doi:10.1177/0261927X02250063

10   *leaders in these vocal transformations:* Eckert, P. (2011). Language and power in the preadolescent heterosexual market. *American Speech, 86*, 85–97.

11   *an expert on implicit attitudes:* Banaji, M. R., & Greenwald, A. G. (2013). Blindspot: Hidden biases of good people. New York: Delacorte Press.

12   *recognize it more when women do it:* Davidson, L. (2017). Detection of creaky voice as a function of speaker pitch and gender. *The Journal of the Acoustical Society of America, 141*, 3981.
     undermine professional success: Anderson, R. C., Klofstad, C. A., Mayew, W. J., & Venkatachalam, M. (2014). Vocal fry may undermine the success of young women in the labor market. *PLOS ONE, 9*(5), e97506–e97506. doi:10.1371/journal.pone.0097506
     going somewhere: One linguistics paper presented some undergraduates from UC Berkeley and the University of Iowa with a typical vocal-y fry-y voice, and they didn't find it negative. This raises the possibility that in the future, this feature of speech may catch on even more. Yuasa, I. P. (2010). Creaky voice: A new feminine voice quality for young urban-oriented upwardly mobile American women? *American Speech, 85*(3), 315–37. doi:10.1215/00031283-2010-018
     sound like other kids: Harris, J. R. (1998). *The nurture assumption: Why children turn out the way they do.* New York: Simon & Schuster.

13   *My former college roommate Joey:* Thanks to Joey Lee for sharing this story.

native American accent: DeJesus, J., Dautel, J., Hwang, H. G., & Kinzler, K. D. (2017). Bilingual children's social preferences hinge on accent. *Journal of Experimental Child Psychology, 164,* 178–91; for a related finding, see Souza, A., Byers-Heinlein, K., & Poulin-Dubois, D. (2013). Bilingual and monolingual children prefer native-accented speakers. *Frontiers Psychology, 4*(953).

15 *sound like their peers:* Harris, *The nurture assumption.*

speak the same way: Howard Giles's communication accommodation theory describes how language shifts to signal social affiliation. Giles, H. (2016). *Communication accommodation theory: Negotiating personal relationships and social identities across contexts.* New York: Cambridge University Press.

follows suit: Chartrand, T. L., & Bargh, J. A. (1999). The chameleon effect: The perception-behavior link and social interaction. *Journal of Personality and Social Psychology, 76*(6), 893–910. doi:10.1037/0022-3514.76.6.893

16 *this VOT feature:* Yu, A. C. L., Abrego-Collier, C., & Sonderegger, M. (2013). Phonetic imitation from an individual-difference perspective: Subjective attitude, personality, and "autistic" traits. *PLOS One, 8*(9), e74746. doi:10.1371/journal.pone.0074746; see also Abrego-Collier, C., Grove, J., Sonderegger, M., & Yu, A. C. L. (2011). Effects of speaker evaluation on phonetic convergence. *Proceedings of the International Congress of the Phonetic Sciences, 17,* 19–195.

17 *language game:* The linguist Molly Babel studied New Zealanders' accommodation to Australian English. Babel, M. (2010). Dialect divergence and convergence in New Zealand English. *Language in Society, 39*(4), 437–56.

key personality traits: Yu, Abrego-Collier, & Sonderegger, Phonetic imitation from an individual-difference perspective.

19 *Justice Ginsburg's voice:* Shapp, A., LaFave, N., & Singler, J. V. (2014). Ginsburg v. Ginsburg: A longitudinal study of regional features in a Supreme Court justice's speech. University of Pennsylvania Working Papers in Linguistics, *20*(2).

My Cousin Vinny: Launer, D., & Schiff, P. (Producers) & Lynn, J. (Director). (1992). [Motion picture]. United States: Twentieth Century Fox.

"Hello Muddah": Sherman, A., Busch, L., & Ponchielli, A. (1963). Hello Muddah, hello Fadduh (A Letter from Camp). Warner Brothers Records.

20 *"In general, New Yorkers":* Labov, W. (1966). *The social stratification of English in New York City.* Washington, D.C.: Center for Applied Linguistics; Labov, W. (1972). The social stratification of (r) in New York City department stores. In *Sociolinguistic patterns* (Chap. 2). Philadelphia: University of Pennsylvania Press.

21 *four . . . economic classes:* Labov, W. (1972). Hypercorrection by the lower middle class as a factor in linguistic change. In *Sociolinguistic patterns* (Chap. 5). Philadelphia: University of Pennsylvania Press.

Time *magazine:* Steinmetz, K. (2016). Ruth Bader Ginsburg found her voice: A new study of the Supreme Court justice's accent says something about the way we all talk. *Time.* Retrieved from https://time.com/ruth-bader-ginsburg-supreme-court/

Elizabeth II's speech: Harrington, J., Palethorpe, S., & Watson, C. (2000). Does the Queen speak the Queen's English? *Nature, 408,* 927–28. doi:10.1038/35050160

22   *according to the* Telegraph: Derbyshire, D. (2000, December 20). Blimey, what became of the Queen's English? *The Telegraph.* Retrieved from https://www.telegraph.co.uk/news/uknews/1378951/Blimey-what-became-of-the-Queens-English.html

"The Queen's English Dethroned": Adam, D. (2000). The queen's English dethroned. *Nature* doi:10.1038/news001221-9. Retrieved at https://www.nature.com/articles/news001221-9

more than one language: Werker, J. F., & Byers-Heinlein, K. (2008). Bilingualism in infancy: First steps in perception and comprehension. *Trends in Cognitive Sciences, 12*(4), 144–51. doi:10.1016/j.tics.2008.01.008; Grosjean, F. (2010). *Bilingual: Life and reality.* Cambridge, MA: Harvard University Press.

23   *tied up in language:* In many cases, language and culture are intertwined; clearly differentiating the effects of "language" without "culture" or "culture" without "language" can be difficult.

Sayuri recalls that: Thanks to Sayuri Hayakawa for sharing this story.

"basic" set of emotions: Ekman, P. (1970). Universal facial expressions of emotion. *California Mental Health Research Digest, 8*(4), 151–58.

24   *"emotional dialect":* Elfenbein, H. A., & Ambady, N. (2003). Universals and cultural differences in recognizing emotions. *Current Directions in Psychological Science, 12*(5), 159–64. doi:10.1111/1467-8721.01252

decode other people's emotions: Matsumoto, D., Anguas-Wong, A. M., & Martinez, E. (2008). Priming effects of language on emotion judgments in Spanish-English bilinguals. *Journal of Cross-Cultural Psychology, 39*(3), 335–42. doi:10.1177/0022022108315489

a famous study: MaMarian, V., & Neisser, U. (2000). Language-dependent recall of autobiographical memories. *Journal of Experimental Psychology: General, 129*(3), 361–68. doi:10.1037/0096-3445.129.3.361

25   *the sense of self is shaped:* Markus, H. R., & Kitayama, S. (1991). Culture and the self: Implications for cognition, emotion, and motivation. *Psychological Review, 98,* 224–53.

tied up in language: Wang, Q., Shao, Y., & Li, Y. J. (2010). "My way or Mom's way?" The bilingual and bicultural self in Hong Kong Chinese children and adolescents. *Child Development, 81*(2), 555–67. doi:10.1111/j.1467-8624.2009.01415.x

26   *a student I know, Paola:* Thanks to Paola Ocampo for sharing this story.

2. NATIVE TONGUES

28   *Native Tongues*: For simplicity, this book uses the terms "native" and "non-native" to describe languages learned at different times in development. Some applied linguists raise concerns that these terms create an artificial binary distinction among languages, and suggest that early-learned languages are necessarily higher in fluency than later-learned languages, when they may not be. An alternative would be to call languages L1 (early-learned) and L2/LX (later-learned). See Dewaele, J. M. (2018). Why the dichotomy "L1 versus LX user" is better than "native versus non-native speaker." *Applied Linguistics, 39*, 236–40.

whom I'll call Gloria: The story of Gloria was told to me by a former student; names and details are fictionalized to protect the individuals' identities.

31   *Polish and later French:* Najder, Z., & Najder, H. (2007). *Joseph Conrad: A life.* Rochester, NY: Camden House.

"he talked English": Ibid., 447.

Vladimir Nabokov: Roper, R. (2015). *Nabokov in America: On the road to Lolita.* New York: Bloomsbury.

told the New York Times: Breit, H. (1951). Talk with Mr. Nabokov. *New York Times.* Retrieved from https://archive.nytimes.com/www.nytimes.com/books/97/03/02/lifetimes/nab-v-talk.html

32   *Andrei Cimpian:* Thanks to Andrei Cimpian for sharing this story.

33   *children can learn new languages:* Werker, J. F., & Hensch, T. K. (2015). Critical periods in speech perception: New directions. *Annual Review of Psychology, 66*, 173–96. Pinker, S. (1994). *The language instinct.* New York: William Morrow and Company.

34   *miraculously resilient:* In the 1960s, the linguist and neurologist Eric Lenneberg wrote of the human-specific biological capacity for language, and in particular for keeping language in the face of trauma. He drew largely on studies of brain injury to document that younger children were able to recover language abilities after a traumatic brain injury in a way that older people were not. Lenneberg, E. H. (1967). *Biological foundations of language.* Oxford, UK: Wiley.

a high school acquaintance: Details fictionalized to protect the individual's identity.

young human brain: Lenneberg, *Biological foundations;* Bates, E. (1999). Plasticity, localization, and language development. In *The changing nervous system: Neurobehavioral consequences of early brain disorders* (pp. 214–53). New York: Oxford University Press; Binder, J. R., Frost, J. A., Hammeke, T. A., Cox, R. W., Rao, S. M., & Prieto, T. (1997). Human brain language areas identified by functional magnetic resonance imaging. *The Journal of Neuroscience, 17*(1), 353. doi:10.1523/JNEUROSCI.17-01-00353.1997

35   *acquiring a new language:* Flege, J. E., Munro, M. J., & Mackay, I. R. A. (1995). Effects of age of second-language learning on the production of English consonants. *Speech Communication, 16*(1), 1–26. doi:https://doi.org/10 .1016/0167-6393(94)00044-B; Weber-Fox, C. M., & Neville, H. J. (1996). Maturational constraints on functional specializations for language processing: ERP and behavioral evidence in bilingual speakers. *Journal of Cognitive Neuroscience, 8*(3), 231–56. doi:10.1162/jocn.1996.8.3.231
     "Isabelle" and "Genie": Gleitman, L. R., & Newport, E. L. (1995). The invention of language by children: Environmental and biological influences on the acquisition of language. In L. R. Gleitman & M. Liberman (Eds.), *Language: An invitation to cognitive science* (pp. 1–24). Cambridge, MA: The MIT Press.

36   *that of "Chelsea":* Ibid.
     Elissa Newport: Newport, E. L. (1990). Maturational constraints on language learning. *Cognitive Science, 14*(1), 11–28. doi:10.1207/ s15516709cog1401_2

37   *born to hearing parents:* US Department of Health & Human Services, National Institute on Deafness and Other Communication Disorders (NIDCD), Quick Statistics About Hearing. Retrieved at https://www .nidcd.nih.gov/health/statistics/quick-statistics-hearing#2
     Molly Flaherty: Thanks to Molly Flaherty for sharing this story.

40   *didn't stop there:* Senghas, A., & Coppola, M. (2001). Children creating language: How Nicaraguan Sign Language acquired a spatial grammar. *Psychological Science, 12*(4), 323–28; Senghas, R. J., Senghas, A., and Pyers, J. E. (2005). The emergence of Nicaraguan Sign Language: Questions of development, acquisition, and evolution. In J. Langer, S. T. Parker, & C. Milbrath (Eds.), *Biology and knowledge revisited: From neurogenesis to psychogenesis.* Mahwah, NJ: Lawrence Erlbaum Associates; Senghas, A., Kita, S., and Özyürek, A. (2004). Children creating core properties of language: Evidence from an emerging sign language in Nicaragua. *Science, 305*(5691), 1779–82.
     Nicaraguan Sign Language: Senghas, R. J. (2003). New ways to be deaf in Nicaragua: Changes in language, personhood, and community. In *Many ways to be deaf: International variation in deaf communities* (pp. 260–82). Washington, D.C.: Gallaudet University Press.

41   *a woman, Anna:* Name changed to protect her identity.

42   *from East Asian countries:* Johnson, J. S., & Newport, E. L. (1989). Critical period effects in second language learning: The influence of maturational state on the acquisition of English as a second language. *Cognitive Psychology, 21*(1), 60–99. doi:10.1016/0010-0285(89)90003-0
     after the age of seven: Some evidence suggests that the parameters of the "critical period" for first-language acquisition are stricter than those for learning a second language. For second languages, proficiency declines

with increasing age of initial exposure, yet this decline may be gradual. Hakuta, K., Bialystok, E., & Wiley, E. (2003). Critical evidence: A test of the critical-period hypothesis for second-language acquisition. *Psychological Science, 14*(1), 31–38. Other research suggests that the decline may begin later in age (at least for grammatical learning) than previously thought — in adolescence rather than childhood. Hartshorne, J. K., Tenenbaum, J. B., & Pinker, S. (2018). A critical period for second-language acquisition: Evidence from 2/3 million English speakers. *Cognition, 177,* 263–77. doi:https://doi.org/10.1016/j.cognition.2018.04.007

43 *eastern European countries:* Glennen, S., & Bright, B. J. (2005). Five years later: Language in school-age internationally adopted children. *Seminars in Speech and Language, 26,* 86–101. doi:10.1055/s-2005-864219; Glennen, S., & Masters, M. G. (2002). Typical and atypical language development in infants and toddlers adopted from Eastern Europe. *American Journal of Speech-Language Pathology;* Snedeker, J., Geren, J., & Shafto, C. L. (2007). Starting over: International adoption as a natural experiment in language development. *Psychological Science, 18*(1), 79–87. doi:10.1111/j.1467-9280.2007.01852.x

   adopted a child from Russia: This story amalgamates those told by two individuals, whose experiences were remarkably similar. Details changed to protect their identities.

44 *any Korean at all:* Pallier, C., Dehaene, S., Poline, J. B., LeBihan, D., Argenti, A. M., Dupoux, E., & Mehler, J. (2003). Brain imaging of language plasticity in adopted adults: Can a second language replace the first? *Cerebral Cortex, 13*(2), 155–61. doi:10.1093/cercor/13.2.155

   Korean children adopted in France: Ibid.

   French-speaking homes in Canada: Pierce, L. J., Chen, J. K., Delcenserie, A., Genesee, F., & Klein, D. (2015). Past experience shapes ongoing neural patterns for language. *Nature Communications, 6,* 10073. doi:10.1038/ncomms10073

45 *processed in the brain:* Pallier et al., Brain imaging; Pierce et al., Past experience.

   Researchers hypothesize: Pierce et al., Past experience.

46 *remnant of the native language:* Choi, J., Broersma, M., & Cutler, A. (2017). Early phonology revealed by international adoptees' birth language retention. *Proceedings of the National Academy of Sciences, 114*(28), 7307. doi:10.1073/pnas.1706405114

47 *as children age:* Hakuta, Bialystok, & Wiley, Critical evidence.

   ultimate mastery: Johnson & Newport, Critical period effects in second language learning. But for evidence that declines may still be found with age on grammatical learning, see Hartshorne, Tenenbaum, & Pinker, A critical period for second-language acquisition.

48 *aroused by curse words:* Harris, C. L. (2010). Bilingual speakers in

the lab: Psychophysiological measures of emotional reactivity. *Journal of Multilingual and Multicultural Development, 25.* doi:10.1080/01434630408666530

49   *"the real Lola":* Thanks to Maria Dolores (Lola) de Hevia for sharing this story.

they feel different: Dewaele, J. M. (2010). *Emotions in multiple languages.* Basingstoke, UK: Palgrave Macmillan; Pavlenko, A. (2005). *Emotions and multilingualism.* Cambridge, UK: Cambridge University Press. Although most people feel more emotion when using their first language, this principle is not set in stone. Emotions related to experiences occurring in the context of a later-learned language may be subsequently evoked by speaking that language.

feeling less themselves: Dewaele, J. M., & Nakano, S. (2012). Multilinguals' perceptions of feeling different when switching languages. *Journal of Multilingual and Multicultural Development, 34,* 107–20. doi:10.1080/01434632.2012.712133

Russian, his first language: Pavlenko, A. (2014). Poetry and the language of the heart. *Psychology Today.* Retrieved at https://www.psychologytoday.com/us/blog/life-bilingual/201410/poetry-and-the-language-the-heart

50   *an example:* Tversky, A., & Kahneman, D. (1981). The framing of decisions and the psychology of choice. *Science, 211*(4481), 453–58. doi:10.1126/science.7455683

51   *much more* rational: Keysar, B., Hayakawa, S. L. & An, S. G. (2012). The foreign-language effect: Thinking in a foreign tongue reduces decision biases. *Psychological Science, 23,* 661-668.

52   *kill one to save five:* Costa, A., Foucart, A., Hayakawa, S., Aparici, M., Apesteguia, J., Heafner, J., & Keysar, B. (2014). Your morals depend on language. *PLOS One, 9*(4), e94842. doi:10.1371/journal.pone.0094842. Hayakawa, S., Costa, A., Foucart, A., & Keysar, B. (2016). Using a foreign language changes our choices. *Trends in Cognitive Sciences, 20*(11), 791–93. doi:https://doi.org/10.1016/j.tics.2016.08.004

3. HOW LANGUAGE DIVIDES US

54   *Murphy Morobe:* "Interview with Murphy Morobe." Gerhart, G. M. (interviewer) and Morobe, M. (interviewee), 5/04/1991; "Soweto 1996: An Audio History," National Public Radio All Things Considered, 6/16/2006. https://www.npr.org/templates/story/story.php?storyId=5489490

55   *in peaceful protest:* "I saw a Nightmare . . .": Doing violence to memory, the Soweto Uprising, June 16, 1973. Radio 702 Talk Radio commemorating June 16, 1976 (13 years later). The John Robbie Show. Featuring Guest, Murphy Morobe.   http://www.gutenberg-e.org/pohlandt-mccormick/pmh06c.html; see also "South African history online: Towards a people's history: The June 16 Soweto Youth Uprising." https://www.sahistory.org.za/article/june-16-soweto-youth-uprising

57   *make this observation effortlessly:* Wagner, L., Clopper, C. G., & Pate, J. K. (2014). Children's perception of dialect variation. *Journal of Child Language, 41*(5), 1062–84. doi:10.1017/S0305000913000330

regions of France: Girard, F., Floccia, C., & Goslin, J. (2008). Perception and awareness of accents in young children. *British Journal of Developmental Psychology, 26,* 409–33. doi:10.1348/026151007X251712

British kids can pick out: Floccia, C., Butler, J., Girard, F., & Goslin, J. (2009). Categorization of regional and foreign accent in 5- to 7-year-old British children. *International Journal of Behavioral Development, 33*(4), 366–75. https://doi.org/10.1177/0165025409103871

stand out as most different: Floccia, C., Goslin, J., Girard, F., & Konopczynski, G. (2006). Does a regional accent perturb speech processing? *Journal of Experimental Psychology: Human Perception and Performance, 32*(5), 1276–93. doi:10.1037/0096-1523.32.5.1276

do not have discrete breaks: Trudgill, P. (2000). *Sociolinguistics: An introduction to language and society* (4th ed.). London: Penguin; Cohen, E. (2012). The evolution of tag-based cooperation in humans: The case for accent. *Current Anthropology, 53,* 588–616. doi:10.1086/667654

58   *sound kind of the same:* Ikeno, A., & Hansen, J. H. L. (2007). The effect of listener accent background on accent perception and comprehension. *EURASIP Journal on Audio, Speech, and Music Processing, 2007*(1), 076030. doi:10.1155/2007/76030

replicate a non-native accent: Hollien, H. F. (2002). *Forensic voice identification.* San Diego, CA: Academic Press.

"own race" advantage: Malpass, R. S., & Kravitz, J. (1969). Recognition for faces of own and other race. *Journal of Personality and Social Psychology, 13*(4), 330–34. Though note that this may be more accurately described as a "familiar race" advantage. Sangrigoli, S., Pallier, C., Argenti, A. M., Ventureyra, V. A., & de Schonen, S. (2005). Reversibility of the other-race effect in face recognition during childhood. *Psychological Science, 16*(6), 440–44. doi:10.1111/j.0956-7976.2005.01554.x

"own accent" advantage: Kerstholt, J. H., Jansen, N. J. M., Van Amelsvoort, A. G., & Broeders, A. P. A. (2006). Earwitnesses: Effects of accent, retention, and telephone. *Applied Cognitive Psychology, 20*(2), 187–97. doi: 10.1002/acp.1175

59   *"army brats":* Clopper, C. G., & Pisoni, D. B. (2004). Homebodies and army brats: Some effects of early linguistic experience and residential history on dialect categorization. *Language Variation and Change, 16*(1), 31–48. doi:10.1017/S0954394504161036

60   *not extremely different:* For a discussion of how regional accents first perturb speech processing, but then are normalized with a short-term adjustment, see Floccia, Goslin, Girard, & Konopczynski, Does a regional accent perturb speech processing? But see Floccia, C., Butler, J., Goslin, J., & Ellis, L. (2009). Regional and foreign accent processing in English:

Can listeners adapt? *Journal of Psycholinguistic Research, 38*(4), 379–412, for evidence that adaptation effects may be more complex.

capably process the speech: Clarke, C. M., & Garrett, M. F. (2004). Rapid adaptation to foreign-accented English. *Journal of the Acoustical Society of America, 116*(6), 3647–58. doi:10.1121/1.1815131. But see Floccia, Butler, Goslin, & Ellis, Regional and foreign accent processing in English.

The Gileadites captured: Judges 12:5–6, *The Holy Bible, New International Version.*

code word lollapalooza: Gramling, O., & Press, A. (1942). *Free men are fighting: The story of World War II.* New York: Farrar and Rinehart.

61 *native-sounding accent:* Asher, J. J., & Garcia, R. (1969). The optimal age to learn a foreign language. *The Modern Language Journal, 53,* 334–41.

62 *"spoke the same language":* Hamilton, A., Madison, J., Jay, J., Dunn, J., Horowitz, D., & Botting, E. (2009). *The federalist papers* (I. Shapiro, Ed.). New Haven, CT: Yale University Press. Retrieved from http://www.jstor.org/stable/j.ctt5vm398; see also Jay, J. (1787). Concerning dangers from foreign force and influence. *Independent Journal.*

settlers in Pennsylvania spoke German: Shell, M. (2001). Language wars. *CR: The New Centennial Review, 1,* 1–17. doi:10.1353/ncr.2003.0059

"the diversities of languages": Webster, N. (1843). *A collection of papers on political, literary, and moral subjects* (p. 119). New York: Webster & Clark.

63 *"Many people maintain":* Shell, Language wars.

Evolutionary linguistics: Atkinson, Q. D., Meade, A., Venditti, C., Greenhill, S. J., & Pagel, M. (2008). Languages evolve in punctuational bursts. *Science, 319*(5863), 588. doi:10.1126/science.1149683

64 *"Whan that aprill":* Chaucer, G., & Benson, L. D. (1987). *The Riverside Chaucer.* Boston: Houghton Mifflin.

banned entirely: Wheeler, M. (2010). Catalan. *Concise encyclopedia of languages of the world* (pp. 188–92). Oxford, UK: Elsevier.

65 *an independent Catalonia:* Dewan, A. (2017, December 19). *The millennials voting for Catalan independence.* CNN. Retrieved from http://www.cnn.com/2017/12/19/europe/catalonia-youth-election-spain-intl/index.html

depend on language: Reizábal, L., Valencia, J., & Barrett, M. (2004). National identifications and attitudes to national ingroups and outgroups amongst children living in the Basque Country. *Infant and Child Development, 13*(1), 1–20. doi:10.1002/icd.328; for additional detail and examples of children in other nations, see Barrett, M. (2007). *Children's knowledge, beliefs, and feelings about nations and national groups.* Hove, UK: Psychology Press.

66 *form more generally:* DeGraff, M. (2005). Linguists' most dangerous myth: The fallacy of Creole exceptionalism. *Language in Society, 34,* 533–91; see also Mufwene, S. S. (2001). *The ecology of language evolution* (p. 1).

Cambridge, UK: Cambridge University Press: "Creoles have developed by the same restructuring processes that mark the evolutions of noncreole languages." More generally, the question of whether the process by which Creoles form is different from how any language forms is an area of debate in the field of linguistics. See Mufwene, S. S. (2015). Pidgin and Creole languages. In James D. Wright (Ed.), *International encyclopedia of the social and behavioral sciences* (2nd ed., vol. 18, pp. 133–45). Oxford, UK: Elsevier.

a "bastard" language: Bickerton, D. (2008). *Bastard tongues: A trailblazing linguist finds clues to our common humanity in the world's lowliest languages.* New York: Hill and Wang.

how people mistakenly: DeGraff, M. (2003). Against Creole exceptionalism. *Language, 79*(2), 391–410.

"When we teach in Creole": DeGraff, M., & Ruggles, M. (2014, August 1). A Creole solution for Haiti's woes. *New York Times,* p. 17. Retrieved from https://www.nytimes.com/2014/08/02/opinion/a-Creole-solution-for -haitis-woes.html

67 *"Language is a central element":* Rita Izsák of the UN Human Rights Council, quoted in *United Nations News.* (2013, March 12). Protection of minority languages is a human rights obligation, UN expert says. Retrieved from http://www.un.org/apps/news/story.asp?NewsID=44352# .WkfcS1Q-fOQ

"in those States": United Nations Human Rights Committee, Office of the High Commissioner. (1966). *International covenant on civil and political rights.* Retrieved from http://www.ohchr.org/EN/ProfessionalInterest/ Pages/CCPR.aspx

situations are indeed diverse: Buhmann, D., & Trudell, B. (2008). Mother tongue matters: Local language as a key to effective learning. Paris: United Nations Educational Cultural and Scientific Organization (UNESCO). Retrieved from https://unesdoc.unesco.org/ark:/48223/pf0000161121

68 *"bad" English:* Lippi-Green, R. (2007). *English with an accent: Language, ideology, and discrimination in the United States.* New York: Routledge; for an overview, see S. S. Mufwene, J. R. Rickford, G. Balley, & J. Baugh (Eds.), *African-American English: Structure, history, and use.* (1998). New York: Routledge.

a dialect of English: Rickford, J. R. (1999). *African American Vernacular English: Features and use, evolution, and educational implications.* Oxford, UK: Blackwell; Bloomquist, J., Green, L. J., & Lanehart, S. L. (Eds.), *The Oxford handbook of African American language.* Oxford, UK: Oxford University Press, 2015.

"Languages, other than": Meyer v. State of Nebraska, 262 U.S. 390 (1923).

69 *Bible verses in German:* Pusey, A. (2017, February 1). Feb. 23, 1923: Justices hear a challenge to "English-only" laws. *American Bar Association Journal.* Retrieved from http://www.abajournal.com/magazine/article/ precedents_meyer_v._nebraska

upheld the teacher's conviction: Meyer v. State of Nebraska, 107 Neb. 657 (1922).

made its way to the Supreme Court: Meyer v. State of Nebraska.

it was reversed: Nebraska may be the most (in)famous, but it isn't the only state to come up with a similar idea during this era. For instance, Iowa and Ohio enacted similar laws at around the same time, prohibiting the teaching of foreign languages to children in grade school. In both states, teachers of parochial schools (typically full of German-speaking parishioners) were convicted of teaching German to young students. In Ohio, *Pohl v. State,* 102 Ohio 474 (1921); in Iowa, *State v. Bartels,* 191 Iowa 1060 (1921). Reversing decisions in Iowa and Ohio, following *Meyer v. State of Nebraska.* Reversals following *Meyer,* 262 U.S. 404, decided June 4, 1923.

70   *Xenophobic comments:* Poniewozik, J. (2014). Coca-Cola's "It's Beautiful" Super Bowl ad brings out some ugly Americans. *Time.* Retrieved from https://time.com/3773/coca-colas-its-beautiful-super-bowl-ad-brings -out-some-ugly-americans/

more beautiful than German: Bauer, L., Trudgill, P., & Trudgill, P.S.P. (1998). *Language myths.* New York: Penguin Books.

71   *"My British accent":* Avery, K., and Co. (Writers), & Pennolino, P., and Co. (Directors). (2017). Episode 108: Alex Jones and InfoWars [Television series episode]. In Oliver, J. (Producer), *Last Week Tonight with John Oliver.* New York: HBO.

Voice and Personality: Pear, T. H. (1931). *Voice and personality.* London: Chapman and Hall, Limited.

the answer is no: Giles, H., & Billings, A. (2008). Assessing language attitudes: Speaker evaluation studies. In A. Davies & C. Elder (Eds.) *The handbook of applied linguistics* (pp. 187–209). Malden, MA: Blackwell Publishing.

72   *Lambert and his colleagues:* Lambert, W., Hodgson, R., Gardner, R., & Fillenbaum, S. (1960). Evaluational reactions to spoken languages. *Journal of Abnormal and Social Psychology, 60,* 44–51; Lambert, W. E., Frankel, H., & Tucker, G. R. (1966). Judging personality through speech: A French-Canadian example. *Journal of Communication, 16,* 305–21.

Official Languages Act: See https://www.clo-ocol.gc.ca/en/lang uage_rights/act

Royal Commission on Bilingualism: See https://www.thecanadian encyclopedia.ca/en/article/royal-commission-on-bilingualism-and -biculturalism

73   *this dual perception:* Fiske, S. T., Cuddy, A. J. C., & Glick, P. (2007). Universal dimensions of social cognition: Warmth and competence. *Trends in Cognitive Sciences, 11*(2), 77–83. doi:10.1016/j.tics.2006.11.005; for another example of speech in Montreal following this similar warmth/ competence split, Canadian adults who were both Jewish and Christian evaluated "Jewish-accented" speech: Anisfeld, M., Bogo, N., & Lambert,

W. E. (1962). Evaluational reactions to accented English speech. *Journal of Abnormal and Social Psychology, 65*(4), 223–31. doi:10.1037/h0045060

74 *pro-English biases:* Lambert et al., Judging personality.

implicit and explicit attitudes: Greenwald, A. G., & Banaji, M. R. (1995). Implicit social cognition: Attitudes, self-esteem, and stereotypes. *Psychological Review, 102*(1), 4–27.

a guy named Tu: Thanks to Tu Tu for sharing this story.

varieties of Chinese dialects: LaPolla, R. J., & Thurgood, G. (2003). The Chinese dialects: Phonology. In *The Sino-Tibetan languages* (pp. 72–83). New York: Routledge.

75 *speakers of Putonghua:* Yang, C. (2014). Language attitudes toward Northeastern Mandarin and Putonghua (PTH) by young professionals. *Chinese Language and Discourse, 5*(2), 211–30. doi:https://doi.org/10.1075/cld.5.2.04yan

All over the globe: Giles, H., & Watson, B. M. (2012). *The social meanings of language, dialect, and accent*: International Perspectives on Speech Styles. New York: Peter Lang; Rakić, T., & Steffens, M. C. Language attitudes in Western Europe. In ibid.; Schieffelin, B. B., Woolard, K. A., & Koskrity, P. V. (Eds.), (1998). *Language ideologies: Practice and theory*. New York: Oxford University Press.

shut down or stop listening: Cargile, A., Giles, H., Ryan, E., & Bradac, J. (1994). Language attitudes as a social process: A conceptual model and new directions. *Language & Communication — LANG COMMUN, 14,* 211–236. doi:10.1016/0271-5309(94)90001-9

does not feel good: Gluszek, A., & Dovidio, J. F. (2010). Speaking with a nonnative accent: Perceptions of bias, communication difficulties, and belonging. *Journal of Language and Social Psychology, 29(2)*, 224–34; Gluszek, A., & Dovidio, J. F. (2010). The way they speak: A social psychological perspective on the stigma of nonnative accents in communication. *Personality and Social Psychology Review, 14*(2), 214–37.

non-native speaker of English: Identifying details changed to protect this person's identity.

76 *former student of mine:* Name changed to protect this person's identity.

77 *"Linguistic insecurity":* Bucci, W., & Baxter, M. (1984). Problems of linguistic insecurity in multicultural speech contexts. *Annals of the New York Academy of Sciences, 433*(1), 185–200. doi:10.1111/j.1749-6632.1984.tb14767.x

two (or more) people: Cargile, A., Giles, H., Ryan, E., & Bradac, J. (1994). Language attitudes as a social process: A conceptual model and new directions. *Language & Communication, 14,* 211–36. doi:10.1016/0271-5309(94)90001-9

78 *negative listening attitude:* Lindemann, S. (2002). Listening with an attitude: A model of native-speaker comprehension of non-native speak-

ers in the United States. *Language in Society, 31,* 419–41. doi:10.1017/
S0047404502020286

79   *better self-control:* Gluszek & Dovidio, The way they speak.

4. DEEP TALK

81   *"Languages are organisms":* Schleicher, A. S. (1869). *Darwinism tested by
      the science of language,* A. V. W. Bikkers (Trans.) (pp. 20–21). London: J. C.
      Hotten.

82   *groups of speakers:* McIntosh, J. (2005). Language essentialism and
      social hierarchies among Giriama and Swahili. *Journal of Pragmatics,
      37*(12), 1919–44. https://doi.org/10.1016/j.pragma2005.01.010; Gal, S., &
      Irvine, J. T. (2019). *Signs of difference: Language and ideology in social
      life.* Cambridge, UK: Cambridge University Press.

      the relevant language: McIntosh, Language essentialism (p. 1921 for dis-
      cussion); see also Henrich, J., & Henrich, N. (2007). *Why humans cooper-
      ate: A cultural and evolutionary explanation.* Oxford, UK: Oxford Univer-
      sity Press.

      known as essentialism: Gelman, *The essential child.*

83   *"linguistic transfer":* McIntosh, Language essentialism.

      Meyer v. State of Nebraska: 107 Neb. 657 (1922).

      ingrained assumption: Gal & Irvine, *Signs of difference.*

      retell the ancient story: Gleitman, L. R., & Newport, E. L. (1995). The in-
      vention of language by children: Environmental and biological influences
      on the acquisition of language. In L. R. Gleitman & M. Liberman (Eds.),
      Language: An invitation to cognitive science (pp. 1–24). Cambridge, MA:
      MIT Press.

84   *"This folk myth is pervasive":* Pinker, S. (1994). *The language instinct* (p.
      258). New York: Harper Perennial Modern Classics.

85   *twin African American girls:* This story has been heavily edited to pro-
      tect the identities of the people involved.

86   *Susan Gelman and Lawrence Hirschfeld:* Hirschfeld, L. A., & Gelman,
      S. A. (1997). What young children think about the relationship between
      language variation and social difference. *Cognitive Development, 12*(2),
      213–38.

87   *Songbirds are the classic:* Marler, P. (1970). Birdsong and speech develop-
      ment: Could there be parallels? There may be basic rules governing vocal
      learning to which many species conform, including man. *American Sci-
      entist, 58*(6), 669–73. New research with neuroscience techniques are re-
      vealing the genetic links between songbirds' brains and their song learn-
      ing, which can help us understand the biology behind how humans learn
      and transmit language: Clayton, D. F., Balakrishnan, C. N., & London,
      S. E. (2009). Integrating genomes, brain, and behavior in the study of
      songbirds. *Current Biology, 19*(18), R865–73.

      "Acoustic clans": Yurk, H., Barrett-Lennard, L., Ford, J. K. B., & Mat-

kins, C. O. (2002). Cultural transmission within maternal lineages: Vocal clans in resident killer whales in southern Alaska. *Animal Behaviour, 63,* 1103–19.

88   *dolphins have names:* Janik, V. M., Sayigh, L. S., & Wells, R. S. (2006). Signature whistle shape conveys identity information to bottlenose dolphins. *Proceedings of the National Academy of Sciences, 103*(21), 8293–97.

kinship and social status: Seyfarth, R. M., & Cheney, D. L. (2015). The evolution of concepts about agents: Or, what do animals recognize when they recognize an individual? In E. Margolis & S. Laurence (Eds.), *The conceptual mind: New directions in the study of concepts* (pp. 57–76). Cambridge, MA: MIT Press.

Horses and crows: Proops, L., McComb, K., & Reby, D. (2009). Crossmodal individual recognition in domestic horses (*Equus caballus*). *Proceedings of the National Academy of Sciences of the United States of America, 106,* 947–51; see also Kondo, N., Izawa, E., & Watanabe, S. (2012). Crows cross-modally recognize group members but not non-group members. *Proceedings: Biological Sciences, 279,* 1937–42.

comes from beadwork: Cohen, E. (2012). The evolution of tag-based cooperation in humans: The case for accent. *Current Anthropology, 53,* 588–616.

a team of archeologists: Vanhaeren, M., & d'Errico, F. (2006). Aurignacian ethno-linguistic geography of Europe revealed by personal ornaments. *Journal of Archeological Science, 33,* 1105–28; d'Errico, F., & Vanhaeren, M. (2011). Linguistic implications of the earliest personal ornaments. In K. Gibson & M. Tallerman (Eds.), *The Oxford handbook of language evolution.* Oxford, UK: Oxford University Press.

90   *would also be wrong:* For an overview of the disconnect between the psychological categorization of race and the biological reality of genetic processes, see Henrich, J. (2017). *The secret of our success: How culture is driving human evolution, domesticating our species, and making us smarter.* Princeton, NJ: Princeton University Press.

91   *descended from an ancestral group:* Thomson, J. (2000, December 7). Humans did come out of Africa, says DNA. *Nature News.* doi:10.1038/news001207-8 Retrieved from https://www.nature.com/news/2000/001207/full/news001207-8.html

eventually the Americas: National Geographic. (2019). *Map of human migration* [interactive graphic]. Retrieved from https://genographic.nationalgeographic.com/human-journey/

"Lightness" in skin tone: Henrich, *The secret of our success;* Gibbons, A. (2015, April 2). How Europeans evolved white skin. *Science.* Retrieved from http://www.sciencemag.org/news/2015/04/how-europeans-evolved-white-skin

92   *small amount of genetic:* Ibid.

most genetic diversity: Ramachandran, S., Omkar, D., Roseman, C. C.,

Rosenberg, N. A., Feldman, M. W., & Cavalli-Sforza, L. L. (2005). Support from the relationship of genetic and geographic distance in human populations for a serial founder effect originating in Africa. *Proceedings of the National Academy of Sciences, 102*(44), 15, 942–47.

Ethiopians with Swedes: Cosmides, L., Tooby, J., & Kurzban, R. (2003). Perceptions of race. *Trends in Cognitive Sciences, 7*(4), 173–79.

93   *People's psychological perception:* Jobling, M. A., Rasteiro, R., & Wetton, J. H. (2016). In the blood: The myth and reality of genetic markers of identity. *Ethnic and Racial Studies, 39*(2), 142–61; see also Henrich, *The secret of our success.*

    the psychology of race: Kurzban, R., Tooby, J., & Cosmides, L. (2001). Can race be erased?: Coalitional computation and social categorization. *Proceedings of the National Academy of Sciences, 98*, 15387–92; Pietraszewski, D., Cosmides, L., & Tooby, J. (2014). The content of our cooperation, not the color of our skin: An alliance detection system regulates categorization by coalition and race, but not sex. *PLOS One 9*(2): e88534. doi: 10.1371/journal.pone.0088534; Pietraszewski, D., Curry, O. S., Petersen, M. B., Cosmides, L., & Tooby, J. (2015). Constituents of political cognition: Race, party politics, and the alliance detection system. *Cognition, 140*, 24–39. doi:10.1016/j.cognition.2015.03.007

94   *"who said what" game:* Taylor, S. E., Fiske, S. T., Etcoff, N. L., & Ruderman, A. J. (1978). Categorical and contextual bases of person memory and stereotyping. *Journal of Personality and Social Psychology, 36*(7), 778–93.

    errors in this same pattern: Hewstone, M., Hantzi, A., & Johnston, L. (1991). Social categorization and person memory: The pervasiveness of race as an organizing principle. *European Journal of Social Psychology, 21*(6), 517–28. http://dx.doi.org/10.1002/ejsp.2420210606

95   *hard to turn off:* Ibid.

    attention to race wanes: Kurzban, Tooby, & Cosmides, Can race be erased? For related findings, see Pietraszewski, Cosmides, & Tooby, The content of our cooperation, and Pietraszewski et al., Constituents of political cognition.

    team membership with accent: Pietraszewski, D., & Schwartz, A. (2014). Evidence that accent is a dedicated dimension of social categorization, not a byproduct of coalitional categorization. *Evolution and Human Behavior, 35*(1), 51–57.

    two different accents: Pietraszewski, D., & Schwartz, A. (2014). Evidence that accent is a dimension of social categorization, not a byproduct of perceptual salience, familiarity, or ease-of-processing. *Evolution and Human Behavior, 35*(1), 43–50.

96   *accent matters more to us:* Rakić, T., Steffens, M. C., & Mummendey, A. (2011). Blinded by the accent!: The minor role of looks in ethnic categorization. *Journal of Personality and Social Psychology, 100*(1), 16–29.

memory-confusion game: Weisman, K., Johnson, M. V., & Shutts, K. (2015). Young children's automatic encoding of social categories. *Developmental Science, 18,* 1036–43.

97 *children automatically encoded:* Vasquez, N. M., Kalish, C. W., & Shutts, K. (2019). *Children's automatic categorization of language and preference information.* Poster presented at the meeting of the Society for Research in Child Development, Baltimore, MD.

98 *moral circles:* Singer, P. (1981). *The expanding circle: Ethics, evolution, and moral progress.* Princeton, NJ: Princeton University Press; see also Bloom, P. (2004). *Descartes' baby: How the science of child development explains what makes us human.* New York: Basic Books.

hurricanes Harvey and Irma: Levenson, E. (2017, September 27). 3 storms, 3 responses: Comparing Harvey, Irma and Maria. CNN. Retrieved from https://www.cnn.com/2017/09/26/us/response-harvey -irma-maria/index.html; see also Mehta, D. (2017, September 28). The media really has neglected Puerto Rico. *FiveThirtyEight.* Retrieved from https://fivethirtyeight.com/features/the-media-really-has-neglected -puerto-rico/

moral circles start early: Rhodes, M., & Chalik, L. (2013). Social categories as markers of intrinsic interpersonal obligations. *Psychological Science, 24*(6), 999–1006.

"One day, a Zaz": Ibid., 1001.

99 *two moralities:* Greene, J. (2013). *Moral tribes: Emotion, reason, and the gap between us and them.* New York: Penguin Books.

Hobbes wrote of life: Hobbes, T. (1969). *Leviathan, 1651.* Menston, UK: Scolar Press; for a summary, see Yale Books Blog. (2013, April 5). Thomas Hobbes: "Solitary, poor, nasty, brutish, and short" [web log post]. Retrieved from https://yalebooksblog.co.uk/2013/04/05/thomas-hobbes -solitary-poor-nasty-brutish-and-short

innately compassionate: Rousseau, J. (1984). *A discourse on the origin of inequality* (M. Cranston, Trans.). London: Penguin Books. (Original work published 1754); Bertram, C. (2018). Jean Jacques Rousseau. In E. N. Zalta (Ed.). *The Stanford encyclopedia of philosophy.* Retrieved from https://plato.stanford.edu/entries/rousseau/

social, collaborative, and intuitively moral: Darwin, C., Bonner, J. Y., & May, R. M. C. (1981). *The descent of man, and selection in relation to sex* (vol. 1, pp. 70, 84). Princeton, NJ: Princeton University Press.

"It is no argument": Ibid., 85.

"between members of the same": Ibid., 95.

"are utterly indifferent": Ibid., 94.

Our evolved linguistic: Hagen, L. K. (2008). The bilingual brain: Human evolution and second language acquisition. *Evolutionary Psychology, 6*(1), 43–63; Hirschfeld, L. A. (2008). The bilingual brain revisited: A comment on Hagen. *Evolutionary Psychology, 6*(1), 182–85.

100 *similar allegiances:* For a related argument, see Pietraszewski &
     Schwartz, Evidence that accent . . .

5. LITTLE BIGOTS?

101 *bad guys in some movies:* Lippi-Green, R. (1997). *English with an accent:
     Language, ideology, and discrimination in the United States.* New York:
     Routledge.

     movies and television: Dragojevic, M., Mastro, D., Giles, H., & Sink,
     A. (2016). Silencing nonstandard speakers: A content analysis of accent
     portrayals on American prime-time television. *Language in Society, 45,*
     59–85.

     less good, less complete: Ibid.

102 *Jacques Mehler started:* Dupoux, E. (Ed.). (2001). *Language, brain, and
     cognitive development: Essays in honor of Jacques Mehler.* Cambridge,
     MA: MIT Press.

103 *change in sucking:* Byers-Heinlein, K. (2014). High-amplitude sucking
     procedure. In P. J. Brooks & V. Kempe (Eds.), *Encyclopedia of language
     development* (pp. 263–64). Thousand Oaks, CA: SAGE.

     studies in the baby lab: Mehler, J., Jusczyk, P., Lambertz, G., Halsted,
     N., Bertoncini, J., & Amiel-Tison, C. (1988). A precursor of language ac-
     quisition in young infants. *Cognition, 29*(2), 144–78. See also Moon, C.,
     Cooper, R. P., & Fifer, W. P. (1993). Two-day-olds prefer their native lan-
     guage. *Infant Behavior & Development,* 16(4), 495–500. https://doi.org/
     10.1016/0163-6383(93)80007-U

104 *different in rhythm:* Nazzi, T., Bertoncini, J., & Mehler, J. (1998). Lan-
     guage discrimination by newborns: Toward an understanding of the role
     of rhythm. *Journal of Experimental Psychology: Human Perception and
     Performance, 3,* 756–66.

     distinguish their own language: Mehler et al., A precursor of language.

     babies get further calibrated: Nazzi, T., Jusczyk, P. W., & Johnson, E. K.
     (2000). Language discrimination by English-learning 5-month-olds: Ef-
     fects of rhythm and familiarity. *Journal of Memory and Language, 43,*
     1–19.

     Seminal research: Werker, J. F., & Tees, R. C. (1984). Cross-language
     speech perception: Evidence for perceptual reorganization during the
     first year of life. *Infant Behavior and Development, 7*(1), 49–63.

     over the first year of life: Ibid.

105 *"citizens of the world":* Gervain, J., & Mehler, J. (2010). Speech percep-
     tion and language acquisition in the first year of life. *Annual Review of
     Psychology, 61,* 191–218.

106 *design was simple:* Kinzler, K. D., Dupoux, E., & Spelke, E. S. (2007). The
     native language of social cognition. *Proceedings of the National Academy
     of Sciences of the United States of America, 104*(30), 12577–80.

108 *In another study:* Shutts, K., Kinzler, K. D., McKee, C., & Spelke, E. S.

(2009). Social information guides infants' selection of foods. *Journal of Cognition and Development, 10,* 1–17.

110 *across language lines:* Liberman, Z., Woodward, A. L., & Kinzler, K. D. (2017). Preverbal infants infer third-party social structure based on linguistic group. *Cognitive Science, 41*(S3), 622–34.

eat one of two foods: Liberman, Z., Woodward, A., Sullivan, K., & Kinzler, K. D. (2016). Early emerging system for reasoning about the social nature of food. *Proceedings of the National Academy of Sciences of the United States of America, 113*(34), 9480–85.

111 different *in other meaningful ways:* Hirschfeld & Gelman, What young children think about the relationship between language variation and social difference; Weatherhead, D., White, K. S., & Friedman, O. (2016). Where are you from? Preschoolers infer background from accent. *Journal of Experimental Child Psychology, 143,* 171–78.

112 *babies tend to imitate:* Buttelmann, D., Daum, M., Zmyj, N., & Carpenter, M. (2013). Selective imitation of in-group over out-group members in 14-month-old infants. *Child Development, 84,* 422–28.

good sources of information: Begus, K., Gliga, T., & Southgate, V. (2016). Infants' preferences for native speakers are associated with an expectation of information. *PNAS, 113,* 12397–402.

how you move a new object: Kinzler, K. D., Corriveau, K. H., & Harris, P. L. (2011). Children's selective trust in native-accented speakers. *Developmental Science, 14,* 106–11.

local social environment: Henderson, A. M. A., Sabbagh, M. A., & Woodward, A. (2012). Preschoolers' selective learning is guided by the principle of relevance. *Cognition, 126,* 246–57; for a related finding, showing that children's sensitivity to linguistic diversity depends on the composition of their local social environment, see Howard, L. H., Carrazza, C., & Woodward, A. L. (2014). Neighborhood linguistic diversity predicts infants' social learning. *Cognition, 133*(2), 474–79.

pretty reliable cues: Nevertheless, children can quickly overcome a preference for learning from "native" in favor of learning from a particularly reliable foreigner, if the native-accented speaker is unreliable: Corriveau, K., Kinzler, K. D., & Harris, P. (2013). Accuracy trumps accent in children's endorsement of object labels. *Developmental Psychology, 49,* 470–79.

113 *meaningful for social grouping:* Tajfel, H. (2001). Experiments in intergroup discrimination. In M. A. Hogg & D. Abrams (Eds.), *Intergroup relations: Essential readings* (pp. 178–87). London: Psychology Press. (Original work published 1971); see also Dunham, Y., Baron, A. S., & Carey, S. (2011). Consequences of "minimal" group affiliations in children. *Child Development, 82*(3), 793–811.

114 *familiar racial group membership:* Bar-Haim, Y., Ziv, T., Lamy, D., & Hodes, R. M. (2006). Nature and nurture in own-race face processing. *Psychological Science, 17*(2), 159–63.

telling apart faces: Kelly, D. J., Quinn, P. C., Slater, A. M., Lee, K., Ge, L., & Pascalis, O. (2007). The other-race effect develops during infancy. *Psychological Science, 18*(12), 1084–89.

regardless of skin color: Kinzler, K. D., & Spelke, E. S. (2011). Do infants show social preferences for people differing in race? *Cognition, 119*(1), 1–9.

did not matter to the toddlers: Ibid. Kinzler, K. D., Dupoux, E., & Spelke, E. S. (2012). "Native" objects and collaborators: Infants' object choices and acts of giving reflect favor for native over foreign speakers. *Journal of Cognition and Development, 13*(1), 67–81.

This body of evidence: Clark, K., & Clark, M. (1940). Skin color as a factor in racial identification of Negro preschool children. *Journal of Social Psychology, 11,* 159–69.

115   *the time they enter kindergarten:* Dunham, Y., Baron, A. S., & Banaji, M. R. (2008). The development of implicit intergroup cognition. *Trends in Cognitive Science, 12,* 248–53.

they picked the native speakers: Kinzler, K. D., Shutts, K., DeJesus, J., & Spelke, E. S. (2009). Accent trumps race in guiding children's social preferences. *Social Cognition, 27,* 623–34.

"grow-up task": Kinzler, K. D., & Dautel, J. (2012). Children's essentialist reasoning about language and race. *Developmental Science, 15*(1), 131–38.

116   *means speaking English:* DeJesus, J., Dautel, J., Hwang, H. G., Park, C., & Kinzler, K. D. (2018). American = English-speaker before American = white: The development of children's reasoning about national identity. *Child Development, 89*(5), 1752–67.

deep and nefarious: Prentice, D. A., & Miller, D. T. (2007). Psychological essentialism of human categories. *Current Directions in Psychological Science, 16*(4), 202–6; see also Haslam, N., Rothschild, L., & Ernst, D. (2000). Essentialist beliefs about social categories. *British Journal of Social Psychology, 39,* 113–27.

117   *Julie was white:* For narrative simplicity, I described the story of "Julie" as one example. However, this anecdote is reflective of many interactions with children and parents and does not pinpoint any particular individual participant in my study.

119   *"high status" way of speaking:* Labov, W. (1972). *Sociolinguistic patterns.* Philadelphia: University of Pennsylvania Press; see also Day, R. (1980). The development of linguistic attitudes and preferences. *TESOL Quarterly, 14,* 27–37; Kinzler, K. D., Shutts, K., & Spelke, E. S. (2012). Language-based social preferences among multilingual children in South Africa. *Language Learning and Development, 8,* 215–32.

119   *the "worst" English:* Preston, D. R. (1998). They speak really bad English down south and in New York City. In Bauer & Trudgill (Eds.), *Language myths* (pp. 139–49).

Southern voices sounded nicer: Kinzler, K. D., & DeJesus, J. M. (2013).

Northern = smart and Southern = nice: The development of accent attitudes in the U.S. *Quarterly Journal of Experimental Psychology, 66,* 1146–58.

120 *incorporating views of status:* Labov, *Sociolinguistic patterns* (discussion, p. 138).

devalue their native tongue: Day, Development of linguistic attitudes.

as legitimate as any other: For the complexity and stigma of AAE in classrooms, and how educational policy could better address this, see Baugh, J. (1995). The law, linguistics, and education: Educational reform for African American language minority students. *Linguistics and Education, 7,* 87–105.

121 *"It's barbaric, but, hey, it's home":* Ashman, H. (Writer). (1992). Arabian nights [Recorded by B. Adler]. On *Aladdin: Original motion picture soundtrack* [CD]. Burbank, CA: Walt Disney.

122 *"While the Aladdin":* Fox, D. J. (1993, July 10). Disney will alter song in "Aladdin" movies: Changes were agreed upon after Arab-Americans complained that some lyrics were racist; Some Arab groups are not satisfied. *Los Angeles Times.* Retrieved from https://www.latimes.com/archives/la -xpm-1993-07-10-ca-11747-story.html

not-so-subtle linguistic bias: Lippi-Green, R. (2012). *English with an accent: Language, ideology, and discrimination in the United States.* New York: Routledge.

accents are depicted differently: Gidney, C., & Dobrow, J. (1998) The good, the bad, and the foreign: The use of dialect in children's animated television. *Annals of the American Academy of Political and Social Science, 557,* 105–19.

across American children's media: Ibid.; see also Lippi-Green, *English with an accent.*

123 *dehumanization:* Haslam, N. (2006). Dehumanization: An integrative review. *Personality and Social Psychology Review, 10*(3), 252–64.

dramatically overrepresented: Dragojevic, M., Mastro, D., Giles, H., & Sink, A. (2016). Silencing nonstandard speakers: A content analysis of accent portrayals on American prime-time television. *Language in Society, 45,* 59–85.

6. ON THE BASIS OF SPEECH

125 *overlooked. Neutralized:* For a description of the Trayvon Martin case and discussion of Jeantel's dialect, and how it was neutralized, see Bloom, L. (2014). *Suspicion nation: The inside story of the Trayvon Martin injustice and why we continue to repeat it* (chap. 5). Berkeley, CA: Counterpoint Press.

126 *dialect of African American English:* Also called African American Vernacular English, and African American Language; referred to here as Af-

rican American English. Rickford, *African American Vernacular English;* Bloomquist, Green, & Lanehart, *The Oxford handbook of African American language.*

"hard to understand": Rickford, J. R., & King, S. (2016). Language and linguistics on trial: Hearing Rachel Jeantel (and other vernacular speakers) in the courtroom and beyond. *Language, 92*(4), 950, 948–88; this juror's testimony is also discussed in Bloom, *Suspicion nation.*

not a single African American: Ibid., 977.

speaks in a standard accent: Frumkin, L. (2007). Influences of accent and ethnic background on perceptions of eyewitness testimony. *Psychology, Crime, and Law, 13,* 317–31.

sounding less guilty: Dixon, J. A., Mahoney, B., & Cocks, R. (2002). Accents of guilt? Effects of regional accent, race, and crime type on attributions of guilt. *Journal of Language and Social Psychology, 21*(2), 162–68.

127   *more controllable than it is:* For a discussion of misperception of controllability and associated stigma, see Gluszek, A., & Dovidio, J. F. (2010). The way they speak: A social psychological perspective on the stigma of nonnative accents in communication. *Personality and Social Psychology Review, 14*(2), 222, 214–37.

has become routinized: Ng, S. H. (2007). Language-based discrimination: Blatant and subtle forms. *Journal of Language and Social Psychology, 26*(2), 106–22.

129   *Even people who know sign languages:* Hall, S. (1983). Train-gone-sorry: The etiquette of social conversations in American Sign Language. *Sign Language Studies,* 41, 291–309.

129   *more likely to underestimate:* Gluszek & Dovidio, The way they speak; for related discussion, see also Hansen, K., & Dovidio, J. F. (2016). Social dominance orientation, nonnative accents, and hiring recommendations. *Cultural Diversity and Ethnic Minority Psychology, 22*(4), 544–51.

linguists presented English speakers: Munro, M. J., & Derwing, T. M. (1995). Foreign accent, comprehensibility, and intelligibility in the speech of second language learners. *Language Learning, 45,* 73–97.

130   *Subjective and objective:* See the discussion in Gluszek & Dovidio, The way they speak.

may feel stigmatized: Gluszek, A., & Dovidio, J. F. (2010). Speaking with a nonnative accent: Perceptions of bias, communication difficulties, and belonging. *Journal of Language and Social Psychology, 29*(2), 224–34.

"They can't even speak English": Marchetti-Bowick, E. (2015, March 31). Incoherent and incompetent: The consequences of accent discrimination. *Stanford Daily.* Retrieved from https://www.stanforddaily.com/ 2015/03/31/incoherent-and-incompetent-the-consequences-of-accent -discrimination/

131 *presented undergraduates:* Rubin, D. L., & Smith, K. A. (1990). Effects of accent, ethnicity, and lecture topic on undergraduates' perceptions of nonnative English-speaking teaching assistants. *International Journal of Intercultural Relations, 14,* 337–53.

In the next study: Rubin, D. L. (1992). Nonlanguage factors affecting undergraduates' judgments of nonnative English-speaking teaching assistants. *Research in Higher Education, 33*(4), 511–31.

132 *accent that did not exist:* For an overview of related research, see Rubin, D. (2012). The power of prejudice in accent perception: Reverse linguistic stereotyping and its impact on listener judgments and decisions. In Levis, J., & LeVelle, K. (Eds.), *Social factors in pronunciation acquisition.* Proceedings of the 3rd Pronunciation in Second Language Learning and Teaching Conference, 10.13140/RG.2.1.1465.4485.

a poor evaluation: Rubin, D. (1998). Help! My professor (or doctor or boss) doesn't talk English! In J. N. Martin, T. K. Makayama, & L. A. Flores (Eds.), *Readings in cultural contexts* (pp. 149–60). Mountain View, CA: Mayfield.

classrooms across the nation: Subtirelu, N. C. (2015). "She does have an accent but . . .": Race and language ideology in students' evaluations of mathematics instructors on RateMyProfessors.com. *Language in Society, 44,* 35–62.

133 *"feel compelled to comment":* Ibid., 54.

134 *Shiri Lev-Ari and Boaz Keysar:* Lev-Ari, S., & Keysar, B. (2010). Why don't we believe non-native speakers? The influence of accent on credibility. *Journal of Experimental Social Psychology, 46,* 1093–96.

Karolina Hansen and John Dovidio: Hansen & Dovidio, Social dominance orientation.

Social Dominance Orientation: Sidanius, J., & Pratto, F. (1999). *Social dominance: An inter-group theory of social hierarchy and oppression.* New York: Cambridge University Press.

"It's probably a good thing": These statements are taken from Thomsen, L., Gree, E. G., Ho, A. K., Levin, S., van Laar, C., Sinclair, S., & Sidanius, J. (2010). Wolves in sheep's clothing: SDO asymmetrically predicts perceived ethnic victimization among white and Latino students across three years. *Personality and Social Psychology Bulletin, 36*(2), 22–238; the same items were subsequently used by Hansen and Dovidio (Hansen & Dovidio, Social dominance orientation).

135 *who were measured to be high in SDO:* Hansen & Dovidio, Social dominance orientation.

biases can come into play: For a related finding on how people who are high in ethnocentrism also trust foreign-accented speech less, see Neuliep, J. W., & Speten-Hansen, K. (2013). The influence of ethnocentrism on social perceptions of nonnative accents. *Language and Communication, 33*(3), 167–76.

"Listening to these and": Matsuda, M. J. (1991). Voices of America: Accent, antidiscrimination, law, and a jurisprudence for the last reconstruction. *Yale Law Journal, 100,* 1348.

136   *"paired testing"*: Also referred to as "audit" studies.

137   *large-scale housing study:* Zhoa, B., Ondrich, J., & Yinger, J. (2006). Why do real estate brokers continue to discriminate? Evidence from the 2000 housing discrimination study. *Journal of Urban Economics, 59,* 394–419. *What predicted whether:* For a related finding of accents devalued in a housing study, see Purnell, T., Isardi, W., & Baugh, J. (1999). Perceptual and phonetic experiments on American English dialect identification. *Journal of Language and Social Psychology, 18,* 10–30.
The economist Jeffrey Grogger: For the study discussed here, Grogger, J. (2011). Speech patterns and racial wage inequality. *Journal of Human Resources, 46,* 1–25; for a replication and extension, see Grogger, J. (2019). Speech and wages. *Journal of Human Resources, 54,* 926–52.

138   *by how they sounded:* For a related finding with Mexican American workers, see Dávila, A., Bohara, A. K., & Saenz, R. (1993). Accent penalties and the earnings of Mexican Americans. *Social Sciences Quarterly, 74,* 902–16; this study shows that Mexican American workers' earnings are predicted by people's perceptions of their accent more than their actual overall proficiency in English or the lightness or darkness of their skin.
accent discrimination: The emerging field of raciolinguistics highlights the connections between language and race. For related evidence that Indian call centers try to "whiten" their voices to sound more appealing to customers, see Ramjattan, V. A. (2019). Raciolinguistics and the aesthetic labourer. *Journal of Industrial Relations, 61*(5), 726–38. https://doi.org/10.1177/0022185618792990. See also Rosa, J. (2018). *Looking like a language, sounding like a race: Raciolinguistic ideologies and the learning of Latinidad.* New York: Oxford University Press.

139   *Fragante, an army veteran:* Matsuda, Voices of America.

140   *"inability to orally communicate"*: Fragante appellate brief filed on behalf of the city of Honolulu, p. 8. Brief filed in the Ninth Circuit: *Fragante v. City and County of Honolulu,* 888 F.2d 591, 597 (9th Cir. 1989).
"He has 37 years": The DMV's notes come from *Fragante v. City and County of Honolulu,* 699 F. Supp. 1429, 1431 (D. Haw. 1987). They are also included in the Ninth Circuit's decision: *Fragante v. City and County of Honolulu,* 888 F.2d 591, 597 (9th Cir. 1989).
"Attorneys for both sides": Matsuda, Voices of America, 1338.

141   *a two-way street: Fragante v. City and County of Honolulu,* 888 F.2d 591, 597 (9th Cir. 1989).
"failed to produce any": The City of Honolulu's brief filed in the Ninth Circuit.

142   *particular "native" American accents:* Some have proposed expanding Title VII's protection of "national origin" to include regional origin within

the United States; Diaz, J. G. (2014). The divided states of America: Reinterpreting Title VII's national origin provision to account for subnational
discrimination within the United States. *University of Pennsylvania Law
Review, 162*, 649–81.

when trying to figure out: U.S. Equal Employment Opportunity Commission, Office of Legal Counsel. (2016). *EEOC Enforcement Guidance on
National Origin Discrimination, (V.)*. Retrieved from https://www.eeoc
.gov/laws/guidance/national-origin-guidance.cfm#_Toc451518822

143 *Burlington Coat Factory: Albert-Aluya v. Burlington Coat Factory Warehouse Corp.*, 470 F. App'x 847 (11th Cir. 2012); for her description of events,
see Complaint for Race & Gender Discrimination, Retaliation/Retaliatory Discharge, Negligent Supervision and Retention, and Intentional
Infliction of Emotional Distress, *Albert-Aluya v. Burlington Coat Factory
Corp.*, No. 1:09-CV-2111-JE (N.D. Ga. Aug. 4, 2009).

*Filipino American hospital workers: EEOC v. Cent. Cal. Found. for
Health* d/b/a DelanoReg'l Med. Ctr, No. 1:10-CV-01492-LJO-JLT (E.D.
Cal., consent decree entered Sept. 17, 2012); for an EEOC press release
about the case: U.S. Equal Employment Opportunity Commission. (2012,
September 17). *Delano regional medical center to pay nearly $1 million
in EEOC National Origin Discrimination suit* [Press release]. Retrieved
from https://www.eeoc.gov/eeoc/newsroom/release/9-17-12a.cfm

144 *case of Yili Tseng: Tseng v. Fla. A&M Univ.*, No. 4:08-CV-91-SPM-WCS,
2009 WL 3163126 (N.D. Fla. Sept. 30, 2009).

145 *discrimination because of their accent:* Going back to the case against
Burlington Coat Factory, involving a Nigerian woman fired for not "speaking like an American," I added this in the "win" column for accent discrimination cases, because the appellate court ultimately said she could
proceed with her case in the district court. Yet the lower court that first
reviewed her case actually sided with Burlington Coat Factory. This was
because the woman failed to directly connect the accent discrimination to
her national origin, which is covered by Title VII.

"multiple protected bases": U.S. Equal Employment Opportunity Commission, Office of Legal Counsel. (2016). *EEOC Enforcement Guidance on
National Origin Discrimination* (C. 1.). Retrieved from https://www.eeoc
.gov/laws/guidance/national-origin-guidance.cfm#_ftn35

146 *As Matsuda describes:* Matsuda, Voices of America.

some sort of standardized test: Ngyuen, B. B.-D. (1993). Accent discrimination and the test of spoken English: A call for an objective assessment
of the comprehensibility of nonnative speakers. *California Law Review,
81*(5), 1325–61.

in educational contexts: For instance, the TOEFL (Test of English as a
Foreign Language) tests spoken English, along with written and listening
comprehension skills.

147 *a reasonable accommodation:* Accent should not be considered a disabil-

ity, since everyone who speaks a language has an accent. Nevertheless, the
theory of and procedures for reasonable accommodations from disability
law might be profitably considered in thinking about possible reasonable
accommodations for communication skills. See Matsuda, Voice of America, for a proposal and in-depth discussion of this idea. The general idea of
considering an accommodation might be pursued informally by employers too, even in the absence of any legal changes.

148   norm setting: McAdams, R. (2017). *The expressive powers of law: Theo-*
      ries and limits. Cambridge, MA: Harvard University Press.
      "atmosphere of inferiority": 29 C.F.R. § 1606.7(a); or 45 Fed. Reg. 85,632,
      85,636 (Dec. 29, 1980).
      a hospital can require: Montes v. Vail Clinic, Inc., 497 F.3d 1160, 1171
      (10th Cir. 2007).
      engaging in other contexts: As discussed in *EEOC v. Cent. Cal. Found. for*
      Health.

149   *"An employer's preference": Chimm v. Spring Branch Indep. Sch. Dist.,* No.
      H-09-3032, 2009 WL 5170214. (The quote is from the district court deci-
      sion; decision later affirmed by the court of appeals.)
      Dionisio Hernandez: Hernandez v. New York, 500 U.S. 352 (1991). Jury
      selection occurred in 1986: *Hernandez v. New York,* Brief for Petitioner at
      *2 (U.S. Nov. 28, 1990).

150   *"It is a harsh paradox": Hernandez v. New York,* 500 U.S. 352 (1991).
      legal system as a whole: Soltero, C. R. (2006). *Latinos and American law:*
      Landmark Supreme Court cases. Austin: University of Texas Press.
      Some have proposed: Rickford & King, *Language and linguistics on*
      trial.

7. A LINGUISTICS REVOLUTION

152   *skepticism about bilingualism:* For discussion of myths about bilingual-
      ism, and general insight on bilingual language development, see Gros-
      jean, F. (2010). *Bilingual: Life and reality.* Cambridge, MA: Harvard Uni-
      versity Press; Beardsmore, H. B. (2003). Who's afraid of bilingualism? In
      J. M. Dewaele, A. Housen, & L. Wei (Eds.), *Bilingualism: Beyond basic*
      principles (pp. 10–27). Tonawanda, NY: Multilingual Matters; Genesee,
      F. H. (2009). Early childhood bilingualism: Perils and possibilities. *Jour-*
      nal of Applied Research on Learning, 2, 1–21.

153   *Scientists used to think:* Powers, F. F. (1929). Psychology of language
      learning. *Psychological Bulletin, 26*(5), 261–74; see also Saer, D. J. (1923).
      The effect of bilingualism on intelligence. *British Journal of Psychology,*
      14(1), 25–38; Darcy, N. T. (1953). A review of the literature on the effects
      of bilingualism upon the measurement of intelligence. *Journal of Genetic*
      Psychology, 82, 21–57.

154   *math whiz growing up:* Identifying details changed to protect my friend's
      identity.

156 *can safely be exposed:* Kay-Raining Bird, E., Genesee, F., & Verhoeven, L. (2016). Bilingualism in children with developmental disorders: A narrative review. *Journal of Communication Disorders, 63,* 1–14.

advice I got was misguided: Grosjean, F. (2017). Supporting bilingual children with special education needs: An interview with Elizabeth Kay-Raining Bird. *Psychology Today.* Retrieved at https://www.psychology-today.com/intl/blog/life-bilingual/201701/supporting-bilingual-children-special-education-needs

when they surveyed: Marinova-Todd, S. H., Colozzo, P., Mirenda, P., Stahl, H., Kay-Raining Bird, E., Parkington, K., . . . & Genesee, F. (2016). Professional practices and opinions about services available to bilingual children with developmental disabilities: An international study. *Journal of Communication Disorders, 63,* 15–31.

157 *most of the world's children:* Grosjean, *Bilingual.*

number of multilingual kids: Commission on Language Learning. (2017). *America's languages: Investing in language education for the 21st century.* Cambridge, MA: American Academy of Arts & Sciences. Retrieved from https://www.amacad.org/sites/default/files/publication/downloads/ Commission-on-Language-Learning_Americas-Languages.pdf

new opportunities: See Genesee, Early childhood bilingualism, for a discussion of the benefits of bilingualism in a globalizing society.

completely natural: Werker, J. F., & Byers-Heinlein, K. (2008). Bilingualism in infancy: First steps in perception and comprehension. *Trends in Cognitive Sciences, 14*(1), 144–51; see also Grosjean, *Bilingual.*

milestones are remarkably similar: Petitto, L. A., Katerelos, M., Levy, B. G., Gauna, K., Tétreault, K., & Ferraro, V. (2001). Bilingual signed and spoken language acquisition from birth: Implications for the mechanisms underlying early bilingual language acquisition. *Journal of Child Language, 28*(2), 453–96; see also Werker & Byers-Heinlein, Bilingualism in infancy, and Grosjean, *Bilingual.*

seems a little slower: Hoff, E., Core, C., Place, S., Rumiche, R., Señor, M., & Parra, M. (2012). Dual language exposure and early bilingual development. *Journal of Child Language, 39*(1), 1–27. doi:10.1017/ S0305000910000759; Hoff, E., & Ribot, K. M. (2017). Language growth in English monolingual and Spanish-English bilingual children from 2.5 to 5 years. *The Journal of Pediatrics, 190,* 241–45.e1. doi:10.1016/j.jpeds.2017 .06.071

158 *size of vocabulary:* Junker, D. A., & Stockman, I. J. (2002). Expressive vocabulary of German-English bilingual toddlers. *American Journal of Speech-Language Pathology, 11,* 381–94; see also Poulin-Dubois, D., Bialystok, E., Blaye, A., Polonia, A., & Yott, J. (2013). Lexical access and vocabulary development in very young bilinguals. *International Journal of Bilingualism, 17*(1), 57–70, and Hoff & Ribot, Language growth in English monolingual and Spanish-English bilingual children.

have a smaller vocabulary: For research on bilingual language development milestones, see Werker & Byers-Heinlein, Bilingualism in infancy,
and Grosjean, *Bilingual.*

complementarity principle: Grosjean, *Bilingual.*

the "home words": Bialystok, E., Luk, G., Peets, K. F., & Yang, S. (2010).
Receptive vocabulary differences in monolingual and bilingual children.
Bilingualism: Language and Cognition, 13(4), 525–31.

159 *in more flexible ways:* Byers-Heinlein, K., & Werker, J. F. (2009). Monolingual, bilingual, trilingual: Infants' language experience influences
the development of a word learning heuristic. *Developmental Science, 12,*
815–23.

the more hours a child: Hoff, E., Core, C., Place, S., Rumiche, R., Señor,
M., & Parra, M. (2012). Dual language exposure and early bilingual devel-
opment. *Journal of Child Language, 39*(1), 1–27; see also Hoff, E., & Core,
C. (2015). What clinicians need to know about bilingual development.
Seminars in Speech and Language, 36(2), 89–99.

160 *diverse vocabulary:* Huttenlocher, J., Haight, W., Bryk, A., Seltzer, M., &
Lyons, T. (1991). Early vocabulary growth: Relation to language input and
gender. *Developmental Psychology, 27*(2), 236–48.

concepts that are abstract: Hoff, E. (2006). How social contexts support
and shape language development. *Developmental Review, 26*(1), 55–88;
see also Rowe, M. L. (2012). A longitudinal investigation of the role of
quantity and quality of child-directed speech in vocabulary development.
Child Development, 83(5), 1762–74.

Input from a native speaker: Hoff & Core, What clinicians need to know;
see also Place, S., & Hoff, E. (2011). Properties of dual language exposure that influence 2-year-olds' bilingual proficiency. *Child Development,
82*(6), 1834–49.

161 *whatever arrangement:* Hoff & Core, What clinicians need to know; see
also Grosjean, *Bilingual.*

where she needs to speak French: For helpful strategies for parents raising children in bilingual environments, see Grosjean, F. (2012). Keeping
a language alive: Ways of maintaining a language. *Psychology Today.*
Retrieved at https://www.psychologytoday.com/intl/blog/life-bilingual/
201202/keeping-language-alive

children standardize the speech: Newport, E. L. (2016). Statistical language learning: Computational, maturational, and linguistic constraints.
Language and Cognition, 8(3), 447–61.

162 *cognitive advantages:* For a seminal study on bilingual advantages
rather than disadvantages, changing the discourse in the field, see Peal,
E., & Lambert, W. E. (1962). The relation of bilingualism to intelligence.
Psychological Monographs: General and Applied, 76(27), 1–23; for more
modern research, see Bialystok, E., Craik, F. I. M., & Luk, G. (2012). Bilingualism: Consequences for mind and brain. *Trends in Cognitive Sci-*

ences, 16(4), 240–50; see also Bialystok, E. (2017). The bilingual adaptation: How minds accommodate experience. *Psychological Bulletin, 143*(3), 233–62.

attention systems: For a general overview, see Petersen, S. E., & Posner, M. I. (2012). The attention system of the human brain: 20 years after. *Annual Review of Neuroscience, 35,* 73–89.

from different angles: Kharkhurin, A. V. (2009). The role of bilingualism in creative performance on divergent thinking and Invented Alien Creatures tests. *Journal of Creative Behavior, 43*(1), 59–71.

163 *do better academically:* Best, J. R., Miller, P. H., & Naglieri, J. A. (2011). Relations between executive function and academic achievement from ages 5 to 17 in a large representative national sample. *Learning and Individual Differences, 21*(4), 327–36.

decline in executive control: Glisky, E. L. (2007). Changes in cognitive function in human aging. In D. R. Riddle (Ed.), *Brain aging: Models, methods, and mechanisms* (chap. 1). Boca Raton, FL: CRC Press/Taylor & Francis. Retrieved from https://www.ncbi.nlm.nih.gov/books/NBK3885/

no clear differences: Dunabeitia, J. A., Hernandez, J. A., Anton, E., Macizo, P., Estevez, A., Fuentes, L. J., & Carreiras, M. (2014). The inhibitory advantage in bilingual children revisited: Myth or reality? *Experimental Psychology, 61,* 234–51. doi:10.1027/1618-3169/a000243; Antón, E., Carreiras, M., & Duñabeitia, J. A. (2019). The impact of bilingualism on executive function and working memory in young adults. *PLOS One, 14*(2): e0206770. https://doi.org/10.1371/journal.pone.0206770

ongoing research and debate: Antoniou, M. (2019). The advantages of bilingualism debate. *Annual Review of Linguistics, 5,* 395–15.

consistently observed differences: Bialystok et al., Bilingualism.

differences in cognitive flexibility: Kovács, A. M., & Mehler, J. (2009). Cognitive gains in 7-month-old bilingual infants. *Proceedings of the National Academy of Sciences of the United States of America, 106*(16), 6556–60.

sharp until late in life: Anderson, J. A., Grundy, J. G., Frutos, J. D., Barker, R. M., Grady, C. L., & Bialystok, E. (2018). Effects of bilingualism on white matter integrity in older adults. *NeuroImage, 167,* 143–50; Bialystok, E., Craik, F. I., & Freedman, M. (2007). Bilingualism as a protection against the onset of symptoms of dementia. *Neuropsychologia, 45*(2), 459–64; Bialystok, E., Craik, F. I. M., Binns, M. A., Ossher, L., & Freedman, M. (2014). Effects of bilingualism on the age of onset and progression of MCI and AD: Evidence from executive function tests. *Neuropsychology, 28*(2), 290–304.

However, some studies find no differences in onset of dementia among older adults: Zahodne, L. B., Schofield, P. W., Farrell, M. T., Stern, Y., & Manly, J. J. (2014). Bilingualism does not alter cognitive decline or dementia risk among Spanish-speaking immigrants. *Neuropsychology,*

28(2), 238–46; Mukadam, N., Sommerlad, A., & Livingston, G. (2017). The relationship of bilingualism compared to monolingualism to the risk of cognitive decline or dementia: A systematic review and meta-analysis. *Journal of Alzheimer's Disease, 58*(1), 45–54.

But see commentary responding to this negative evidence: Grundy, J. G., & Anderson, J.A.E. (2017). Commentary: The relationship of bilingualism compared to monolingualism to the risk of cognitive decline or dementia: A systematic review and meta-analysis. *Frontiers in Aging Neuroscience, 9,* 344; Konnikova, M. (2015, January 22). Is bilingualism really an advantage? *New Yorker.* Retrieved from https://www.newyorker .com/science/maria-konnikova/bilingual-advantage-aging-brain

the incidence of Alzheimer's: Klein, R. M., Christie, J., & Parkvall, M. (2016). Does multilingualism affect the incidence of Alzheimer's disease? A worldwide analysis by country. *SSM—Population Health, 2,* 463–67.

164   *sharing a linguistic past:* Oh, J. S., & Fuligni, A. J. (2010). The role of heritage language development in the ethnic identity and family relationships of adolescents from immigrant backgrounds. *Social Development, 19,* 202–20; see also Hoff & Core, What clinicians need to know.

165   *adept perspective-taking:* Interlocutor sensitivity, or responding to people based on which language they speak, emerges by age two in bilinguals: Deuchar, M., & Quay, S. (1999). Language choice in the earliest utterances: A case study with methodological implications. *Journal of Child Language, 26,* 461–75.

navigating linguistic complexity: Genesee, F., Boivin, I., & Nicoladis, E. (1996). Talking with strangers: A study of bilingual children's communicative competence. *Applied Psycholinguistics, 17,* 427–42.

167   *the bilingual kids:* Fan, S., Liberman, Z., Keysar, B., & Kinzler, K. D. (2015). The exposure advantage: Early exposure to a multilingual environment promotes effective communication. *Psychological Science, 26,* 1090–97; for a related finding, see Yow, W. Q., & Markman, E. M. (2015). A bilingual advantage in how children integrate multiple cues to understand a speaker's referential intent. *Bilingualism, 18*(3), 391–99.

168   *a little over a year in age:* Liberman, Z., Woodward, A. L., Keysar, B., & Kinzler, K. D. (2017). Exposure to multiple languages enhances communication skills in infancy. *Developmental Science, 20*(1), 1–11.

inconstancies, redundancies: Siegal, M., Iozzi, L., & Surian, L. (2009). Bilingualism and conversational understanding in young children. *Cognition, 110*(1), 115–22.

169   *use the emotional tone:* Yow, W. Q., & Markman, E. M. (2011). Bilingualism and children's use of paralinguistic cues to interpret emotion in speech. *Bilingualism, 14*(4), 562–69.

verbal and nonverbal channels: Yow, W. Q., & Markman, E. M. (2011). Young bilingual children's heightened sensitivity to referential cues. *Jour-*

nal of Cognition and Development, 12(1), 12–31; Yow & Markman, A bilingual advantage.

a little bit of exposure: Yow, W. Q., & Markman, E. M. (2016). Children increase their sensitivity to a speaker's nonlinguistic cues following a communicative breakdown. *Child Development, 87*(2), 85–394.

others' mental states: Kovács, A. M. (2009). Early bilingualism enhances mechanisms of false belief reasoning. *Developmental Science, 12*(1), 48–54.

degree of empathizing: Erle, T. M., & Topolinski, S. (2015). Spatial and empathic perspective-taking correlate on a dispositional level. *Social Cognition, 33*(3), 187–210.

their thoughts and feelings: Erle, T. M., & Topolinski, S. (2017). The grounded nature of psychological perspective-taking. *Journal of Personality and Social Psychology, 112*(5), 683–95.

bilingual kids prefer: DeJesus, Dautel, Hwang, & Kinzler, Bilingual children's social preferences hinge on accent; Souza, Byers-Heinlein, & Poulin-Dubois, Bilingual and monolingual children prefer native-accented speakers; Kinzler, Shutts, & Spelke, Language-based social preferences among multilingual children in South Africa.

170 *breakdowns in communication:* Comeau, L., Genesee, F., & Mendelson, M. (2007). Bilingual children's repairs of breakdowns in communication. *Journal of Child Language, 34*(1), 159–74; Wermelinger, S., Gampe, A., & Daum, M. M. (2017). Bilingual toddlers have advanced abilities to repair communication failure. *Journal of Experimental Child Psychology, 155,* 84–94; Comeau, L., Genesee, F., & Mendelson, M. (2010). A comparison of bilingual and monolingual children's conversational repairs. *First Language, 30,* 354–74.

can be valuable: For additional evidence that bilingual children may be more socially flexible, see Byers-Heinlein, K., Behrend, D., Said, L. M., Giris, H., & Poulin-Dubois, D. (2017). Monolingual and bilingual children's social preferences for monolingual and bilingual speakers. *Developmental Science, 20*(4), e12392; DeJesus, Dautel, Hwang, & Kinzler, Bilingual children's social preferences hinge on accent; Byers-Heinlein, K. & Garcia, B. (2015), Bilingualism changes children's beliefs about what is innate. *Dev Sci,* 18: 344–50. doi:10.1111/desc.12248

171 *Justice Clarence Thomas:* Wagner, L. (2016, February 29). Clarence Thomas asks 1st question from Supreme Court bench in 10 years. *NPR: The Two-Way.* Retrieved from https://www.npr.org/sections/thetwo -way/2016/02/29/468576931/clarence-thomas-asks-1st-question-from -supreme-court-bench-in-10-years

"When I was 16": The 43rd president: In his own words. (2000, December 14). *The New York Times.* Retrieved from http://www.nytimes.com/ 2000/12/14/us/the-43rd-president-in-his-own-words.html

172 *"made African American students":* Baugh, J. (2017). Linguistic profiling.

In Ball, A., Makoni, S., Smitherman, G., & Spears, A. K. (2005). *Black linguistics: Language, society, and politics in Africa and the Americas* (p. 166). London: Routledge.

compositions and drawings: Giles, H., & Billings, A. C. (2008). Assessing language attitudes: Speaker evaluation studies. In A. Davies & C. Elder (Eds.), *The handbook of applied linguistics* (pp. 187–209). Malden, MA: Blackwell Publishing; see also Seligman, C., Tucker, G. R., & Lambert, W. E. (1972). The effects of speech style and other attributes on teachers' attitudes toward pupils. *Language in Society, 1,* 131–42.

"the relationship between": Text of the letter sent by members of Congress to the AAAS, appended to Commission on Language Learning, *America's languages.*

173 *"It is critical that":* Ibid., 6.

American school systems: American Academy of Arts and Sciences. (2016). *The state of languages in the U.S.: A statistical portrait* (p. 11). Cambridge, MA: American Academy of Arts and Sciences.

174 *opportunities for employment:* See Commission on Language Learning, *America's languages,* p. 6 and n. 62, which states that "recent surveys of state and local job markets reveal a significant increase in the number of job postings that list language skills as a requirement." See also American Academy of Arts and Sciences, *State of languages* (p. 17).

America's linguistic diversity: National Center for Education Statistics (2019). *English language learners in public schools* [Report]. Retrieved from https://nces.ed.gov/programs/coe/indicator_cgf.asp; Sanchez, C. (2017, February 23). English language learners: How your state is doing. NPR Ed, *5 million voices.* Retrieved from https://www.npr.org/sections/ed/2017/02/23/512451228/5-million-english-language-learners-a-vast-pool-of-talent-at-risk

most linguistically diverse: Buhmann, D., & Trudell, B. (2008). Mother tongue matters: Local language as a key to effective learning. Paris: United Nations Educational Cultural and Scientific Organization (UNESCO). Retrieved from https://unesdoc.unesco.org/ark:/48223/pf0000161121

both Welsh and English: Baker, C. (2003). Language planning: A grounded approach. In J. M. Dewaele, A. Housen, & L. Wei (Eds.), *Bilingualism: Beyond basic principles* (chap. 6). Tonawanda, NY: Multilingual Matters.

different subjects and time periods: Jones, G. M. (2003). Accepting bilingualism as a language policy: An unfolding Southeast Asian story. In Dewaele, Housen, & Wei (Eds.), *Bilingualism* (chap. 7).

175 *dual-immersion classrooms:* Commission on Language Learning, *America's languages,* for recent examples of successes; Steele, J. L., Slater, R., Zamarro, G., Miller, T., Li, J. J., Burkhauser, S., & Bacon, M. (2017). *Dual-language immersion programs raise student achievement in English.* Santa Monica, CA: RAND Corporation. Retrieved from https://www.rand.org/

pubs/research_briefs/RB9903.html; Buhmann & Trudell, Mother tongue matters; Fausset, R. (2019, August 21). Louisiana says "oui" to French, amid explosion in dual-language schools. *The New York Times*. Retrieved from https://www.nytimes.com/2019/08/21/us/louisiana-french-dual -language.html

cultural misperception: Cummins, J. (2003). Bilingual education: Basic principles. In Dewaele, Housen, & Wei (Eds.), *Bilingualism* (chap. 4).

AFTERWORD: IT'S ~~NOT~~ WHAT YOU SAY

177 *"blue eyes/brown eyes" experiment:* Peters, W., & Cobb, C. (1985). A class divided. [Television program transcript]. PBS Frontline. Retrieved from http://www.pbs.org/wgbh/pages/frontline/shows/divided/etc/script .html

179 stereotype threat: Shih, M., Pittinsky, T. L., & Ambady, N. (1999). Stereotype susceptibility: Identity salience and shifts in quantitative performance. *Psychological Science, 10*(1), 81–84.

180 *differences in an adult's language:* Rhodes, M., Leslie, S. J., & Tworek, C. M. (2012). Cultural transmission of social essentialism. *Proceedings of the National Academy of the United States of America, 109,* 13526–31. For related evidence of the link between language and social categorization, see Waxman, S. R. (2010), Names will never hurt me? Naming and the development of racial and gender categories in preschool aged children. *Eur. J. Soc. Psychol., 40:* 593–610. doi:10.1002/ejsp.732

181 *essentialized group:* Gelman, S. A. (2005). *The essential child: Origins of essentialism in everyday thought.* New York: Oxford University Press.

182 *Rebecca Bigler:* Bigler, R. S. (1995). The role of classification skill in moderating environmental influences on children's gender stereotyping: A study of the functional use of gender in the classroom. *Child Development, 66*(4), 1072–87.

184 *Stereotypes and prejudice about race:* Mandalaywala, T. M., Ranger-Murdock, G., Amodio, D. M., & Rhodes, M. (2019). The nature and consequences of essentialist beliefs about race in early childhood. *Child Development* 90, e437–e453; Pauker, K., Xu, Y., Williams, A., & Biddle, A. M. (2016). Race essentialism and social contextual differences in children's racial stereotyping. *Child Development* 87(5), 1409–22; Roberts, S. O., & Rizzo, M. T. (2020). The psychology of American racism. *American Psychologist.*

185 *"colorblind" approaches:* Perry, S. P., Skinner, A. L., & Abaied, J. L. (2019). Bias awareness predicts color conscious racial socialization methods among White parents. *Journal of Social Issues* 1075, 1035–56.

unjust narratives: Roberts & Rizzo, The psychology of American racism.

talk about race: Hughes, D., Rodriguez, J., Smith, E. P., Johnson, D. J., Stevenson, H. C., & Spicer, P. (2006). Parents' ethnic-racial socialization practices: A review of research and directions for future study. *Developmental Psychology* 42, 747–70; Perry, Skinner, & Abaied, Bias awareness predicts color conscious racial socialization methods among White parents.

186 *concrete-to-abstract trajectory:* Semin, G. R., & Fiedler, K. (1988). The cognitive functions of linguistic categories in describing persons: Social cognition and language. *Journal of Personality and Social Psychology, 54,* 558–68.

linguistic intergroup bias: Maass, A., Salvi, D., Arcuri, L., & Semin, G. (1989). Language use in intergroup contexts: The linguistic intergroup bias. *Journal of Personality and Social Psychology, 57,* 981–93.

also how they listen: Porter, S. C., Rheinschmidt-Same, M., & Richeson, J. A. (2016). Inferring identity from language: Linguistic intergroup bias information and social categorization. *Psychological Science, 27,* 94–102.

INDEX

abstract language, 185–86
abuse, 35–36
accent
    becoming accustomed to, 59–60, 199
    children's preferences and, 115, 117–19
    difficulty of faking/replicating, x, 58
    difficulty of mastering, 61
    infant preferences for, 107
    in media, 121–24
    misperceptions regarding, 128–30
    proposed changes to employment laws and, 145–48
    sensitivity to, 57–58
    social effects of, xiv–xv
    social groups and, xi–xii
    when speaking foreign languages, x, xi
    "who said what" game and, 95
    workers' earnings and, 214
accent attitudes, 71–79
accent bias/discrimination, 126–27, 130–33, 134–48
accent groups, animals and, 87–88
acoustic clans, 87

actors, accents and, 61–62
adolescents
    bilingual, 25–26
    speech of, 8–12
    See also children; infants
African American English, xiv, 68, 77, 120, 122, 126, 142, 211
Afrikaan Medium Decree, 55
age
    discarding languages and, 42–44
    language acquisition and, 41–42, 47–48
    See also children; infants
Aladdin, 121–22
Albert-Aluya, Adesuwa, 143, 215
"America the Beautiful" ad, 70
American Academy of Arts and Sciences, 172
American Sign Language (ASL), 36–39
American-Arab Anti-Discrimination Committee (ADC), 121–22
Americans, The, 61–62
animal communications, 87–88
apartheid, 54–56
appearance, recollections of, 3–4
Australians, 16–17

autobiographical memories, 25
avoidance strategies, 78–79

Babel, 63
Babel, Molly, 17, 193
babies. *See* infants
Balkans, xii–xiii
Banaji, Mahzarin, 11–12
Basque country, 65
Baugh, John, 171–72, 211
beadwork, 88–90
Bialystok, Ellen, 163, 197, 217–19
bias
    effects of, 78–79, 126–27
    linguistic, 101, 117–24, 127–28,
        149–51
    linguistic intergroup, 185–86
    non-standard dialects and, 101
    See also accent attitudes; accent
        bias/discrimination
Bible, xi–xii
Bigler, Rebecca, 182–84
bilingual and bicultural children,
        13–15, 23, 26–27, 153–61, 164
bilingual bonus, 162–64
bilingualism, 22–23, 24, 148–50,
        152–57, 169, 170, 216, 218,
        219–20
"biological linguistic roots," myth of,
        83–87
biological reasons for speech changes,
        lack of in gay men, 2
"blue eyes brown eyes" experiment,
        177–80
brain structure, language acquisition
        and, 45–46
Broca's area, 45
Burlington Coat Factory case, 143,
        215
burnouts, 10
Bush, George W., 17–18

Canterbury Tales, The (Chaucer), 64
Catalan, 64–65

categories
    children and, 111–12
    creation of, 180–81
    prism of, 4
    See also social groups
Chaucer, 64
children
    bilingual and bicultural, 13–15,
        23, 26–27, 153–61, 164
    categorization by language by,
        111–12
    deaf, 36–39
    discarding languages and,
        42–43
    of immigrants, 12–15, 28–30
    learning in native language and,
        66, 68–69
    local social environments and,
        112–13
    race and, 113–17, 184–85
    See also adolescents; infants
Chinese dialects, 74–75
Cimpian, Andrei, 32–33, 52–53,
        61
Civil Rights Act (1964; United
        States), 138–39, 149
Class Divided, A, 178–79
Clinton, Hillary, 17–18
Clueless, 11
code-switching, 77
"colorblind" parenting approaches,
        184–85
communication, biases and,
        78–79
communication accommodation
        theory, 193
communication skills, assessments of,
        146–47
competence, judgments of, 73–74
complementarity principle, 158
conceptual vocabulary, 159
Conrad, Joseph, 31, 61
Constitution Act (1867; Canada),
        72

Constitution Project, 67
content of speech, 177–86
controllability, perception of, 79, 127, 212
Corriveau, Kathleen, 112
Cosmides, Leda, 92, 206
Creoles, 65–66, 120, 201
Croatian, xii–xiii, 190
culture, language and, 62–63, 64–65, 194
curse words, 48, 52–53

Danes, Claire, 11
Darwin, Charles, 81, 99–100
Dautel, Jocelyn, 115
deaf children, 36–39
decision making, native-language emotions and, 50–52
DeGraff, Michel, 66
dehumanization, 123
DeJesus, Jasmine, 13–14, 116, 119
Descent of Man, The (Darwin), 99–100
dipthongs, Martha's Vineyard studies and, 7–8
discarding languages
    children and, 42–43
    effects on adults of, 45–46
discrimination
    employment, 128, 137–48
    housing, 136–37, 214
    language, 66–67
    national, 142–44
    See also accent bias/discrimination
Do I Sound Gay?, 1–2
Dovidio, John, 134, 212
dual-language classrooms, 173–75
Dumbo, 122
Dupoux, Emmanuel, 107

Eckert, Penelope, 9–10
education. See schools

Ekman, Paul, 23–24
Elizabeth II, 21–22
Elliott, Jane, 178–80
emotional dialect theory, 24
emotions
    "basic," 23–24
    emotional dialect theory of, 24
    native language and, 48–52
empathy, 169
employment discrimination, 128, 137–48, 214
employment law, 148–49
English as a second language, 174–76
English-only policies, 148
Equal Employment Opportunity Commission (EEOC), 142, 143
essentialism, 82–83, 116–17, 181, 184–185
Eye of the Storm, The, 178

facial expressions, 23–24
Fair Housing Act (1968; United States), 136
Fan, Samantha, 166
Federalist Papers, 62
Fey, Tina, 9
Fiske, Susan, 73
Flaherty, Molly, 37
fMRI testing, 45
foreign language
    detecting accents in, 58
    fear of, 69–70
    "voice lineups" and, 58–59
Fragante, Manuel, 139–42, 147, 214
Franco, Francisco, 64–65

Geechee, 171
Gelman, Susan, 86
gender
    generic language and, 182–84
    vocal transformations and, 10–11

generic language, 181–82
genetic diversity, 92
Giles, Howard, 193
Ginsburg, Ruth Bader, 18–20, 21,
    171
girls
    as leaders of vocal transforma-
        tions, 10–11. *see also* gender
Grogger, Jeffrey, 137–38, 214
Grosjean, François, 156, 158, 216,
    217, 218
Gullah, 171

Haitian Creole, 66
Hansen, Karolina, 134, 212
Harris, Paul, 112
Hawaiian Creole, 120
Hayakawa, Sayuri, 23–24, 51–52
Henrich, Joseph, 90
Hernandez, Dionisio, 149–50
Herodotus, 83–84
high school studies, 9–10
Hirschfeld, Lawrence, 86
Hobbes, Thomas, 99
Homeland, 11
homosexuality, 1–2, 32–33
House, 61
housing discrimination, 136–37
humor, native language and, 49
Hurricane Maria, 98
hyperarticulation, 2

immigrants
    children of, 12–15, 28–30
    language acquisition and age of,
        47–48
implicit attitudes, 11–12
inequality in society, 134–35
infants
    native language preference and,
        102–4, 106–8, 112
    social group preferences of,
        xiii–xiv
    social group study and, 108–11

as universal listeners, 104–5
    See also adolescents; children
international adoptions, studies on,
    42–45, 85
International Covenant on Civil and
    Political Rights, 67

Jay, John, 62–63
Jeantel, Rachel, 125–26, 150
jocks, 10
Jungle Book, The, 122
jurors, 149–50

Kahneman, Daniel, 50
Keysar, Boaz, 51–52, 134, 166
King, Sharese, 126

Labov, Bill, 6–8, 20–21, 70, 74
Lambert, Wallace, 72–74
language
    abstract, 185–86
    creation of categories with,
        180–81
    culture and, 62–63, 64–65, 194
    discarding, 42–43, 45–46
    effect of on social groups, x
    minority, 54–56, 67
    as natural organism, 81–82
    non-standard dialects, x–xi,
        77, 101, 121–24, 150–51,
        171–72
    restrictions on, 64–65
    See also bilingual and bicul-
        tural children; bilingualism;
        foreign language; native
        language
language acquisition
    absence of, 35–36
    adults and, 30–33
    age and, 41–42
    children and, 28–30, 33–40
    neuroscience findings on, 45–46
    quality of exposure and, 159–60
language discrimination, 66–67

Language Instinct, The (Pinker), 84–85
language loyalty, 64
language policies
  in schools, 55, 67, 68–69, 171–72, 173–75, 202
  in work place, 148
Last Week Tonight, 71
Laurie, Hugh, 61
Lenneberg, Eric, 195
Lev-Ari, Shiri, 134
linguistic bias, 101, 117–24, 127–28, 149–51
linguistic diversity, studies of, 88–90, 209
linguistic geniuses, 30–32
linguistic groups, 4–6
linguistic insecurity, 75–79, 171–72
linguistic intergroup bias, 185–86
linguistic prejudice/discrimination, xii, xiv, 97, 118, 138
linguistic shibboleths, 60–61
linguistic sway, 17–18
linguistic transfer, 83
Lion King, The, 122
Lippi-Green, Rosina, 122–23
local social environments, children and, 112–13
lollapalooza, 60–61
loss aversion, 50–51

Markman, Ellen, 168, 220–21
Martha's Vineyard studies, 7–8
Martin, Trayvon, 125–26, 150
Master of None, 13
Matched Guise Technique, 72–74
Matsuda, Mari, 135, 140, 146
McIntosh, Janet, 82–83
Mean Girls, 9
Mehler, Jacques, 102–3, 106
memory, 24–27, 49
mental states, understanding of, 169
Meyer v. State of Nebraska, 69, 83
Middle English, 64

minority languages
  protections for, 67
  suppression of, 54–56
Modern Standard Mandarin, 75
monolingual myth, 152–57, 161
Montreal, study in, 72–74
moral circles, 98–100
morality, 52
Morobe, Murphy, 54–55
Mufwene, Salikoko, 65, 201
Munson, Benjamin, 2

Nabokov, Vladimir, 31, 49
National Longitudinal Survey of Youth, 137–38
national origin discrimination, 142–44
native language
  critical or sensitive period and, x, 47, 196, 197
  decision making and emotions of, 50–52
  detecting accents in, 57–58
  emotions and, 48–52, 198
  humor and, 49
  infant preferences for, 102–4, 106–8, 112
  learning in, 66, 68–69
  permanence of, 27, 30–31
  terminology for, 195
Netanyahu, Benjamin, 31–32
neuroscience findings on language acquisition, 45–46
New Yorkers, 19–21
New Zealanders, 16–17
Newport, Elissa, 36–39, 41–42, 47, 161
Nicaraguan Sign Language, 39–40, 64, 81
non-standard dialects
  bias and, 101
  in legal system, 150–51
  linguistic insecurity and, 21, 75–77

non-standard dialects (*cont.*)
   in media, 121–24
   in schools, 171–72
   stigmatization and, x–xi
nonverbal communication, bilingualism and, 169, 170
norm setting, 148
Northeastern Mandarin (NEM), 75
Northern American accents, 17–18,
   58, 101–2, 119–20, 121

Obama, Barack, 17–18
Official Languages Act (1969;
   Canada), 72
Old English, 64
Oliver, John, 70–71
openness, 17, 22
overgeneralizations, 4
"own race" face processing, 58, 199

paired testing, housing
   discrimination and, 136–37
Pavlenko, Aneta, 49
Pear, Tom Hatherly, 71–72
perspective-taking, 165–68, 169
Pietraszewski, David, 95, 206, 208
Pinker, Steven, 9, 84–85
Pohl v. State, 202
politicians, 17–18
prejudice, creation of, 177–80
Psammetichus, 83–84
Putonghua, 75

race, 90–97, 113–17, 136–37, 184–85
raciolinguistics, 214
racism, systemic, xiv, 90, 93, 97, 115,
   184–85
reasonable accommodations, 147,
   215–16
Received Pronunciation (R. P.)
   accent, 75
Rhodes, Marjorie, 98, 180–81
Rhys, Matthew, 61–62

Rickford, John, 126
Rousseau, Jean-Jacques, 99
Royal Commission on Bilingualism
   and Biculturalism (Canada),
   72
r's
   dropping of, 19–20, 21
   length of, 7
Rubin, Don, 131–33, 213

Schindler's List, 123
Schleicher, August, 81
schools
   accent discrimination and,
      130–33, 144–45
   bilingual education and, 153
   high school studies, 9–10
   language policies in, 55, 67,
      68–69, 171–72, 173–75, 202
Senghas, Ann, 40
Senghas, Richard, 40
Sense of Style, The (Pinker), 9
Serbian, xii–xiii
Shell, Marc, 63
shibboleth story, xii, 60
Shutts, Kristin, 96, 115
sign languages, 36–40
Siman Act, 68–69
slang, 8–9
Smyth, Ron, 2, 190–91
Social Dominance Orientation
   (SDO), 134–35, 213
social groups
   abstract language and, 185–86
   creation of new, 177–80
   effect of language on, x
   impact of, 3–4
   infant preferences for, xiii–xiv
   infant study on, 108–11
   moral circles and, 98–100
   as part of human nature, ix
   race and, 90–97
   See also categories

social mirroring, 15–17
songbirds, 87, 204
South Africa, 54–56
South African Student's Movement
    (SASM), 54
Southern American accents, 17–18,
    58, 101–2, 119–20, 121–22, 142
Specific Language Impairment,
    155–56
Spelke, Elizabeth, 105–6, 114–15
Standard American English, x, 123
State v. Bartels, 202
stereotype threat, 177–79
stereotypes
    accents and, 70–72
    language and, 183–85
    in media, 118–22
    pervasiveness of, 101–2
superior temporal sulcus, 46
"switched at birth" task, 86
systemic racism, xiv, 90, 93, 97, 115,
    184–85

teachers, accent discrimination and,
    130–33, 144–45. *See also*
    schools
Thomas, Clarence, 171–72
Thorpe, David, 1–2, 6
"thought vowel" raising, 19–20, 21
Title VII, 138–39, 149, 214–15
traumatic brain injuries, 34
tribes/tribalism, ix, xii, 80, 99–100.
    See also social groups
"trolley problem" thought experiment,
    51–53

trust, 133–35
Truth and Reconciliation Commis-
    sion (South Africa), 55
Tseng, Yili, 144–45
Tversky, Amos, 50
24, 62

UN Human Rights Council, 67
United Nations, 66–67
upspeak, 10–11
US Constitution, 68

vocabulary in bilingual children,
    158–59, 217–18
vocal fry, 10, 12, 192
Voice and Personality (Pear), 71
voice onset timing (VOT), 16

wages, 136, 137–38
warmth, judgments of, 73–74
Webster, Noah, 62–63
Werker, Janet, 104, 217–18
Wernicke's area, 45
"who said what" game, 94–97
Woodward, Amanda, 108–9
World War I, 68
World War II, 60–61

Xenophobia, 70, 112, 118, 120, 124,
    152

Yow, Quin, 168, 220–21
Yugoslavia, breakup of, xii–xiii

Zimmerman, George, 125

CPSIA information can be obtained
at www.ICGtesting.com
Printed in the USA
LVHW091824180422
716534LV00017B/2444